Korean
Phrase Book
&
Dictionary

Berlitz Publishing
New York   Munich   Singapore

No part of this book may be reproduced, stored in a retrieval system or transmitted in any form or means electronic, mechanical, photocopying, recording or otherwise, without prior written permission from APA Publications.

Contacting the Editors
Every effort has been made to provide accurate information in this publication, but changes are inevitable. The publisher cannot be responsible for any resulting loss, inconvenience or injury. We would appreciate it if readers would call our attention to any errors or outdated information. We also welcome your suggestions; if you come across a relevant expression not in our phrase book, please contact Berlitz Publishing. email: comments@berlitzpublishing.com

All Rights Reserved
© 2009 Berlitz Publishing/APA Publications GmbH & Co. Verlag KG, Singapore Branch, Singapore

Berlitz Trademark Reg. U.S. Patent Office and other countries. Marca Registrada. Used under license from Berlitz Investment Corporation.

Printed in China by CTPS, April 2011

Publishing Director: Sheryl Olinsky Borg
Senior Editor/Project Manager: Lorraine Sova
Editor: Chung Hwa Kim
Proofreader: Hyunju Noh McDonald
Cover Design: Claudia Petrilli
Interior Design: Derrick Lim, Juergen Bartz
Production Manager: Elizabeth Gaynor
Composition: Datagrafix, Inc.
Cover Photo: © Makoto Watanabe/Getty Images/MIXA
Interior Photos: p. 14 © Studio Fourteen/Brand X Pictures/age fotostock; p. 19 © UKraft/Alamy; p. 27 © Pixtal/age fotostock; p. 41 © Corbis/fotosearch.com; p. 52 © Purestock/Alamy; p. 58 © Clement K.L. Cheah, 2008. Used under license from Shutterstock, Inc.; p. 74 © WizData, Inc., 2008. Used under license from Shutterstock, Inc.; p. 80 © ImageDJ/Alamy; p. 83 © Netfalls/2003-2007 Shutterstock, Inc.; p. 95 © WizData, Inc., Used under license from Shutterstock, Inc.; p. 99 © BananaStock Ltd.; p. 105 © Daniel Thistlethwaite/PictureQuest; p. 106 © ImageGap/Alamy; p. 109, 113 © 2008 Jupiterimages Corporation; p. 119 © Sz Akos, 2008. Used under license from Shutterstock, Inc.; p. 134 © Jupiterimages/Brand X/Corbis; p. 136 © Stockbyte/Fotosearch.com; p. 139 © Corbis/2006 Jupiterimages Corporation; p. 142 © David McKee/2003-2007 Shutterstock, Inc.; p. 143, 153, 162 © 2007 Jupiterimages Corporation

Distribution
UK & Ireland: GeoCenter International Ltd., Meridian House, Churchill Way West, Basingstoke, Hampshire RG21 6YR. email: sales@geocenter.co.uk

United States: Ingram Publisher Services, One Ingram Boulevard, PO Box 3006, La Vergne, TN 37086-1986. email: customer.service@ingrampublisherservices.com

Worldwide: APA Publications GmbH & Co., Verlag KG (Singapore branch), 7030 Ang Mo Kio Avenue 5, 08-65 Northstar @ AMK, Singapore 569880
email: apasin@singnet.com.sg

Contents

Food

People

Fun

Special Needs

Resources

Dictionary

Pronunciation

This section is designed to make you familiar with the sounds of Korean using our simplified phonetic transcription*. You'll find the pronunciation of the Korean letters and sounds explained below, together with their "imitated" equivalents. This system is used throughout the phrase book; simply read the pronunciation as if it were English, noting any special rules below.

Beginning Consonants

Letter	Approximate Pronunciation	Symbol	Example	Pronunciation
ㄱ	g as in girl	g	감	gahm
ㄴ	n as in no	n	나	nah
ㄷ	d as in dog	d	돈	dohn
ㄹ	between English r and l**	l	나라	nah·lah
ㅁ	m as in moon	m	물	mool
ㅂ	b as in book	b	불	bool
ㅅ	s as in sand	s	산	sahn

*The Korean Ministry of Culture and Tourism has its own Korean romanization system, which you will see on road signs, place names and certain legal documents.

**In Korean, the sounds l and r are pronounced similarly. The position of the tongue when pronouncing the letter ㄹ is somewhere between the position of the tongue when pronouncing r and l in English. It is pronounced more like l when it appears at the end of a syllable, as in 물 mool, and like an r when it is between two vowels, as in 머리 muree. For the sake of simplicity, this sound appears as "l" in the pronunciation.

Letter	Approximate Pronunciation	Symbol	Example	Pronunciation
ㅇ	silent		이	ee
ㅈ	j as in jam	j	줄	jool
ㅊ	ch as in chin	ch	춤	choom
ㅋ	k as in kite	k	콩	kohng
ㅌ	t as in table	t	탈	tahl
ㅍ	p as in park	p	팔	pahl
ㅎ	h as in hill	h	한	hahn
ㄲ	sharp k as in sky	kk	꼬리	kkoh·lee
ㄸ	sharp t as in stop	tt	또	ttoh
ㅃ	sharp p as in spy	pp	빵	ppahng
ㅆ	sharp s as in sun	ss	쌀	ssahl
ㅉ	tz as in pretzel	tz	찐	tzeen

Final Consonants

Letter	Approximate Pronunciation	Symbol	Example	Pronunciation
ㄱ, ㄲ, ㅋ	k as in pick	k	목	mohk
ㄴ	n as in pin	n	산	sahn

Letter	Approximate Pronunciation	Symbol	Example	Pronunciation
ㄷ,ㅌ,ㅅ, ㅆ,ㅈ,ㅊ, ㅎ	t as in pot	t	빛	beet
ㄹ	l as in pool	l	풀	pool
ㅁ	m as in jam	m	곰	gohm
ㅂ,ㅍ	p as in top	p	집	jeep
ㅇ	ng as in ring	ng	공	gohng

 Besides the basic final consonants listed above, there are also complex final consonants made by combining two basic consonants. If a complex final consonant is used at the end of a syllable or before a consonant, only one basic consonant of the two is pronounced.

Vowels

Letter	Approximate Pronunciation	Symbol	Example	Pronunciation
ㅏ	a as in father	ah	안	ahn
ㅑ	ya as in yacht	yah	야구	yah·goo
ㅓ	u as in nut	uh	섬	suhm
ㅕ	yu as in yum	yuh	여자	yuh·jah
ㅗ	o as in no	oh	소	soh

Letter	Approximate Pronunciation	Symbol	Example	Pronunciation
ㅛ	yo as in yoga	yo	표	pyo
ㅜ	oo as in boot	oo	줄	jool
ㅠ	like the word you	yoo	유리	yoo·lee
ㅡ	a short u as in put	u	은	un
ㅣ, ㅢ	ee as in feet	ee	비	bee
ㅐ, ㅔ	e as in end	eh	새	seh
ㅒ, ㅖ	ye as in yes	yeh	예	yeh
ㅘ	wa as in watt	wah	사과	sah·gwah
ㅙ, ㅚ, ㅞ	we as in wet	weh	왜	weh
ㅝ	wo as in won	wuh	원	wuhn
ㅟ	wi as in twig	wih	쥐	jwih

There are ten basic vowels in Korean. There are also additional compound vowels made by combining basic vowels. The compound vowels are supposed to be distinguishable in pronunciation, but in casual Korean speech, the distinction between ㅐ/ㅔ, ㅒ/ㅖ and ㅙ/ㅞ/ㅚ has been lost.

Korean is the official language of both North and South Korea. There are about 80 million Korean speakers worldwide. In South Korea, Korean is referred to as 한국어 **hahn·goo·guh**. In North Korea, Korean is most often called 조선말 **joh·suhn·mahl**. There are several dialects of Korean, but the standard dialect in South Korea, which is featured in this phrase book, is 서울 **suh·ool** (Seoul), and in North Korea, it is the dialect of 평양 **pyuhng·yahng** (Pyongyang).

Korean has formal polite, informal polite and casual forms. The form used is dependent on the situation. This phrase books applies both the formal polite and informal polite forms, as dictated by the context.

How to Use This Book

These essential phrases can also be heard on the audio CD.

Sometimes you see two alternatives in italics, separated by a slash. Choose the one that's right for your situation.

Essential

I'm on *vacation [holiday]/business*.	휴가로/일 때문에 왔습니다. *hyoo·gah·loh/ eel tteh·moo·neh* waht·ssum·nee·dah
I'm going to...	···갑니다. ...gahm·nee·dah
I'm staying at the... Hotel.	···호텔에 머물고 있습니다. ...hoh·teh·leh muh·mool·goh eet·ssum·nee·dah

You May See...

도착 doh·chahk	arrivals
출발 chool·bahl	departures
수하물 찾는 곳 soo·hah·mool chahn·nun goht	baggage claim

Finding Lodging

Can you recommend...?	···추천해 주시겠습니까? ...choo·chuhn·heh joo·see·geht·ssum·nee·kkah
– a hotel	– 호텔 hoh·tehl
– a hostel	– 호스텔 hoh·su·tehl
– a campsite	– 캠핑장 kehm·peeng·jahng

Any of the words or phrases preceded by dashes can be plugged into the sentence above.

Words you may see are shown in *You May See* boxes.

12

Korean phrases appear in red.

Read the simplified pronunciation as if it were English. For more on pronunciation, see page 7.

Relationships

How old are you?	나이가 어떻게 되십니까? nah·ee·gah uh·ttuh·keh dweh·seem·nee·kkah
I'm…	저는… juh·nun…

▶ For numbers, see page 159.

Are you married?	결혼하셨습니까? gyuh·lohn·hah·syuht·ssum·nee·kkah
I'm…	저는… juh·nun…
– single/in a relationship	– 미혼입니다/사귀는 사람이 있습니다. mee·hoh·neem·nee·dah/sah·gwih·nun sah·lah·mee eet·ssum·nee·dah
– widowed	– 사별했습니다. sah·byuhl·heht·ssum·nee·dah

The arrow indicates a cross reference where you'll find related phrases.

Information boxes contain relevant country, culture and language tips.

In formal Korean, 씨 **ssee** (Mr., Mrs. or Miss) is said after a colleague's or subordinate's name and 님 **neem** (an honorific form added to a kinship term, a job title or a personal name) is used for one's superiors or distant adults to show respect.

You May Hear…

영어 조금 밖에 못 합니다. yuhng·uh joh·gum bah·kkeh moh tahm·nee·dah	I only speak a little English.
영어 못 합니다. yuhng·uh moh tahm·nee·dah	I don't speak English.

Expressions you may hear are shown in *You May Hear* boxes.

Color-coded side bars identify each section of the book.

▼ Survival

Arrival and Departure

Essential

I'm on *vacation* [*holiday*]/*business*.	휴가로/일 때문에 왔습니다. *hyoo·gah·loh/ eel tteh·moo·neh waht·ssum·nee·dah*
I'm going to…	…갑니다. …*gahm·nee·dah*
I'm staying at the… Hotel.	…호텔에 머물고 있습니다. …*hoh·teh·leh muh·mool·goh eet·ssum·nee·dah*

You May Hear…

여권 좀 보여주십시오. *yuh·kkwun johm boh·yuh·joo·seep·ssee·yo*	Your passport, please.
방문 목적이 무엇입니까? *bahng·moon mohk·tzuh·gee moo·uh·seem·nee·kkah*	What's the purpose of your visit?
어디에 묵으실 겁니까? *uh·dee·eh mook·gu·seel kkuhm·nee·kkah*	Where are you staying?
얼마나 계실 겁니까? *uhl·mah·nah geh·seel kkuhm·nee·kkah*	How long are you staying?
누구하고 같이 오셨습니까? *noo·goo·hah·goh gah·chee oh·shut·ssum·nee·kkah*	Who are you here with?

Passport Control and Customs

I'm just passing through.	통과 여객입니다. *tohng·gwah yuh·geh·geem·nee·dah*
I'd like to declare…	…신고하고 싶습니다. …*seen·goh·hah·goh seep·ssum·nee·dah*
I have nothing to declare.	신고할 것이 없습니다. *seen·goh·hahl kkuh·see uhp·ssum·nee·dah*

You May Hear...

신고하실 물건이 있습니까?
seen·goh·hah·seel mool·guh·nee
eet·ssum·nee·kkah

Anything to declare?

이것은 관세를 내야 합니다. ee·guh·sun
gwahn·seh·lul neh·yah hahm·nee·dah

You must pay duty on this.

이 가방을 열어 보십시오. ee
gah·bahng·ul yuh·luh boh·seep·ssee·oh

Open this bag.

You May See...

세관 seh·gwahn	customs
면세품 myuhn·seh·poom	duty-free goods
자진 신고 jah·jeen seen·goh	goods to declare
면세 myuhn·seh	nothing to declare
입국 심사 eep·kkook seem·sah	passport control
경찰 gyuhng·chahl	police

Money and Banking

Essential

Where's...?	...어디 있습니까? ...uh·dee eet·ssum·nee·kkah
– the ATM	– 현금 인출기 hyuhn·gum een·chool·gee
– the bank	– 은행 un·hehng
– the currency exchange office	– 환전소 hwahn·juhn·soh

When does the bank *open/close*?	은행 언제 엽니까/닫습니까? un·hehng uhn·jeh *yuhm·nee·kkah/ daht·ssum·nee·kkah*
I'd like to change *dollars/pounds* into Won.	달러를/파운드를 원화로 바꾸고 싶습니다. *dahl·luh·lul/pah·oon·du·lul* wuhn·hwah·loh bah·kkoo·goh seep·ssum·nee·dah
I'd like to cash traveler's checks [cheques].	여행자 수표를 현금으로 바꾸고 싶습니다. yuh·hehng·jah soo·pyo·lul hyuhn·gu·mu·loh bah·kkoo·goh seep·ssum·nee·dah

ATM, Bank and Currency Exchange

I'd like to...	…싶습니다. ...seep·ssum·nee·dah
– change money	– 환전하고 hwahn·juhn·hah·goh
– change *dollars/ pounds* into Won	– 달러를/파운드를 원화로 바꾸고 *dal·luh·lul/pah·oon·du·lul* wuhn·hwah·loh bah·kkoo·goh
– cash *traveler's checks [cheques]/ Eurocheques*	– 여행자 수표를/유로체크를 현금으로 바꾸고 yuh·hehng·jah soo·pyo·lul/ yoo·loh·cheh·ku·lul hyuhn·gu·mu·loh bah·kkoo·goh
– get a cash advance	– 현금 서비스 받고 hyuhn·gum ssuh·bee·su baht·kkoh
What's the *exchange rate/fee*?	환율이/환전 수수료가 얼마입니까? hwahn·yoo·lee/hwahn·juhn soo·soo·lyo·gah uhl·mah·eem·nee·kkah
I think there's a mistake.	착오가 있는 것 같습니다. chah·goh·gah een·nun guht gaht·ssum·nee·dah
I lost my traveler's checks [cheques].	여행자 수표를 잃어버렸습니다. yuh·hehng·jah soo·pyo·lul ee·luh·buh·lyuht·ssum·nee·dah

My card…	제 카드를… jeh kah·du·lul…
– was lost	– 잃어버렸습니다 ee·luh·buh·lyuht·ssum·nee·dah
– was stolen	– 도난당했습니다 doh·nahn·dahng·heht·ssum·nee·dah
– doesn't work	– 쓸 수 없습니다 ssul ssoo uhp·ssum·nee·dah
The ATM ate my card.	현금 인출기가 제 카드를 먹어버렸습니다. hyuhn·gum een·chool·gee·gah jeh kah·du·lul muh·guh·buh·lyuht·ssum·nee·dah

▶ For numbers, see page 159.

Banks are open Monday through Friday, 9:30 a.m. to 4:30 p.m. At some banks, cash can be obtained from ATMs with many international bank and credit cards. Keep in mind, though, that most banks allow ATM transactions only if the user has an account at a Korean bank. For cash withdrawals only, 현금 인출기 **hyuhn·gum een·chool·gee** (automatic cash dispensers) are available at some public transportation terminals and convenience stores.

You May See…

카드를 넣어 주십시오 kah·du·lul nuh·uh joo·seep·ssee·oh	insert card here
취소 chwih·soh	cancel
확인 hwah·geen	enter
비밀번호 bee·meel buhn·hoh	PIN
출금 chool·gum	withdrawal
영수증 yuhng·soo·jung	receipt

You May See...

Korean currency is the 원 **wuhn** (Won, abbreviated as W).

Coins: 십 원 **see bwuhn** (10 Won), 오십 원 **oh·see bwuhn** (50 Won), 백 원 **beh gwuhn** (100 Won), 오백 원 **oh·beh gwuhn** (500 Won)

Bills: 천 원 **chuh nwuhn** (1,000 Won), 오천 원 **oh·chuh nwuhn** (5,000 Won), 만 원 **mah nwuhn** (10,000 Won)

Transportation

Essential

How do I get to town?	시내로 어떻게 갑니까? see·neh·loh uh·ttuh·keh gahm·nee·kkah
Where's...?	…어디 있습니까? ...uh·dee eet·ssum·nee·kkah
– the airport	– 공항 gohng·hahng

Where's…?	…어디 있습니까? …uh·dee eet·ssum·nee·kkah
– the train [railway] station	– 기차역 gee·chah·yuhk
– the bus station	– 버스 정류장 buh·su juhng·nyoo·jahng
– the subway [underground] station	– 지하철 역 jee·hah·chuhl lyuhk
How far is it?	얼마나 멉니까? uhl·mah·nah muhm·nee·kkah
Where do I buy a ticket?	표 어디서 삽니까? pyo uh·dee·suh sahm·nee·kkah
A *one-way/round-trip [return]* ticket to…	…로 가는 편도표/왕복표. …loh gah·nun *pyuhn·doh·pyo/wahng·bohk·pyo*
How much?	얼마입니까? uhl·mah·eem·nee·kkah
Is there a discount?	할인됩니까? hah·leen·dwehm·nee·kkah
Which…?	어떤…? uh·ttuhn…
– gate	– 탑승구 tahp·ssung·goo
– line	– 노선 noh·suhn
– platform	– 승강장 sung·gahng·jahng
Where can I get a taxi?	택시 어디서 잡습니까? tehk·ssee uh·dee·suh jahp·ssum·nee·kkah
Take me to this address.	이 주소로 가 주십시오. ee joo·soh·loh gah joo·seep·ssee·oh
Where's the car rental [hire]?	렌터카 어디 있습니까? len·tuh·kah uh·dee eet·ssum·nee·kkah
Can I have a map?	지도 하나 주시겠습니까? jee·doh hah·nah joo·see·geht·ssum·nee·kkah

Ticketing

When's...to Seoul?	서울로 가는…언제 있습니까? suh·ool·loh gah·nun…uhn·jeh eet·ssum·nee·kkah
– the (first) bus	– (첫) 차 (chuht) chah
– the (next) flight	– (다음) 비행기 (dah·um) bee·hehng·gee
– the (last) train	– (마지막) 기차 (mah·jee·mahk) gee·chah
Is there...trip?	…가는 교통편이 있습니까? …gah·nun gyo·tohng·pyuh·nee eet·ssum·nee·kkah
– an earlier	– 더 일찍 duh eel·tzeek
– a later	– 더 늦게 duh nut·kkeh
– an overnight	– 밤새 bahm·seh
– a cheaper	– 더 싸게 duh ssah·geh
Where do I buy a ticket?	표 어디서 삽니까? pyo uh·dee·suh sahm·nee·kkah
One ticket/two tickets, please.	표 한장/두장 주세요. *pyo hahn·jahng/ doo·jahng* joo·seh·yo
For *today/tomorrow*.	오늘/내일 거요. *oh·nul/neh·eel* kkuh·yo

▶ For days, see page 162.

▶ For time, see page 161.

...ticket.	…표. …pyo
– A one-way	– 편도 pyuhn·doh
– A round-trip [return]	– 왕복 wahng·bohk
– A first class	– 일등석 eel·ttung·suhk
– A business class	– 비지니스석 bee·jee·nee·su·suhk
– An economy class	– 이코노미석 ee·koh·noh·mee·suhk
How much?	얼마입니까? uhl·mah·eem·nee·kkah

Is there…discount?	…할인 됩니까? …hah·leen dwehm·nee·kkah
– a child	– 어린이 uh·lee·nee
– a senior citizen	– 노인 noh·een
– a student	– 학생 hahk·ssehng
– a tourist	– 관광객 gwahn·gwahng·gehk
I have an e-ticket.	전자티켓이 있습니다. juhn·jah·tee·keh·see eet·ssum·nee·dah
Can I buy a ticket on the *bus/train*?	버스/기차 안에서 표 살 수 있습니까? *buh·su/gee·chah* ah·neh·suh pyo sahl ssoo eet·ssum·nee·kkah
I'd like to…my reservation.	예약을…싶습니다. yeh·yah·gul… seep·ssum·nee·dah
– cancel	– 취소하고 chwih·soh·hah·goh
– change	– 변경하고 byuhn·gyuhng·hah·goh
– confirm	– 확인하고 hwah·geen·hah·goh

Plane ————————————————

Getting to the Airport

How much is a taxi to the airport?	공항으로 가는 택시 얼마입니까? gogng·hagng·u·loh gah·nun tehk·ssee uhl·mah·eem·nee·kkah
To…Airport, please.	…공항으로 가 주십시오. …gohng·hahng·u·loh gah joo·seep·ssee·oh
My airline is…	제 항공사는… jeh hahng·gohng·sah·nun…
My flight leaves at…	제 비행기는…에 출발합니다. je bee·hehng·gee·nun…eh chool·bahl·hahm·nee·dah
I'm in a rush.	급합니다. gu·pahm·nee·dah

▶ For time, see page 161.

| Can you take an alternate route? | 다른 길로 갈 수 았습니까? dah·lun geel·loh gahl ssoo eet·ssum·nee·kkah |
| Can you drive *faster/ slower*? | 더 빨리/천천히 가 주시겠습니까? duh *ppahl·lee/chuhn·chuh·nee* gah joo·see·geht·ssum·nee·kkah |

You May Hear...

어느 항공사로 가십니까? uh·nu hahng·gohng·sah·loh gah·seem·nee·kkah	What airline are you flying?
국내선입니까, 국제선입니까? goong·neh·suh·neem·nee·kkah gook·tzeh·suh·neem·nee·kkah	Domestic or international?
어느 터미널입니까? uh·nu tuh·mee·nuh·leem·nee·kkah	What terminal?

You May See...

도착 doh·chahk	arrivals
출발 chool·bahl	departures
수하물 찾는 곳 soo·hah·mool chahn·nun goht	baggage claim
검색대 guhm·sehk·tteh	security
국내선 항공 goong·neh·suhn hahng·gohng	domestic flights
국제선 항공 gook·tzeh·suhn hahng·gohng	international flights
탑승 수속대 tahp·ssung soo·sohk·tteh	check-in
전자티켓 체크인 juhn·jah·tee·keht cheh·ku·een	e-ticket check-in
출발 탑승구 chool·bahl tahp·ssung·goo	departure gates

Check-in and Boarding

Where's check-in?	어디서 탑승 수속 합니까? uh·dee·suh tahp·ssung soo·sohk hahm·nee·kkah
My name is…	제 이름은…입니다. jeh ee·lu·mun… eem·nee·dah
I'm going to…	…갑니다. …gahm·nee·dah
I have…	…있습니다. …eet·ssum·nee·dah
– one suitcase	– 가방 하나 gah·bahng hah·nah
– two suitcases	– 가방 두 개 gah·bahng doo geh
– one carry-on [piece of hand luggage]	– 휴대 수하물 하나 hyoo·deh soo·hah·mool hah·nah
How much luggage is allowed?	짐은 얼마나 허용됩니까? jee·mun uhl·mah·nah huh·yong dwehm·nee·kkah
Which *terminal/gate*?	어느 터미널입니까/탑승구입니까? uh·nu *tuh·mee·nuh·leem·nee·kkah/ tahp·ssung·goo·eem·nee·kkah*
I'd like *a window/ an aisle* seat.	창문쪽/통로쪽 좌석으로 주십시오. *chahng·moon·tzohk/tohng·noh·tzohk* jwah·suh·gu·loh joo·seep·ssee·oh
When do we *leave/ arrive*?	우리 언제 출발합니까/도착합니까? oo·lee uhn·jeh *chool·bahl·hahm·nee·kkah/ doh·chah·kahm·nee·kkah*
Is the flight delayed?	비행기가 연착됐습니까? bee·hehng·gee·gah yuhn·chahk·dweht·ssum·nee·kkah
How late?	얼마나 늦습니까? uhl·mah·nah nut·ssum·nee·kkah

You May Hear…

다음! dah·um	Next!
여권을/비행기표를 보여 주십시오. *yuh·kkwuh·nul/bee·hehng·gee·pyo·lul* boh·yuh joo·seep·ssee·oh	Your *passport/ ticket*, please.

부치실 짐이 있습니까? boo·chee·seel jee·mee eet·ssum·nee·kkah	Are you checking any luggage?
짐이 너무 많습니다. jee·mee nuh·moo mahn·ssum·nee·dah	You have excess luggage.
기내에 휴대하기에는 너무 큽니다. gee·neh·eh hyoo·deh·hah·gee·eh·nun nuh·moo kum·nee·dah	That's too large for a carry-on [to carry on board].
이 짐들 직접 싸셨습니까? ee jeem·dul jeek·tzuhp ssah·syuht·ssum·nee·kkah	Did you pack these bags yourself?
누군가 물건을 맡긴 적이 있습니까? noo·goon·gah mool·guh·nul maht·kkeen juh·gee eet·ssum·nee·kkah	Did anyone give you anything to carry?
신발을 벗어 주십시오. seen·bah·lul buh·suh joo·seep·ssee·yo	Take off your shoes.
…탑승해 주십시오. …tahp·ssung·heh joo·seep·ssee·oh	Now boarding…

Luggage

Where *is/are*…?	…어디 있습니까? …uh·dee eet·ssum·nee·kkah
– the luggage carts [trolleys]	– 카트 kah·tu
– the luggage lockers	– 짐 보관함 jeem boh·gwahn·hahm
– the baggage claim	– 수하물 찾는 곳 soo·hah·mool chahn·nun goht
My luggage has been *lost/stolen*.	제 짐을 분실했습니다/도난 당했습니다. jeh jee·mul *boon·seel·heht·ssum·nee·dah/ doh·nahn dahng·heht·ssum·nee·dah*
My suitcase is damaged.	제 가방이 손상되었습니다. jeh gah·bahng·ee sohn·sahng dweh·uht·ssum·nee·dah

Finding Your Way

Where *is/are*...?	···어디 있습니까? ...uh·dee eet·ssum·nee·kkah
– the currency exchange	– 환전소 hwahn·juhn·soh
– the car rental [hire]	– 렌터카 lehn·tuh·kah
– the exit	– 출구 chool·goo
– the phones	– 전화 juhn·hwah
– the taxis	– 택시 tehk·ssee
Is there...into town?	시내로 가는··· 있습니까? see·neh·loh gah·nun...eet·ssum·nee·kkah
– a bus	– 버스 buh·su
– a train	– 기차 gee·chah
– a subway [underground]	– 지하철 jee·hah·chuhl

▶ For directions, see page 36.

Train ————————————————————

Where's the train [railway] station?	기차역이 어디 있습니까? gee·chah·yuh·gee uh·dee eet·ssum·nee·kkah
How far is it?	얼마나 멉니까? uhl·mah·nah muhm·nee·kkah
Where *is/are*...?	···어디 있습니까? ...uh·dee eet·ssum·nee·kkah
– the ticket office	– 매표소 meh·pyo·soh
– the information desk	– 안내 ahn·neh
– the luggage lockers	– 짐 보관함 jeem boh·gwahn·hahm
– the platforms	– 승강장 sung·gahng·jahng

▶ For ticketing, see page 21.

You May See...

안내 ahn·neh	information
예약 yeh·yahk	reservations
도착 doh·chahk	arrivals
출발 chool·bahl	departures

Questions

Can I have a schedule [timetable]?	시간표 하나 주시겠습니까? see·gahn·pyo hah·nah joo·see·geht·ssum·nee·kkah
How long is the trip?	얼마나 걸립니까? uhl·mah·nah guhl·leem·nee·kkah
Is it a direct train?	직행 기차입니까? jee·kehng gee·chah·eem·nee·kkah
Do I have to change trains?	기차를 갈아타야 합니까? gee·chah·lul gah·lah·tah·yah hahm·nee·kkah
Is the train on time?	기차가 제시간에 도착합니까? gee·chah·gah jeh·see·gah·neh doh·chah·kahm·nee·kkah

You May Hear...

어디 가십니까? uh·dee gah·seem·nee·kkah	Where to?
표 몇장요? pyo myuht·tzahng·yo	How many tickets?

i The reliable South Korean train network covers all major cities. Most of the signs, especially at larger stations, are displayed in Korean and English; You may also find ticket windows for foreigners at these stations. The Korean National Tourism Organization, travel agencies and hotel staff will be able to provide information about train reservations and times. Schedules, fares, route maps and additional details can be found (in Korean and English) on the Korail website.

▶ For useful websites, see page 166.

Departures

Which track [platform] to...?	어느 승강장이…(으)로 갑니까?* uh·nu sung·gahng·jahng·ee…(u·)loh gahm·nee·kkah
Is this the *track [platform]/train* to...?	여기가…(으)로 가는 승강장입니까/ 기차입니까? yuh·gee·gah…(u·)loh gah·nun *sung·gahng·jahng·eem·nee·kkah/ gee·chah·eem·nee·kkah*
Where is track [platform] to...?	…(으)로 가는 승강장 어디 있습니까? …(u·)loh gah·nun sung·gahng·jahng uh·dee eet·ssum·nee·kkah
Where do I change for...?	…가려면 어디서 갈아탑니까? …gah·lyuh·myuhn uh·dee·suh gah·lah·tahm·nee·kkah

* When the word ends in a consonant, use 으로 u·loh; when the word ends in a vowel, use 로 loh.

Boarding

Can I *sit here/open the window*?	여기 앉아도/창문 열어도 됩니까? *yuh·gee ahn·jah·doh/chahng·moon yuh·luh·doh dwehm·nee·kkah*
That's my seat.	거기 제 자리입니다. guh·gee jeh jah·lee·eem·nee·dah
Here's my reservation.	제 예약표 여기 있습니다. jeh yeh·yahk·pyo yuh·gee eet·ssum·nee·dah

You May Hear...

탑승해 주세요! tahp·ssung·heh joo·seh·yo	All aboard!
표 보여 주세요. pyo boh·yuh joo·seh·yo	Tickets, please.
…에서 갈아 타야 합니다. …eh·suh gah·lah·tah·yah hahm·nee·dah	You have to change at…
다음 정거장은… dah·um juhng·guh·jahng·un…	Next stop is…

Bus

Where's the bus station?	버스 정류장 어디 있습니까? buh·su juhng·nyoo·jahng uh·dee eet·ssum·nee·kkah
How far is it?	얼마나 멉니까? uhl·mah·nah muhm·nee·kkah
How do I get to…?	…어떻게 갑니까? …uh·ttuh·keh gahm·nee·kkah
Is this the bus to…?	…(으)로 가는 버스입니까? …(u·)loh gah·nun buh·su·eem·nee·kkah
Can you tell me where to get off?	어디서 내리는지 말씀해 주시겠 습니까? uh·dee·suh neh·lee·nun·jee mahl·ssum·heh joo·see·geht·ssum·nee·kkah
Do I have to change buses?	버스를 갈아타야 합니까? buh·su·lul gah·lah·tah·yah hahm·nee·kkah

| How many stops to…? | …까지 몇 정거장입니까? …kkah·jee myuht juhng·guh·jahng·eem·nee·kkah |
| Stop here, please! | 여기서 세워 주십시오! yuh·gee·suh seh·wuh joo·seep·ssee·oh |

▶ For ticketing, see page 21.

 South Korea offers two types of bus service: inter-city express and local. Place the fare directly into the fare box next to the bus driver or purchase an electronic card, called T-money, in advance. These cards can be purchased at any convenience store or kiosk that displays the T-money logo. Bus fares are based on the total distance traveled. More information on express bus schedules and fares can be found at the Kobus website.

▶ For useful websites, see page 166.

You May See...

| 버스 정류장 buh·su juhng·nyoo·jahng | bus stop |
| 입구/출구 eep·kkoo/chool·goo | enter/exit |

Subway [Underground]

Where's the subway [underground] station?	지하철 역 어디 있습니까? jee·hah·chuhl lyuhk uh·dee eet·ssum·nee·kkah
A map, please.	노선도 하나 주세요. noh·suhn·doh hah·nah joo·seh·yo
Which line for…?	…은 몇 호선입니까? …un myuht toh·suh·neem·nee·kkah
Do I have to transfer [change]?	갈아타야 합니까? gah·lah·tah·yah hahm·nee·kkah
Is this the subway [train] to…?	…가는 지하철 맞습니까? …gah·nun jee·hah·chuhl maht·ssum·nee·kkah

| How many stops to…? | …까지 몇 정거장입니까? …kkah·jee myuht tzuhng·guh·jahng·eem·nee·kkah |
| Where are we? | 여기가 어디입니까? yuh·gee·gah uh·dee·eem·nee·kkah |

▶ For ticketing, see page 21.

In South Korea, Seoul, Busan, Daegu, Daejeon and Incheon have efficient subways, but they can get very crowded at peak hours. Station signs and route maps—available at subway ticket booths—include English translations. Purchase an electronic card, which can also be used on buses, or buy single-use or multiple-use subway tickets from automatic ticket machines or at ticket booths. Fares vary based on the distance traveled. In North Korea, Pyongyang alone has a subway system.

Boat and Ferry

| When is the ferry to…? | …가는 배가 언제 있습니까? …gah·nun beh·gah uhn·jeh eet·ssum·nee·kkah |
| Where are the life jackets? | 구명 조끼 어디 있습니까? goo·myuhng joh·kkee uh·dee eet·ssum·nee·kkah |

▶ For ticketing, see page 21.

You May See...

| 구명 보트 goo·myuhng boh·tu | life boat |
| 구명 조끼 goo·myuhng joh·kkee | life jacket |

South Korea is a peninsula, and so there are numerous ferry and boat services allowing for domestic travel as well as travel between Korean harbors and China or Japan. The ferry ride to Jeju-do Island, a UNESCO World Natural Heritage site, promises beautiful ocean scenery and a glimpse of volcanic remains and lava tubes. Visit the Korean National Tourism Organization (KNTO) online or in person for details.

▶ For useful websites, see page 166.

Bicycle and Motorcycle

I'd like to rent [hire]…	…빌리고 싶습니다. …beel·lee·goh seep·ssum·nee·dah
– a bicycle	– 자전거 jah·juhn·guh
– a moped	– 소형 오토바이 soh·hyuhng oh·toh·bah·ee
– a motorcycle	– 오토바이 oh·toh·bah·ee
How much per *day/ week*?	하루에/일주일에 얼마입니까? hah·loo·eh/eel·tzoo·ee·leh uhl·mah·eem·nee·kkah
Can I have a *helmet/ lock*?	헬멧/자물쇠 있습니까? hehl·meht/ jah·mool·ssweh eet·ssum·nee·kkah

Taxi

Where can I get a taxi?	택시 어디서 잡습니까? tehk·ssee uh·dee·suh jahp·ssum·nee·kkah
Do you have the number for a *taxi/ van taxi*?	콜택시/콜밴 전화번호 있습니까? kohl·tehk·ssee/kohl·behn juhn·hwah·buhn·hoh eet·ssum·nee·kkah
I'd like a taxi *now/ in an hour*.	지금/한 시간 뒤에 택시를 보내주세요. jee·gum/hahn see·gahn dwih·eh tehk·ssee·lul boh·neh·joo·seh·yo
Pick me up at…	…(으)로 데리러 와 주세요.* …(u·)loh deh·lee·luh wah joo·seh·yo

* When the word ends in a consonant, use 으로 u·loh; when the word ends in a vowel, use 로 loh.

I'm going to...	...갑니다. ...gahm·nee·dah
– this address	– 이 주소로 ee joo·soh·loh
– the airport	– 공항으로 gohng·hahng·u·loh
– the train [railway] station	– 기차역으로 gee·chah·yuh·gu·loh
I'm late.	늦었습니다. nu·juht·ssum·nee·dah
Can you drive *faster/slower*?	더 빨리/천천히 갈 수 있습니까? duh *ppahl·lee/chuhn·chuh·nee* gahl ssoo eet·ssum·nee·kkah
Stop/Wait here.	여기서 세워/기다려 주십시오. yuh·gee·suh *seh·wuh/gee·dah·lyuh* joo·seep·ssee·oh
How much?	얼마입니까? uhl·mah·eem·nee·kkah
You said it would cost...	...원이라고 하셨지 않습니까 ...wuh·nee·lah·goh hah·syuht·tzee ahn·ssum·nee·kkah
Can I have a receipt?	영수증 주세요. yuhng·soo·jung joo·seh·yo
Keep the change.	거스름돈은 됐습니다. guh·su·lum·ttoh·nun dweht·ssum·nee·dah

You May Hear...

어디 가십니까? uh·dee gah·seem·nee·kkah	Where to?
주소가 어떻게 되십니까? joo·soh·gah uh·ttuh·keh dweh·seem·nee·kkah	What's the address?
야간/공항 수수료가 있습니다. *yah·gahn/gohng·hahng* soo·soo·lyo·gah eet·ssum·nee·dah	There's a *nighttime/ airport* surcharge.

i Hail a standard taxi at taxi stands, found in most busy city areas, or on the street. You may reserve a taxi in advance by phone, but the fee may be slightly higher. Nighttime surcharges of about 20% apply. Also available are deluxe taxis, which offer more room per passenger and a higher level of service; look for the black and yellow sign with the words "Deluxe Taxi" on top of the taxi. For high-tech service, try brand taxis; these offer voice interpretation machines and wireless terminals. Finally, for groups of up to eight, van taxis are available.

In North Korea, taxis can be booked only from tourist hotels.

Car

Car Rental [Hire]

Where's the car rental [hire]?	렌터카 어디 있습니까? lehn·tuh·kah uh·dee eet·ssum·nee·kkah
I'd like…	…주세요. …joo·seh·yo
– an automatic	– 오토매틱 oh·toh·meh·teek
– a manual	– 스틱 su·teek
– a car seat	– 카시트 kah·ssee·tu
How much…?	…얼마입니까? …uhl·mah·eem·nee·kkah
– per *day/week*	– 하루에/ 일주일에 hah·loo·eh/eel·tzoo·ee·leh
– for unlimited mileage	– 무제한 마일리지 moo·jeh·hahn mah·eel·lee·jee
– with insurance	– 보험 포함해서 boh·huhm poh·hahm·heh·suh
Are there any discounts?	할인됩니까? hah·leen·dwehm·nee·kkah

You May Hear...

여권 좀 보여주십시오. yuh·kkwuhn johm boh·yuh·joo·seep·ssee·oh	Your passport, please.
보험을 원하십니까? boh·huh·mul wuhn·hah·seem·nee·kkah	Do you want insurance?
보증금이 필요합니다. boh·jung·gu·mee pee·lyo·hahm·nee·dah	I'll need a deposit.
여기에 사인하십시오. yuh·gee·eh ssah·een·hah·seep·ssee·yo	Sign here.

Gas [Petrol] Station

Where's the gas [petrol] station?	주유소가 어디 있어요? joo·yoo·soh·gah uh·dee eet·ssuh·yo
Fill it up.	가득 채워 주세요. gah·duk cheh·wuh joo·seh·yo
…Won worth, please.	…원어치 주세요. …wuh nuh·chee joo·seh·yo
I'll pay *in cash/by credit card*.	현금으로/신용카드로 낼게요. *hyuhn·gu·mu·loh/see·nyong·kah·du·loh* nehl·kkeh·yo

▶ For numbers, see page 159.

You May See...

기름 gee·lum	gas [petrol]
무연 moo·yuhn	unleaded
보통 boh·tohng	regular
고급 goh·gup	super
디젤 dee·jehl	diesel

Asking Directions

Is this the way to…?	이게…(으)로 가는 길입니까?* ee·geh…(u·)loh gah·nun gee·leem·nee·kkah
How far is it to…?	…까지 얼마나 멉니까? …kkah·jee uhl·mah·nah muhm·nee·kkah
Where's *this address/the highway [motorway]*?	…어디 있습니까 이 주소/고속도로? …uh·dee eet·ssum·nee·kkah ee joo·sohl/ goh·sohk·ttoh·roh
Can you show me on the map?	지도에서 보여 주시겠습니까? jee·doh·eh·suh boh·yuh joo·see·geht·ssum·nee·kkah
I'm lost.	길을 잃었습니다. gee·lul ee·luht·ssum·nee·dah

You May Hear…

직진해서 jeek·tzeen·heh·suh	straight ahead
왼쪽 wehn·tzohk	left
오른쪽 oh·lun·tzohk	right
코너에/코너를 돌아서 koh·nuh·eh/koh·nuh·lul doh·lah·suh	*on/around* the corner
맞은편 mah·jun·pyuhn	opposite
뒤에 dwih·eh	behind
옆에 yuh·peh	next to
지나서 jee·nah·suh	after
북쪽/남쪽 book·tzohk/nahm·t zohk	north/south
동쪽/서쪽 dohng·tzohk/suh·t zohk	east/west

---

* When the word ends in a consonant, use 으로 u·loh; when the word ends in a vowel, use 로 loh.

신호등에서 seen·hoh·dung·eh·suh		at the traffic light
교차로에서 gyo·chah·loh·eh·suh		at the intersection

You May See...

정지 juhng·jee	stop
천천히 chuhn·chuh·nee	slow
양보 yahng·boh	yield
진입 금지 jee·neep kkum·jee	do not enter
일방통행 eel·bahng·tohng·hehng	one way
주정차 금지 joo·juhng·chah gum·jee	no parking
입구 eep·kkoo	entrance
출구 chool·goo	exit
추월 금지 choo·wuhl gum·jee	no passing

Parking

Can I park here?	여기에 주차해도 됩니까? yuh·gee·eh joo·chah·heh·doh dwehm·nee·kkah
Where's…?	…어디 있습니까? …uh·dee eet·ssum·nee·kkah
– the parking lot [car park]	– 주차장 joo·chah·jahng
– the parking attendant	– 주차 요원 joo·chah yoh·wuhn
– the parking meter	– 주차 미터기 joo·chah mee·tuh·gee
How much…?	…얼마입니까? …uhl·mah·eem·nee·kkah
– per hour	– 한 시간에 hahn see·gah·neh
– per day	– 하루에 hah·loo·eh
– for overnight	– 야간에 yah·gah·neh

Breakdown and Repairs

My car *broke down/ won't start.*
제 차가 고장났습니다/시동이 안 걸립니다.
jeh chah·gah *goh·jahng·naht·ssum·nee·dah/ see·dohng·ee ahn guhl·leem·nee·dah*

Can you fix it (today)? (오늘) 고칠 수 있습니까? (oh·nul) goh·cheel ssoo eet·ssum·nee·kkah

When will it be ready? 언제 다 됩니까? uhn·jeh dah dwehm·nee·kkah

How much? 얼마입니까? uhl·mah·eem·nee·kkah

Accidents

There was an accident.
사고가 났습니다. sah·goh·gah naht·ssum·nee·dah

Call *an ambulance/ the police.*
구급차/경찰 불러 주세요.
goo·gup·chah/gyuhng·chahl bool·luh joo·seh·yo

Accommodations

Essential

Can you recommend a hotel?
호텔 하나 추천해 주시겠습니까?
hoh·tehl hah·nah choo·chuhn·heh joo·see·geht·ssum·nee·kkah

I have a reservation.
예약했습니다.
yeh·yah·kheht·ssum·nee·dah

My name is...
제 이름은…입니다. jeh ee·lu·mun… eem·nee·dah

Do you have a room...?
…방이 있습니까? …bahng·ee eet·ssum·nee·kkah

– for *one/two*
– 일인용/이인용 ee·leen·nyong/ ee·een·nyong

– with a bathroom	– 화장실 딸린 hwah·jahng·seel ttahl·leen
– with air conditioning	– 냉방 되는 nehng·bahng dweh·nun
How much for…?	…에 얼마입니까? …eh uhl·mah·eem·nee·kkah
– tonight	– 오늘밤 oh·nul·ppahm
– two nights	– 이틀 ee·tul
– one week	– 일주일 eel·tzoo·eel
Is there anything cheaper?	더 싼 방 있습니까? duh ssan bahng eet·ssum·nee·kkah
When's check-out?	언제 체크아웃합니까? uhn·jeh cheh·ku·ah·oot·thahm·nee·kkah
Can I leave this in the safe?	이걸 금고에 보관해 주시겠습니까? ee·guhl gum·goh·eh boh·gwahn·heh joo·see·geht·ssum·nee·kkah
Can I leave my bags?	짐을 맡겨도 됩니까? jee·mul maht·kkyuh·doh dwehm·nee·kkah
Can I have *my bill/ a receipt*?	계산서/영수증 주시겠습니까? *geh·sahn·suh/yuhng·soo·jung* joo·see·geht·ssum·nee·kkah
I'll pay *in cash/by credit card*.	현금으로/신용카드로 지불하겠습니다. *hyuhn·gu·mu·loh/see·nyong·kah·du·loh* jee·bool·hah·geht·ssum·nee·dah

i If you didn't reserve accommodations before your trip, visit the local 관광 안내소 **gwahn·gwahng ahn·neh·soh** (tourist information office) for recommendations on places to stay.

Finding Lodging

Can you recommend...?	…추천해 주시겠습니까? …choo·chuhn·heh joo·see·geht·ssum·nee·kkah
– a hotel	– 호텔 hoh·tehl
– a hostel	– 호스텔 hoh·su·tehl
– a campsite	– 캠핑장 kehm·peeng·jahng
What is it near?	어디 근처입니까? uh·dee gun·chuh·eem·nee·kkah
How do I get there?	거기 어떻게 갑니까? guh·gee uh·ttuh·keh gahm·nee·kkah

i

호텔 **hoh·tehl** (hotels) in South Korea range from luxury to budget. The majority of hotels charge a 10–15% service fee.

In addition to hotels, you will also find inexpensive 모텔 **moh·tehl** (motels) or 여관 **yuh·gwahn** (inns). Most feature rooms with heated floors and sleeping mats.

아파트 임대 **ah·pah·tu eem·deh** (apartment rentals) are available mainly during off-peak travel times; these usually offer kitchen facilities, pools, exercise rooms and more. Prices vary by location and length of stay.

For travelers who are interested in budget accommodations, 게스트 하우스 **geh·su·tu hah·oo·su** (guest houses) and 호스텔 **hoh·su·tehl** (hostels) are popular options.

While in South Korea, you may wish to enjoy a unique cultural experience by reserving 템플 스테이 **tehm·pul su·teh·ee** (a temple stay). Partake in a Buddhist ceremonial service, Zen meditation, tea ceremony and more. For those who would like a glimpse of traditional Korean life, stay at 한옥 **hah·nohk** (a hanok) or 전통 가옥 **juhn·tohng gah·ohk** (traditional home). Here, you will find the surroundings arranged as in traditional times.

Visit the Korean National Tourism Organization (KNTO) online or in person for details and reservations.

▶ For useful websites, see page 166.

At the Hotel

I have a reservation.	예약했습니다. yeh·yah·keht·ssum·nee·dah
My name is...	제 이름은…입니다. jeh ee·lu·mun... eem·nee·dah
Do you have a room...?	…방 있습니까? ...bahng eet·ssum·nee·kkah
– for *one/two*	– 일인용/이인용 ee·leen·nyong/ee·een·nyong
– with a *bathroom [toilet]/shower*	– 화장실/샤워 있는 hwah·jahng·seel/ syah·wuh een·nun
– with air conditioning	– 냉방 되는 nehng·bahng dweh·nun
– with a *single/ double* bed	– 싱글/더블 침대 있는 sseeng·gul/duh·bul cheem·deh een·nun
– that's *smoking/ non-smoking*	– 흡연/금연 hu·byuhn/gu·myuhn
How much for...?	…에 얼마입니까? ...eh uhl·mah·eem·nee·kkah
– tonight	– 오늘밤 oh·nul·ppahm
– two nights	– 이틀 ee·tul
– a week	– 일주일 eel·tzoo·eel

▶ For numbers, see page 159.

Where can I park?	어디에 주차합니까? uh·dee·eh joo·chah·hahm·nee·kkah
Do you have…?	…있습니까? …eet·ssum·nee·kkah
– a computer	– 컴퓨터 kuhm·pyoo·tuh
– an elevator [a lift]	– 엘리베이터 ehl·lee·beh·ee·tuh
– (wireless) internet service	– (무선) 인터넷 (moo·suhn) een·tuh·neht
– room service	– 룸서비스 loom·ssuh·bee·su
– a TV	– 텔레비전 tehl·leh·bee·juhn
– a pool	– 수영장 soo·yuhng·jahng
– a gym	– 헬스클럽 hehl·ssu·kul·luhp
I need…	…필요합니다. …pee·lyo·hahm·nee·dah
– an extra bed	– 보조 침대 boh·joh cheem·deh
– a cot	– 아기용 침대 ah·gee·yong cheem·deh
– a crib	– 아기용 침대 ah·gee·yong cheem·deh

You May Hear…

여권/신용카드 보여주십시오. yuh·kkwuhn/see·nyong·kah·du boh·yuh·joo·seep·ssee·oh	Your *passport/credit card*, please.
이 용지를 작성해 주십시오. ee yong·jee·lul jahk·ssuhng·heh joo·seep·ssee·oh	Fill out this form.
여기 서명해 주십시오. yuh·gee suh·myuhng·heh joo·seep·ssee·oh	Sign here.

Price

How much per *night/ week*?　하룻밤에/일주일에 얼마입니까?
hah·loot·ppah·meh/eel·tzoo·ee·leh uhl·mah·eem·nee·kkah

| Does that include *breakfast /sales tax [VAT]*? | 아침식사/ 부가가치세 포함돼 있습니까? *ah·cheem·seek·ssah/boo·gah gah·chee·seh* poh·hahm·dweh eet·ssum·nee·kkah |
| Are there any discounts? | 할인됩니까? hah·leen·dwehm·nee·kkah |

Decisions

Can I see the room?	방 볼 수 있습니까? bahng·bohl ssoo eet·ssum·nee·kkah
I'd like…room.	…방으로 주십시오. …bahng·u·lo joo·seep·ssee·oh
– a better	– 더 좋은 duh joh·un
– a bigger	– 더 큰 duh kun
– a cheaper	– 더 싼 duh ssahn
– a quieter	– 더 조용한 duh joh·yong·hahn
I'll take it.	이걸로 하겠습니다 ee·guhl·loh hah·geht·ssum·nee·dah
No, I won't take it.	아니요, 이건 안 하겠습니다. ah·nee·yo ee·guhn ahn hah·geht·ssum·nee·dah

Questions

Where's…?	…어디 있습니까? …uh·dee eet·ssum·nee·kkah
– the bar	– 바 bah
– the bathroom [toilet]	– 화장실 hwah·jahng·seel
– the elevator [lift]	– 엘리베이터 ehl·lee·beh·ee·tuh
– the pool	– 수영장 soo·yuhng·jahng
Can I have…?	…주시겠습니까? …joo·see·geht·ssum·nee·kkah
– a blanket	– 담요 dahm·nyo
– an iron	– 다리미 dah·lee·mee

Can I have…?	…주시겠습니까? …joo·see·geht·ssum·nee·kkah
– the *room key/key card*	– 방 열쇠/키카드 bahng yuhl·ssweh/ kee·kah·du
– a pillow	– 베개 beh·geh
– soap	– 비누 bee·noo
– toilet paper	– 화장실 휴지 hwah·jahng·seel hyoo·jee
– a towel	– 수건 soo·guhn
Do you have an adapter for this?	이것에 쓸 어댑터가 있습니까? ee·guh·seh ssul uh·dehp·tuh·gah eet·ssum·nee·kkah
How do I turn on the lights?	불을 어떻게 켭니까? boo·lul uh·ttuh·keh kyuhm·nee·kkah
Can you wake me at…?	…시에 깨워주시겠습니까? …see·eh kkeh·wuh joo·see·geht·ssum·nee·kkah
When does breakfast *start/end*?	아침 식사 언제 시작합니까/끝납니까? ah·cheem seek·ssah uhn·jeh see·ja·kahm·nee·kkah/kkun·nahm·nee·kkah
Can I leave this in the safe?	이걸 금고에 보관해 주시겠습니까? ee·guhl gum·goh·eh boh·gwahn·heh joo·see·geht·ssum·nee·kkah
Can I have my things from the safe?	금고에서 물건을 찾을 수 있겠습니까? gum·goh·eh·suh mool·guh·nul chah·jul ssoo eet·kkeh·ssum·nee·kkah
Is there *mail [post]/ a message* for me?	저한테 온 우편물이/메시지가 있습니까? juh·hahn·teh ohn *oo·pyuhn·moo·lee/ meh·ssee·jee·gah* eet·ssum·nee·kkah

You May See…

미세요/당기세요 mee·seh·yo/dahng·gee·seh·yo	push/pull
화장실 hwah·jahng·seel	restroom [toilet]
샤워실 syah·wuh·seel	shower

엘리베이터 ehl·lee·beh·ee·tuh	elevator [lift]
계단 geh·dahn	stairs
세탁실 seh·tahk·sseel	laundry
방해하지 마시오 bahng·heh·hah·jee mah·see·oh	do not disturb
방화문 bahng·hwah·moon	fire door
(비상) 출구 (bee·sahng) chool·goo	(emergency) exit
모닝콜 moh·neeng·kohl	wake-up call

Problems

There's a problem.	문제가 있습니다. moon·jeh·gah eet·ssum·nee·dah
I lost my *key/key card*.	열쇠를/키카드를 잃어 버렸습니다. *yuhl·ssweh·lul/kee·kah·du·lul* ee·luh buh·lyuht·ssum·nee·dah
I'm locked out of the room.	방에서 열쇠를 안 가지고 나왔습니다. bahng·eh·suh yuhl·ssweh·lul ahn gah·jee·goh nah·waht·ssum·nee·dah
There's no hot water.	온수가 안 나옵니다. ohn·soo·gah ahn nah·ohm·nee·dah
There's no toilet paper.	화장지가 없습니다. hwah·jahng·jee·gah uhp·ssum·nee·dah
The room is dirty.	방이 더럽습니다. bahng·ee duh·luhp·ssum·nee·dah
There are bugs in the room.	방에 벌레가 있습니다. bahng·eh buhl·leh·gah eet·ssum·nee·dah
...doesn't work.	…고장났습니다. ...goh·jahng·naht·ssum·nee·dah
Can you fix...?	…고쳐 주시겠습니까? ...goh·chyuh joo·see·geht·ssum·nee·kkah
– the air conditioning	– 에어컨 eh·uh·kuhn

Can you fix...?	…고쳐 주시겠습니까? …goh·chyuh joo·see·geht·ssum·nee·kkah
– the fan	– 선풍기 suhn·poong·gee
– the heat [heating]	– 난방 nahn·bahng
– the light	– 전등 juhn·dung
– the TV	– 텔레비전 tehl·leh·bee·juhn
– the toilet	– 화장실 hwah·jahng·seel
I'd like another room.	다른 방으로 바꿔 주십시오. dah·lun bahng·u·loh bah·kkwuh joo·seep·ssee·oh

Check-out

When's check-out?	언제 체크 아웃합니까? uhn·jeh cheh·ku ah·oot·thahm·nee·kkah
Can I leave my bags here until...?	…까지 여기에 짐을 맡겨도 되겠습니까? …kkah·jee yuh·gee·eh jee·mul maht·kkyuh·doh dweh·geht·ssum·nee·kkah
Can I have *an itemized bill/a receipt*?	명세서/영수증 주시겠습니까? *myuhng·seh·suh/yuhng·soo·jung* joo·see·geht·ssum·nee·kkah
I think there's a mistake.	착오가 있는 것 같습니다. chah·goh·gah een·nun guht gaht·ssum·nee·dah
I'll pay *in cash/by credit card*.	현금으로/신용카드로 지불하겠습니다. *hyuhn·gu·mu·loh/see·nyong·kah·du·loh* jee·bool·hah·geht·ssum·nee·dah

i

Tipping is not traditionally done in Korea, but feel free to do so if you've received extraordinary service. In most tourist and luxury hotels, a service charge is added to your bill. Furthermore, in some high-end restaurants and bars, a service charge may be included in your bill.

Renting

I reserved *an apartment/a room.*	아파트를/방을 예약했습니다. *ah·pah·tu·lul/bahng·ul* yeh·yah·keht·ssum·nee·dah
My name is…	제 이름은…입니다. jeh ee·lu·mun…eem·nee·dah
Can I have the *key/ key card*?	열쇠/키카드 주시겠습니까? *yuhl·ssweh/kee·kah·du* joo·see·geht·ssum·nee·kkah
Are there…?	…있습니까? …eet·ssum·nee·kkah
– dishes	– 접시 juhp·ssee
– pillows	– 베개 beh·geh
– sheets	– 시트 see·tu
– towels	– 수건 soo·guhn
– utensils	– 식기 seek·kkee
When do I put out the *trash [rubbish]/ recycling*?	쓰레기는/재활용은 언제 내놓습니까? *ssu·leh·gee·nun/jeh·hwah·lyong·un* uhn·jeh neh·noht·ssum·nee·kkah
…is broken.	…고장났습니다. …goh·jahng·naht·ssum·nee·dah
How does…work?	…어떻게 씁니까? …uh·ttuh·keh ssum·nee·kkah
– the air conditioner	– 에어컨 eh·uh·kuhn
– the dishwasher	– 식기 세척기 seek·kkee seh·chuhk·kkee
– the freezer	– 냉동고 nehng·dohng·goh
– the heater	– 히터 hee·tuh
– the microwave	– 전자레인지 juhn·jah·leh·een·jee
– the refrigerator	– 냉장고 nehng·jahng·goh
– the stove	– 가스레인지 kkah·su·leh·een·jee
– the washing machine	– 세탁기 seh·tahk·kkee

Household Items

I need… …필요합니다. …pee·lyo·hahm·nee·dah

– an adapter – 어댑터 uh·dehp·tuh

– aluminum [kitchen] foil – 쿠킹 호일 koo·keeng hoh·eel

– a bottle opener – 병따개 byuhng ttah·geh

– a broom – 빗자루 beet·tzah·loo

– a can opener [tin opener] – 통조림 따개 tohng·joh·leem ttah·geh

– cleaning supplies – 세척용품 seh·chuhng·nyong·poom

– a corkscrew – 코르크 마개뽑이 koh·lu·ku mah·geh·ppoh·bee

– detergent – 세제 seh·jeh

– dishwashing liquid – 주방용 세제 joo·bahng·yong seh·jeh

– garbage [rubbish] bags – 쓰레기 봉투 ssu·leh·gee bohng·too

– a light bulb – 전구 juhn·goo

– matches – 성냥 suhng·nyahng

– a mop – 대걸레 deh·guhl·leh

– napkins – 냅킨 nehp·keen

– paper towels – 종이 타월 johng·ee tah·wuhl

– plastic wrap [cling film] – 랩 lehp

– a plunger – 변기 뚫는 것 byuhn·gee ttool·nun·guht

– scissors – 가위 gah·wee

– a vacuum cleaner – 진공 청소기 jeen·gohng chuhng·soh·gee

▶ For dishes and utensils, see page 67.

▶ For oven temperatures, see page 166.

Hostel

Is there a bed available?	침대 있습니까? cheem·deh eet·ssum·nee·kkah
Can I have…?	…주시겠습니까? …joo·see·geht·ssum·nee·kkah
– a blanket	– 담요 dahm·nyo
– a pillow	– 베개 beh·geh
– sheets	– 시트 see·tu
– a towel	– 수건 soo·guhn
When do you lock up?	문 언제 닫습니까? moon uhn·jeh daht·ssum·nee·kkah
Here's my International Student Card.	제 국제 학생증 여기 있습니다. jeh gook·tzeh hahk·ssehng·tzung yuh·gee eet·ssum·nee·dah

Camping

Can I camp here?	여기서 캠핑해도 됩니까? yuh·gee·suh kehm·peeng·heh·doh dwehm·nee·kkah
Where's the campsite?	캠핑장 어디 있습니까? kehm·peeng·jahng uh·dee eet·ssum·nee·kkah
What is the charge per *day/week*?	하루에/일주일에 얼마입니까? *hah·loo·eh/eel·tzoo·ee·leh* uhl·mah·eem·nee·kkah
Are there…?	…있습니까? …eet·ssum·nee·kkah
– cooking facilities	– 주방 시설 joo·bahng see·suhl
– electric outlets	– 전기 콘센트 juhn·gee kohn·sehn·tu
– showers	– 샤워실 syah·wuh·seel
– tents for rent [hire]	– 텐트 대여 tehn·tu deh·yuh
Where can I empty the chemical toilet?	휴대 변기를 어디서 비울 수 있습니까? hyoo·deh byuhn·gee·lul uh·dee·suh bee·ool ssoo eet·ssum·nee·kkah

> Cabins, cottages, camping grounds and mountain huts can be found at many of South Korea's national parks; such accommodations are popular with hikers and nature lovers, so over-crowding can be a concern during the summer and fall months. Facilities available may include kitchenettes, showers and restrooms. For information and reservations, visit the Korean National Tourism Organization (KNTO) online or in person, or visit the Korea National Park Service website.

▶ For useful websites, see page 166.

You May See...

식수 seek·ssoo	drinking water
캠프파이어/취사 금지 *kehm·pu·pah·ee·uh/ chwih·sah* gum·jee	*no campfires/ barbecues*

Internet and Communications

Essential

Where's an internet cafe?	PC방 어디 있습니까? pee·ssee·bahng uh·dee eet·ssum·nee·kkah
Can I *access the internet/check e-mail*?	인터넷할/이메일 확인할 수 있습니까? *een·tuh·neht·tahl/ee·meh·eel hwah·geen·hahl* ssoo eet·ssum·nee·kkah
How much per *hour/ half hour*?	한 시간에/삼십 분에 얼마입니까? *hahn see·gah·neh/sahm·seep ppoo·neh* uhl·mah·eem·nee·kkah

How do I *connect/ log on*?	어떻게 접속/로그온 합니까? uh·ttuh·keh *juhp·ssohk/loh·gu·ohn* hahm·nee·kkah
A phone card, please.	전화 카드 한 장 주십시오. juhn·hwah kah·du hahn jahng joo·seep·ssee·oh
Can I have your phone number?	전화 번호 주시겠습니까? juhn·hwah buhn·hoh joo·see·geht·ssum·nee·kkah
Here's my *number/ e-mail*.	여기 제 전화번호/이메일 주소 있습니다. yuh·gee jeh *juhn·hwah·buhn·hoh/ ee·meh·eel* joo·soh eet·ssum·nee·dah
Call/E-mail me.	전화/이메일 주십시오. *juhn·hwah/ ee·meh·eel* joo·seep·ssee·oh
Hello. This is…	여보세요. 저는…입니다. yuh·boh·seh·yo juh·nun…eem·nee·dah
Can I speak to…?	…바꿔 주시겠습니까? …bah·kkwuh joo·see·geht·ssum·nee·kkah
Can you repeat that?	다시 말씀해 주시겠습니까? dah·see mahl·ssum·heh joo·see·geht·ssum·nee·kkah
I'll call back later.	다시 전화 드리겠습니다. dah·see juhn·hwah du·lee·geht·ssum·nee·dah
Bye.	안녕히 계세요. ahn·nyuhng·hee geh·seh·yo
Where's the post office?	우체국 어디 있습니까? oo·cheh·gook uh·dee eet·ssum·nee·kkah
I'd like to send this to…	이걸…(으)로 보내고 싶습니다.* ee·guhl…(u)·loh boh·neh·goh seep·ssum·nee·dah

---

* When the word ends in a consonant, use 으로 u·loh; when the word ends in a vowel, use 로 loh.

51

Computer, Internet and E-mail

Where's an internet cafe?	PC방 어디 있습니까? pee·ssee·bahng uh·dee eet·ssum·nee·kkah
Does it have wireless internet?	무선 인터넷 됩니까? moo·suhn een·tuh·neht dwehm·nee·kkah
How do I turn the computer *on/off*?	컴퓨터를 어떻게 켭니까/끕니까? kuhm·pyoo·tuh·lul uh·ttuh·keh *kyuhm·nee·kkah/kkum·nee·kkah*
Can I...?	…수 있습니까? …ssoo eet·ssum·nee·kkah
– access the internet	– 인터넷할 een·tuh·neh·tahl
– burn *CDs/DVDs*	– 씨디/디브이디 구울 *ssee·dee/ dee·bu·ee·dee* goo·ool
– check e-mail	– 이메일 확인할 ee·meh·eel hwah·geen·hahl
– print	– 프린트할 pu·leen·tu·hahl
– use any computer	– 아무 컴퓨터나 쓸 ah·moo kuhm·pyoo·tuh·nah ssul
How do I...?	…어떻게 합니까? …uh·ttuh·keh hahm·nee·kkah
– connect/disconnect	– 접속/접속 끊기 juhp·ssohk/juhp·ssohk kkun·kee
– log *on/off*	– 로그 온/오프 loh·gu *ohn/oh·pu*

– type this symbol	– 이 기호 치는 것 ee gee·hoh chee·nun guht
What's your e-mail?	이메일 주소가 어떻게 되십니까? ee·meh·eel joo·soh·gah uh·ttuh·keh dweh·seem·nee·kkah
My e-mail is…	제 이메일 주소는…입니다. jeh ee·meh·eel joo·soh·nun…eem·nee·dah

i South Korea is a technologically savvy country, and internet services abound. In addition to internet cafes, many public places, such as airports and train and bus stations, offer internet access. Most internet cafes, known as PC방 **pee·ssee·bahng** (PC bangs), are open 24 hours. The Korean National Tourism Organization (KNTO) provides a free PC bang at its location in Joong-gu, Seoul.

You May See…

삭제 sahk·tzeh	delete
이메일 ee·meh·eel	e-mail
종료 johng·nyo	exit
도움말 doh·oom·mahl	help
메신저 meh·sseen·juh	instant messenger
인터넷 een·tuh·neht	internet
로그인 loh·gu·een	login
새 (메시지) seh (meh·ssee·jee)	new (message)
열기 yuhl·gee	open
프린트 pu·leen·tu	print
저장 juh·jahng	save
사용자명/비밀번호 sah·yong·jah·myuhng/ bee·meel·buhn·hoh	username/password
무선 인터넷 moo·suhn een·tuh·neht	wireless internet

Phone

A *phone card/prepaid phone*, please.	전화 카드/선불 휴대폰 주십시오. *juhn·hwah kah·du/suhn·bool hyoo·deh·pohn* joo·seep·ssee·oh
How much?	얼마입니까? uhl·mah·eem·nee·kkah
Can I recharge this phone?	이 전화 요금 충전할 수 있습니까? ee juhn·hwah yo·gum choong·juhn·hahl ssoo eet·ssum·nee·kkah
Where's the pay phone?	공중전화 어디 있습니까? gohng·joong·juhn·hwah uh·dee eet·ssum·nee·kkah
My phone doesn't work here.	여기서는 제 전화가 되지 않습니다. yuh·gee·suh·nun jeh juhn·hwah·gah dweh·jee ahn·ssum·nee·dah
What's the *area/ country* code for…?	…지역/국가 번호가 무엇입니까? …jee·yuhk/gook·kkah buhn·hoh·gah moo·uh·seem·nee·kkah
What's the number for Information?	전화 번호 안내가 몇 번입니까? juhn·hwah·buhn·hoh ahn·neh·gah myuht ppuh·neem·nee·kkah
I'd like the number for…	…전화 번호 부탁합니다. …juhn·hwah·buhn·hoh boo·tah·kahm·nee·dah
I'd like to call collect [reverse the charges].	수신자 부담으로 걸겠습니다. soo·seen·jah boo·dah·mu·loh guhl·geht·ssum·nee·dah
Can I have your number?	전화번호 주시겠습니까? juhn·hwah·buhn·hoh joo·see·geht·ssum·nee·kkah
Here's my number.	여기 제 전화번호있습니다. yuh·gee jeh juhn·hwah·buhn·hoh eet·ssum·nee·dah

▶ For numbers, see page 159.

54

Please *call/text* me.	전화/문자 주십시오. *juhn·hwah/moon·tzah* joo·seep·ssee·oh
I'll *call/text* you.	전화/문자 드리겠습니다. *juhn·hwah/ moon·tzah* du·lee·geht·ssum·nee·dah

On the Phone

Hello. This is…	여보세요. 저는…입니다. yuh·boh·seh·yo juh·nun…eem·nee·dah
Can I speak to…?	…바꿔 주시겠습니까? …bah·kkwuh joo·see·geht·ssum·nee·kkah
Extension…	내선 번호… neh·suhn buhn·hoh…
Speak *louder/more slowly*, please.	더 크게/천천히 말씀해 주십시오. duh *ku·geh/chuhn·chuh·nee* mahl·ssum·heh joo·seep·ssee·oh
Can you repeat that?	다시 말씀해 주시겠습니까? dah·see mahl·ssum·heh joo·see·geht·ssum·nee·kkah
I'll call back later.	나중에 다시 전화 드리겠습니다. nah·joong·eh dah·see juhn·hwah du·lee·geht·ssum·nee·dah
Bye.	안녕히 계세요. ahn·nyuhng·hee geh·seh·yo

You May Hear...

누구세요? noo·goo·seh·yo	Who's calling?
잠시만요. jahm·see·mahn·nyo	Hold on.
지금 자리에 없습니다. jee·gum jah·lee·eh uhp·ssum·nee·dah	He/She is not here.
다시 전화 드리라고 해도 될까요? dah·see juhn·hwah du·lee·lah·goh heh·doh dwehl·kkah·yo	Can he/she call you back?
전화번호가 어떻게 되십니까? juhn·hwah·buhn·hoh·gah uh·ttuh·keh dweh·seem·nee·kkah	What's your number?

Public phones accept coins, credit cards or phone cards; the latter can be purchased in various units at convenience stores and newsstands. Cell phone rentals are another option, though an expensive one.

To call the U.S. or Canada from South Korea, dial 00 + 1 + area code (minus the first 0) + phone number. To call the U.K., dial 00 + 44 + area code (minus the first 0) + number.

Fax

Can I *send/receive* a fax here?	여기서 팩스 보낼 /받을 수 있습니까? yuh·gee·suh pehk·ssu *boh·nehl/bah·dul* ssoo eet·ssum·nee·kkah
What's the fax number?	팩스 번호가 몇 번입니까? pek·su buhn·hoh·gah myuht ppuh·neem·nee·kkah
Please fax this to...	이거…(으)로 팩스 보내 주십시오.* ee·guh...(u·)loh pehk·ssu boh·neh joo·seep·ssee·oh

* When the word ends in a consonant, use 으로 u·loh; when the word ends in a vowel, use 로 loh.

Post Office

Where's the *post office/mailbox [postbox]*?	우체국/우체통 어디 있습니까? *oo·cheh·gook/oo·cheh·tohng* uh·dee eet·ssum·nee·kkah
A stamp for this *postcard/letter* to…	이 엽서를/편지를…(으)로 보낼 우표 주세요. ee *yuhp·ssuh·lul/pyuhn·jee·lul*… (u·)loh boh·nehl oo·pyo joo·seh·yo
How much?	얼마입니까? uhl·mah·eem·nee·kkah
Send this package *by airmail/express*.	이 소포를 항공 우편으로/특급 우편으로 보내주세요. ee soh·poh·lul *hahng·gohng oo·pyuh·nu·loh/tuk·kkup oo·pyuh·nu·loh* boh·neh·joo·seh·yo
A receipt, please.	영수증 주세요. yuhng·soo·jung joo·seh·yo

There are domestic and international mailing services available at 우체국 **oo·cheh·gook** (post offices) throughout North and South Korea. Note that addresses in Korea are written in the reverse of the Western order. The address begins with the postal code, and is followed by country, city, 구 **goo** (urban district), 동 **dohng** (administrative district), street, street number; the name of the recipient is at the end. The post office will deliver your letter even if the address is written in English.

Korea Post has information on locations, hours, services, fees and more on its English-language website.

▶ For useful websites, see page 166.

▼ Food

Eating Out

Essential

Can you recommend a good *restaurant / bar*?	괜찮은 식당/바 추천해 주시겠어요? gwehn·chah·nun *seek·ttahng/bah* choo·chuhn·heh joo·see·geht·ssuh·yo
Is there a *traditional Korean/an inexpensive* restaurant nearby?	이 근처에 전통 한/저렴한 식당 있어요? ee gun·chuh·eh *juhn·tohng hahn/ juh·lyuhm·hahn* seek·ttahng eet·ssuh·yo
A table for *one/two*, please.	한/두 명요. *hahn/doo* myuhng·yo
Can we sit…?	…앉아도 되요? …ahn·jah·doh dweh·yo
– here/there	– 여기/저기 yuh·gee/juh·gee
– outside	– 밖에 bah·kkeh
– in a non-smoking area	– 금연 구역에 gu·myuhn goo·yuh·geh
I'm waiting for someone.	누구 기다리는 중인데요. noo·goo gee·dah·lee·nun joong·een·deh·yo
Where's the restroom [toilet]?	화장실 어디 있어요? hwah·jahng·seel uh·dee eet·ssuh·yo
A menu, please.	메뉴 좀 주세요. meh·nyoo johm joo·seh·yo
What do you recommend?	뭐가 맛있어요? mwuh·gah mah·seet·ssuh·yo
I'd like…	…주세요. …joo·seh·yo
Some more…, please.	…좀 더 주세요. …johm duh joo·seh·yo
Enjoy your meal!	맛있게 드세요! mah·seet·kkeh du·seh·yo
The check [bill], please.	계산서 주세요. geh·sahn·suh joo·seh·yo

Is service included?	봉사료가 포함돼 있어요? bohng·sah·lyo·gah poh·hahm·dweh eet·ssuh·yo
Can I pay by credit card?	신용카드 받으세요? see·nyong·kah·du bah·du·seh·yo
Can I have a receipt?	영수증 주시겠어요? yuhng·soo·jung joo see·geht·ssuh·yo
Thank you!	감사합니다! gahm·sah·hahm·nee·dah

Restaurant Types

Can you recommend...?	…추천해 주시겠어요? ...choo·chuhn·heh joo·see·geht·ssuh·yo
– a restaurant	– 음식점 uhm·seek·tzuhm
– a bar	– 바 bah
– a cafe	– 카페 kkah·peh
– a fast-food place	– 패스트푸드 점 peh·su·tu·poo·du juhm
– a traditional teahouse	– 전통 찻집 juhn·tohng chaht·tzeep

Meal times in Korea are similar to that in the U.S. and U.K.: 아침 ah·cheem (breakfast) is served until about 9 a.m., 점심 juhm·seem (lunch) is served from 12–2 p.m. and 저녁 juh·nyuhk (dinner) is served from 6–9 p.m.

Korean food is traditionally spicy and hot, and garlic is a common ingredient. The cuisine is based on meat, poultry and fish, though vegetarian options are increasingly becoming more popular. Korean food is not served in courses; instead, dishes are served all at the same time. A Korean meal is typically a combination of 밥 bahp (rice), 국 gook (soup) and various 반찬 bahn·chahn (side dishes). Spoons are used for rice and soup dishes, chopsticks for side dishes.

Reservations and Questions

I'd like to reserve a table...	…예약하고 싶습니다. …yeh·yah·kah·goh seep·ssum·nee·dah
– for two	– 두 명 doo myuhng
– for this evening	– 오늘 저녁 oh·nul tzuh·nyuhk
– for tomorrow at...	– 내일…시 neh·eel…see
A table for two, please.	두 명입니다. doo·myuhng·eem·nee·dah
We have a reservation.	예약했습니다. yeh·yah·keht·ssum·nee·dah
My name is...	제 이름은…입니다. jeh ee·lu·mun… eem·nee·dah
Can we sit...?	…앉아도 됩니까? …ahn·jah·doh dwehm·nee·kkah
– by the window	– 창가에 chang·kkah·eh
– here/there	– 여기/저기 yuh·gee/juh·gee
– in a non-smoking area	– 금연 구역에 gu·myuhn goo·yuh·geh
– outside	– 밖에 bah·kkeh
Where's the restroom [toilet]?	화장실 어디 있습니까? hwah·jahng·seel uh·dee eet·ssum·nee·kkah

You May Hear...

주문하시겠습니까? joo·moon·hah·see·geht·ssum·nee·kkah	Are you ready to order?
…추천합니다. …choo·chuhn·hahm·nee·dah	I recommend...
맛있게 드십시오. mah·seet·kkeh du·seep·ssee·yo	Enjoy your meal.

Ordering

Waiter/Waitress!	여기요! yuh·gee·yo
We're ready to order.	주문할게요. joo·moon·hahl·kkeh·yo
The wine list, please.	포도주 리스트 주세요. poh·doh·joo lee·su·tu joo·seh·yo
I'd like a *bottle/glass* of...	…한 병/ 한 잔 주세요. ...*hahn byuhng/ hahn jahn* joo·seh·yo

▶ For alcoholic and non-alcoholic drinks, see page 78.

The menu, please.	메뉴 좀 주세요. meh·nyoo johm joo·seh·yo
Do you have...?	…있어요? ...eet·ssuh·yo
– a menu in English	– 영어 메뉴 yuhng·uh meh·nyoo
– a fixed-price menu	– 세트 메뉴 sseh·tu meh·nyoo
– a children's menu	– 어린이 메뉴 uh·lee·nee meh·nyoo
What do you recommend?	뭐가 맛있어요? mwuh·gah mah·seet·ssuh·yo
What's this?	이건 뭐예요? ee·guhn mwuh·eh·yo
What's in it?	뭐 들어 갔어요? mwuh du·luh·gaht·ssuh·yo
Is it spicy?	매워요? meh·wuh·yo
Without..., please.	… 빼 주세요. ...ppeh joo·seh·yo
It's to go [take away].	싸 주세요. ssah joo·seh·yo

You May See...

정가 juhng·kkah	fixed-price
(오늘의) 특선 메뉴 (oh·nu·leh) tuk·ssuhn meh·nyoo	menu (of the day)
서비스료 (불)포함 ssuh·bee·su·lyo (bool) poh·hahm	service (not) included
특선 tuk·ssuhn	specials

62

Cooking Methods

baked	구운 goo·oon
boiled	삶은 sahl·mun
breaded	빵가루를 입힌 ppahng·kkah·loo·lul ee·peen
deep-fried	튀긴 twih·geen
diced	잘게 썬 jahl·geh ssuhn
grilled	불에 구운 bu·leh goo·oon
poached	데친 deh·cheen
roasted	구운 goo·oon
sautéed	살짝 볶은 sahl·tzahk boh·kkun
smoked	훈제한 hoon·jeh·hahn
steamed	찐 tzeen
stewed	약한 불로 익힌 yah·kahn bool·loh ee·keen
stir-fried	볶은 boh·kkun
stuffed	속을 채운 soh·gul cheh·oon

Special Requirements

I'm *diabetic/lactose intolerant.*	저는 당뇨병/유당 불내증이 있습니다. juh·nun *dahng·nyo·ppyuhng/yoo·dahng bool·leh·tzng·*ee eet·ssum·nee·dah
I'm a vegetarian.	저는 채식주의자입니다. juh·nun cheh·seek·tzoo·ee·jah·eem·nee·dah
I'm allergic to…	…에 알레르기가 있습니다. …eh ahl·leh·lu·gee·gah eet·ssum·nee·dah
I can't eat…	…못 먹습니다. …mohn muhk·ssum·nee·dah
– dairy	– 유제품 yoo·jeh·poom
– gluten	– 글루텐 gul·loo·tehn
– nuts	– 견과류 gyuhn·gwah·lyoo

I can't eat…	…못 먹습니다. …mohn muhk·ssum·nee·dah
– pork	– 돼지고기 dweh·jee goh·gee
– shellfish	– 조개류 joh·geh·lyoo
– spicy foods	– 매운 음식 meh·oon um·seek

Dining with Kids

Do you have children's portions?	어린이 메뉴 있어요? uh·lee·nee meh·nyoo eet·ssuh·yo
A *highchair/child's seat*, please.	높은/어린이용 의자 주세요. *noh·pun/ uh·lee·nee·yong* u·jah joo·seh·yo
Where can I *feed/ change* the baby?	어디서 수유 할/기저귀 갈 수 있어요? uh·dee·suh *soo·yoo hahl/gee·juh·gwih gahl* ssoo eet·ssuh·yo
Can you warm this?	이거 데워 주시겠어요? ee·guh deh·wuh joo·see·geht·ssuh·yo

▶ For travel with children, see page 137.

Complaints

How much longer will our food be?	음식 얼마나 더 기다려야 합니까? um·seek uhl·mah·nah duh gee·dah·lyuh·yah hahm·nee·kkah
We can't wait any longer.	더 이상은 못 기다립니다. duh ee·sahng·un motht kkee·dah·leem·nee·dah
We're leaving.	저희 갑니다. juh·hee gahm·nee·dah
I didn't order this.	이거 주문한 적 없습니다. ee·guh joo·moon·hahn juhk uhp·ssum·nee·dah
I ordered…	저는…시켰습니다. juh·nun… see·kyuht·ssum·nee·dah
I can't eat this.	이거 못 먹습니다. ee·guh mohn muhk·ssum·nee·dah
This isn't *clean/fresh*.	이거 깨끗하지/싱싱하지 않습니다. ee·guh *kkeh·kku·tah·jee/seeng·seeng·hah·jee* ahn·ssum·nee·dah

Paying

The check [bill], please.	계산서 주세요. geh·sahn·suh joo·seh·yo
Separate checks [bills], please.	따로 계산해 주세요. ttah·loh geh·sahn·heh joo·seh·yo
It's all together.	함께 계산해 주세요. hahm·kkeh geh·sahn·heh joo·seh·yo
What's this amount for?	이 금액은 뭐지요? ee gu·meh·gun mwuh·jee·yo
I didn't have that. I had...	저는 그거 안 먹었는데요. 저는…먹었어요. juh·nun gu·guh ahn muh·guhn·nun·deh·yo juh·nun…muh·guht·ssuh·yo
Can I have *a receipt/an itemized bill*?	영수증/명세서 주시겠어요? *yuhng·soo·jung/myuhng·seh·suh* joo·see·geht·ssuh·yo

> Tipping in restaurants is not customary in North or South Korea. Some high-end restaurants and hotels in South Korea might include a service charge and sales tax, or value-added tax (VAT), in the total price.

Market

Where are the *carts [trolleys]/baskets*?	카트/바구니 어디 있어요? *kah·tu/bah·goo·nee* uh·dee eet·ssuh·yo
Where is...?	…어디 있어요? …uh·dee eet·ssuh·yo

▶ For food items, see page TK.

I'd like some of *that/this*.	저거/이거 주세요. *juh·guh/ee·guh* joo·seh·yo
Can I taste it?	먹어 봐도되요? muh·guh bwah·doh dweh·yo
I'd like...	…주세요. …joo·seh·yo
– a bottle of...	– …한 병 …hahn byuhng

I'd like...	···주세요. ...joo·seh·yo
– a *kilo/half-kilo* of...	– ···일 킬로/오백 그램 ...eel *kee·loh*/ *oh·bek gu·lehm*
– a liter of...	– ···일 리터 ...eel lee·tuh
– more/less	– 더 많이/더 조금 duh mah·nee/duh joh·gum
How much?	얼마예요? uhl·mah·yeh·yo
Where do I pay?	어디서 계산해요? uh·dee·suh geh·sahn·heh·yo
A bag, please.	봉지 주세요. bohng·jee joo·seh·yo
I'm being helped.	다른 분이 도와 주고 계세요. dah·lun boo·nee doh·wah joo·goh geh·seh·yo

▶ For conversion tables, see page 164.

You May Hear...

무엇을 도와드릴까요? moo·uh·sul doh·wah·du·leel·kkah·yo	Can I help you?
뭐 드릴까요? mwuh du·leel·kkah·yo	What would you like?
더 필요한 거 없으세요? duh pee·lyo·hahn guh uhp·ssu·seh·yo	Anything else?
···원이에요. ...wuh·nee·yeh·yo	That's...Won.

You May See...

유통 기한···까지 yoo·tohng gee·hahn... kkah·jee	best if used by...
냉장 요 nehng·jahng yo	keep refrigerated
전자레인지 사용 가능 juhn·jah·leh·een·jee sah·yong gah·nung	microwaveable
유통 기한···까지 yoo·tohng gee·hahn... kkah·jee	sell by...

Dishes, Utensils and Kitchen Tools ——————

bottle opener	병따개	byuhng·ttah·geh
bowl	사발	sah·bahl
can opener	통조림 따개	tohng·joh·leem ttah·geh
chopsticks	젓가락	juht·kkah·lahk
corkscrew	코르크 마개뽑이	koh·lu·ku mah·geh·ppoh·bee
cup	컵	kuhp
fork	포크	poh·ku
frying pan	후라이팬	hoo·lah·ee·pehn
glass	유리잔	yoo·lee·jahn
(steak) knife	(스테이크) 칼	(su·teh·ee·ku) kahl
measuring *cup/spoon*	계량 컵/스푼	gyeh·lyahng *kuhp/su·poon*
napkin	냅킨	nehp·keen
plate	접시	juhp·ssee
pot	냄비	nehm·bee
rice bowl	밥 그릇	bahp kku·lut
rice cooker	밥솥	bahp·ssoht
soup bowl	국 그릇	gook kku·lut
spoon	숟가락	soot·kkah·lahk
steamer	찜통	tzeem·tohng

Meals

Western Breakfast ——————

bacon	베이컨	beh·ee·kuhn
bread	빵	ppahng
butter	버터	buh·tuh
cereal	시리얼	ssee·lee·uhl

cheese	치즈 chee·ju
coffee/tea...	...커피/차 ...kuh·pee/chah
– black	– 블랙 bul·lehk
– decaf	– 카페인 없는 kah·peh·een uhm·nun
– with milk	– 우유 넣은 oo·yoo nuh·un
– with sugar	– 설탕 넣은 suhl·tahng nuh·un
– with artificial sweetener	– 인공 감미료 넣은 een·gohng gahm·mee·lyo nuh·un
*hard-/soft-*boiled egg	완숙/반숙 계란 *wahn·sook/bahn·sook* geh·lahn
jam/jelly	잼/젤리 tzehm/jehl·lee
...juice	...주스 ...joo·su
– apple	– 사과 sah·gwah
– grapefruit	– 자몽 jah·mohng
– orange	– 오렌지 oh·lehn·jee
milk	우유 oo·yoo
oatmeal	오트밀 oh·tu·meel
omelet	오물렛 oh·mool·leht
roll	롤빵 lohl·ppahng
sausage	소시지 ssoh·seh·jee
scrambled egg	스크램블 에그 su·ku·lehm·bul eh·gu
toast	토스트 toh·su·tu
yogurt	요구르트 yo·goo·lu·tu

Korean Breakfast

kimchi (pickled vegetables)	김치 geem·chee
poached egg	수란 soo·lahn

I'd like...	...주세요. ...joo·seh·yo
More..., please.	...좀 더 주세요. ...johm duh joo·seh·yo

…pot stew	…찌개 …tzee·geh
– tofu	– 두부 doo·boo
– kimchi	– 김치 geem·chee
– soy bean paste	– 된장 dwehn·jahng
porridge	죽 jook
rice	밥 bahp
roasted seaweed paper	구운 김 goo·oon geem
…soup	…국 …kkook
– bean sprout	콩나물 kohng·nah·mool
– radish	– 무 moo
– seaweed	– 미역 mee·yuhk
– soy bean paste	– 된장 dwehn·jahng
– spinach	– 시금치 see·gum·chee
seasoned, broiled fish	생선 구이 sehng·suhn goo·ee
seasoned vegetable dish with…	…나물 …nah·mool
– green bean sprouts	– 숙주 sook·tzoo
– spinach	– 시금치 see·gum·chee
– squash	– 호박 hoh·bahk
steamed egg, Asian style	계란 찜 gyeh·lahn tzeem

Western-style breakfast is popular, and available at most hotels. A typical Korean breakfast often consists of a bowl of rice, soup and some side dishes—similar to a Korean dinner.

With/Without…	…넣어서/ 빼고. …nuh·uh·suh/ppeh·goh
I can't have…	…못 먹어요. …mohn muh·guh·yo

Side Dishes

dumplings	만두 mahn·doo
...kimchi (pickled vegetables)	...김치 ...geem·chee
– Chinese cabbage	– 배추 beh·choo
– white Chinese cabbage	– 백 behk
– young radish	– 총각 chohng·gahk
mung bean pancake	빈대떡 been·deh·ttuhk
pan-fried and breaded...	...전 ...juhn
– fillet of beef	– 소고기 soh·goh·gee
– fish fillet	– 생선 sehng·suhn
– sliced squash	– 호박 hoh·bahk
rice wrapped in lettuce	상추쌈 sahng·choo·ssahm
scallion pancake	파전 pah·juhn
seasoned, broiled fish dishes	생선 구이 sehng·suhn goo·ee
stir-fried anchovy	멸치 볶음 myuhl·chee bohk·kkum
tofu kimchi	두부 김치 doo·boo geem·chee

 Kimchi is a quintessential Korean side dish, and can be made with a variety of pickled vegetables and spiced with chili pepper, ginger, salted seafood or other flavorings. Various types of kimchi are available, based on the region and season.

I'd like...	...주세요. ...joo·seh·yo
More..., please.	...좀 더 주세요. ...johm duh joo·seh·yo

Soup

beef and bone stew	설렁탕 suhl·luhng·tahng
beef rib soup	갈비탕 gahl·bee·tahng
ginseng chicken soup	삼계탕 sahm·geh·tahng
...soup	···국 ...kkook
– bean sprout	– 콩나물 kohng·nah·mool
– dumpling	– 만두 mahn·doo
– Korean radish	– 무 moo
– rice cake	– 떡 ttuhk
– seaweed	– 미역 mee·yuhk
– soy bean paste	– 된장 dwehn·jahng
– spinach	– 시금치 see·gum·chee

Fish and Seafood

assorted, raw fish	모듬회 moh·dum·hweh
clam	조개 joh·geh
cod fish soup	대구탕 deh·goo·tahng
crab	게 geh
grilled eel	장어 구이 jahng·uh goo·ee
halibut	넙치 nuhp·chee
herring	청어 chuhng·uh
lobster	바닷가재 bah·daht·kkah·jeh
mackerel	고등어 goh·dung·uh
mixed seafood stew	해물 잡탕 heh·mool jahp·tahng
monkfish stew	아구탕 ah·goo·tahng
mussel	홍합 hohng·hahp

With/Without...	···넣어서/ 빼고. ...nuh·uh·suh/ppeh·goh
I can't have...	···못 먹어요. ...mohn muh·guh·yo

octopus	문어	moo·nuh
oyster	굴	gool
pickled crab in soy sauce	간장 게장	gahn·jahng geh·jahng
pollack	명태	myuhng·teh
pufferfish	복어	boh·guh
salmon	연어	yuh·nuh
sea bass	농어	nohng·uh
shrimp	새우	seh·oo
squid	오징어	oh·jeeng·uh
tuna	참치	chahm·chee
whitebait	뱅어	behng·uh
yellow corvina	조기	joh·gee

Meat and Poultry

barbecued beef dish	불고기	bool·goh·gee
beef	소고기	soh·goh·gee
chicken	닭고기	dahk·kkoh·gee
duck	오리고기	oh·lee·goh·gee
grilled breast of chicken	닭가슴살 구이	dahk·kkah·sum·sahl goo·ee
ham	햄	hehm
lamb	양고기	yahng·goh·gee
leg	다리	dah·lee
liver	간	gahn
pork	돼지고기	dweh·jee·goh·gee

I'd like…	…주세요.	…joo·seh·yo
More…, please.	…좀 더 주세요.	…johm duh joo·seh·yo

rib of beef	갈비 gahl·bee
rib of pork	돼지갈비 dweh·jee·gahl·bee
sausage	소시지 ssoh·seh·jee
sirloin steak	등심 스테이크 dung·seem su·teh·ee·ku
steak	스테이크 su·teh·ee·ku
T-bone steak	티본 스테이크 tee·bohn su·teh·ee·ku

rare	덜 익힌 duhl lee·keen
medium	반 쯤 익힌 bahn tzum ee·keen
well-done	완전히 익힌 wahn·juh·nee ee·keen

Rice and Noodles

buckwheat noodles with eggs, vegetables and red pepper paste	비빔냉면 bee·beem·nehng·myuhn
cold buckwheat noodles in broth with beef, eggs, Korean radish and mustard	물냉면 mool·lehng·myuhn
cold noodles with vegetables and red pepper paste	비빔국수 bee·beem·gook·ssoo
five-grain rice	오곡밥 oh·gohk·ppahp
handmade noodles with soup	칼국수 kahl·gook·ssoo
noodle cassorole	국수 전골 gook·ssoo juhn·gohl
rice cooked with bean sprouts	콩나물밥 kohng·nah·mool·ppahp

| With/Without... | …넣어서/ 빼고. ...nuh·uh·suh/ppeh·goh |
| I can't have... | …못 먹어요. ...mohn muh·guh·yo |

rice with nuts and herbs in a stone pot	영양 돌솥밥 yuhng·yahng dohl·soht·ppahp
rice with red beans	팥밥 paht·ppahp
rice with vegetables and fried egg, mixed with red pepper sauce	비빔밥 bee·beem·ppahp
stir-fried noodles with vegetables and meat	잡채 jahp·cheh
stir-fried rice with vegetables	볶음밥 bohk·kkum·bahp
wheat noodles with onions, bean curd, red pepper powder and egg	우동 oo·dohng

| I'd like... | …주세요. ...joo·seh·yo |
| More..., please. | …좀 더 주세요. ...johm duh joo·seh·yo |

Snacks

dumplings	만두 mahn·doo
fish cake	오뎅 oh·dehng
goldfish cake (pastry filled with sweet red bean paste)	붕어빵 boong·uh·ppahng
Korean sausage	순대 soon·deh
rice wrapped in dried seaweed paper	김밥 geem·ppahp
stir-fried rice cake with spicy sauce	떡볶이 ttuhk·ppohk·kkee

Throughout South Korea, you'll find many street vendors selling a variety of delicious snacks; these treats are very popular and often nutritious as well. Stop at a 포장마차 **poh·jahng mah·chah** (literally, covered cart bar) to enjoy some local flavors.

Vegetables and Staples

avocado	아보카도 ah·boh·kah·doh
bean sprouts	콩나물 kohng·nah·mool
bread	빵 ppahng
broccoli	브로콜리 bu·loh·kohl·lee
cabbage	양배추 yahng·beh·choo
carrot	당근 dahng·gun
Chinese bellflower	도라지 doh·lah·jee
Chinese cabbage	배추 beh·choo

With/Without…	…넣어서/ 빼고. …nuh·uh·suh/ppeh·goh
I can't have…	…못 먹어요. …mohn muh·guh·yo

corn	옥수수 ohk·ssoo·soo
cucumber	오이 oh·ee
eggplant [aubergine]	가지 gah·jee
garlic	마늘 mah·nul
green bean	녹두콩 nohk·doo·kohng
green pepper	피망 pee·mahng
kelp	다시마 dah·see·mah
Korean radish	무 moo
kosari (fern)	고사리 goh·sah·lee
lettuce (head/leaf)	양상추/상추 yahng·sahng·choo/sahng·choo
mung bean	녹두 nohk·ttoo
mushroom	버섯 buh·suht
olive	올리브 ohl·lee·bu
onion	양파 yahng·pah
pea	완두콩 wahn·doo·kohng
potato	감자 gahm·jah
potato cakes	감자전 gahm·jah·juhn
red chili pepper	고추 goh·choo
rice (uncooked/cooked)	쌀/밥 ssahl/bahp
seaweed	미역 mee·yuhk
shiitake (mushroom)	표고(버섯) pyo·goh (buh·suht)
spinach	시금치 see·gum·chee
spring onion	파 pah
squash	호박 hoh·bahk
sweet potato	고구마 goh·goo·mah

I'd like…	…주세요. …joo·seh·yo
More…, please.	…좀 더 주세요. …johm duh joo·seh·yo

sweet red pepper	빨간 피망 ppal·gahn pee·mahng
tofu kimchi	두부 김치 doo·boo geem·chee
tomato	토마토 toh·mah·toh
vegetable	채소 cheh·soh

Fruit

apple	사과 sah·gwah
banana	바나나 bah·nah·nah
blueberry	블루베리 bul·loo·beh·lee
cherry	체리 cheh·lee
fruit	과일 gwah·eel
grape	포도 poh·doh
grapefruit	자몽 jah·mohng
Korean melon	참외 chah·mweh
Korean pear	배 beh
lemon	레몬 leh·mohn
lime	라임 lah·eem
mandarin	귤 gyool
orange	오렌지 oh·lehn·jee
peach	복숭아 bohk·ssoong·ah
persimmon	감 gahm
pineapple	파인애플 pah·ee·neh·pul
plum	자두 jah·doo
raspberry	산딸기 sahn·ttahl·gee
strawberry	딸기 ttahl·gee
watermelon	수박 soo·bahk

With/Without…	…넣어서/ 빼고. …nuh·uh·suh/ppeh·goh
I can't have…	…못 먹어요. …mohn muh·guh·yo

Dessert

cinnamon punch	수정과 soo·juhng·gwah
honey cake	약과 yahk·kkwah
ice cream	아이스크림 ah·ee·su·ku·leem
sesame cake	깨- 강정 kkeh·gahng·johng
spiced rice with nuts and raisins	약식 yahk·sseek
square rice cake with bean flour	인절미 een·juhl·mee
steamed rice cake with chestnuts or sesame seeds	송편 sohng·pyuhn
sweet, fried rice cake	화전 hwah·juhn
sweet rice cake dumpling	경단 gyuhng·dahn
sweet rice punch	식혜 seek·keh

Drinks

Essential

The *wine list/drink menu*, please.	와인/주류 메뉴 주세요. *wah·een/joo·lyoo* meh·nyoo joo·seh·yo
What do you recommend?	뭐 추천하세요? mwuh choo·chuhn·hah·seh·yo
I'd like a *glass/bottle* of *red/white* wine.	적/백 포도주 한 잔/병 주세요. *juhk/behk* poh·doh·joo han *jahn/byuhng* joo·seh·yo
The house wine, please.	하우스 와인 주세요. hah·oo·su wah·een joo·seh·yo
Another *bottle/glass*, please.	한 병/잔 더 주세요. hahn *byuhng/jahn* duh joo·seh·yo

I'd like a local beer.	국산 맥주 주세요. gook·ssahn mehk·tzoo joo·seh·yo
Can I buy you a drink?	제가 한 잔 사도 될까요? jeh·gah hahn jahn sah·doh dwehl·kkah·yo
Cheers!	건배! guhn·beh
A *coffee/tea*, please.	커피/차 주세요. *kuh·pee/chah* joo·seh·yo
Black.	블랙으로요. bul·leh·gu·loh·yo
With...	…넣어서 ...nuh·uh·suh
– milk	– 우유 oo·yoo
– sugar	– 설탕 suhl·tahng
– artificial sweetener	– 인공 감미료 een·gohng gahm·mee·lyo
..., please.	…주세요. ...joo·seh·yo
– Juice	– 주스 joo·su
– Soda	– 탄산음료 tahn·sahn·um·nyo
– *Sparkling/Spring* water	– 탄산수/생수 tahn·sahn·soo/sehng·soo
Is the water safe to drink?	물 마시기에 안전해요? mool mah·see·gee·eh ahn·juhn·heh·yo

Non-alcoholic Drinks

coffee	커피 kuh·pee
cola	콜라 kohl·lah
hot chocolate	코코아 koh·koh·ah
juice	주스 joo·su
lemonade	레모네이드 leh·moh·neh·ee·du
milk	우유 oo·yoo
rice punch	식혜 seek·keh
soda	탄산음료 tahn·sahn·um·nyo
soy milk	두유 doo·yoo

sparkling/spring water	탄산수/생수 tahn·sahn·soo/sehng·soo
sweet cinnamon punch	수정과 soo·juhng·gwah
(iced) tea	(아이스) 티 (ah·ee·su) tee
...tea	...차 ...chah
– barley	– 보리 boh·lee
– black	– 홍 hohng
– corn	– 옥수수 ohk·ssoo·soo
– ginger	– 생강 sehng·gahng
– ginseng	– 인삼 een·sahm
– green	– 녹 nohk
– "five-taste" fruit	– 오미자 oh·mee·jah

> *i* Tea has been an integral part of Korean life for nearly 1000 years, and the great variety of tea available would please any palate. Visiting a traditional teahouse, participating in a tea ceremony or enjoying a green tea festival are just a few ways one can experience the tasteful tea culture while in South Korea.

You May Hear...

음료수 갖다 드릴까요? um·nyo·soo gaht·ttah du·leel·kkah·yo	Can I get you a drink?
탄산수요, 생수요? tahn·sahn·soo·yo sehng·soo·yo	Sparkling or spring water?

Aperitifs, Cocktails and Liqueurs

brandy	브랜디 bu·lehn·dee
gin	진 jeen
ginseng liquor	인삼주 een·sahm·joo
mild, unrefined rice liquor	막걸리 mahk·kkuhl·lee
rum	럼 luhm
scotch	스카치 su·kah·chee
soju (Korean liquor similar to vodka)	소주 soh·joo
tequila	테킬라 teh·kkeel·lah
vodka	보드카 boh·du·kah
whisky	위스키 wih·su·kee

Beer

...beer	...맥주 ...mehk·tzoo
– bottled/draft	– 병/생 byuhng/sehng
– dark/light	– 흑/순한 huk/soon·hahn
– local/imported	– 국산/수입 gook·ssahn/soo·eep
– non-alcoholic	– 무알콜 moo·ahl·kohl

I'd like...	...주세요. ...joo·seh·yo
A local..., please.	국산...주세요. gook·ssahn...joo·seh·yo

Wine

fruit wine	과실주 gwah·seel·tzoo
Korean sake	정종 juhng·johng
raspberry wine	복분자주 bohk·ppoon·jah·joo
red/white wine	적/백 포도주 *juhk/behk* poh·doh·joo
rice wine	동동주 dohng·dohng·joo
rice wine of high quality	법주 buhp·tzoo

I'd like...	…주세요. …joo·seh·yo
A local..., please.	국산…주세요. gook·ssahn…joo·seh·yo

Menu Reader

abalone (seafood)	전복 juhn·bohk
almond	아몬드 ah·mohn·du
anchovy	멸치 myuhl·chee
apple	사과 sah·gwah
apricot	살구 sahl·goo
artificial sweetener	인공 감미료 een·gohng gahm·mee·lyo
avocado	아보카도 ah·boh·kah·doh
bacon	베이컨 beh·ee·kuhn
banana	바나나 bah·nah·nah
barbecued beef dish	불고기 bool·goh·gee
barley	보리 boh·lee
bass	농어 nohng·uh
bean sprout soup	콩나물국 kohng·nah·mool·kkook
bean sprouts	콩나물 kohng·nah·mool

beef	소고기 soh·goh·gee
beef and bone soup	곰국 gohm·kkook
beef and bone stew	설렁탕 suhl·luhng·tahng
beef rib soup	갈비탕 gahl·bee·tahng
beef rib stew	갈비찜 gahl·bee·tzeem
beer	맥주 mehk·tzoo
blueberry	블루베리 bul·loo·beh·lee
bread	빵 ppahng
breast (of chicken)	닭가슴살 dahk·kkah·sum·sahl
broth	육수 yook·ssoo
buckwheat noodles	메밀국수 meh·meel·gook·ssoo
buckwheat noodles with eggs, vegetables and red pepper paste	비빔냉면 bee·beem·nehng·myuhn
butter	버터 buh·tuh

cabbage	양배추 yahng·beh·choo
cake	케이크 keh·ee·ku
candy [sweets]	사탕 sah·tahng
caramel	캐러멜 keh·luh·mehl
carrot	당근 dahng·gun
casserole of meat, fish, vegetables, nuts and quail eggs	신선로 seen·suhl·loh
celery	셀러리 ssehl·luh·lee
cereal	시리얼 ssee·lee·uhl
cheese	치즈 chee·ju
cherry	체리 cheh·lee
chestnut	밤 bahm
chicken	닭고기 dahk·kkoh·gee
chicken pan-fried with vegetables and hot spices	닭갈비 dahk·kkahl·bee
chicken stewed with onions, carrots, garlic, black and red pepper, salt or soy sauce	닭찜 dahk·tzeem
chicory	치커리 chee·kuh·lee
chili pepper	고추 goh·choo
Chinese bellflower	도라지 doh·lah·jee
Chinese cabbage	배추 beh·choo
Chinese cabbage kimchi	배추김치 beh·choo·geem·chee
chocolate	초콜릿 choh·kohl·leet
chopped [minced] meat	자른 고기 jah·lun goh·gee
cinnamon	계피 gyeh·pee

clam	조개 joh·geh
cod fish	대구 deh·goo
cod fish soup	대구탕 deh·goo·tahng
coffee	커피 kuh·pee
cold buckwheat noodles in broth with beef, eggs, Korean radish and mustard	물냉면 mool·lehng·myuhn
cold noodles with vegetables and red pepper paste	비빔국수 bee·beem·gook·ssoo
cookie [biscuit]	쿠키 koo·kee
crab	게 geh
crabmeat	게살 geh·ssahl
cracker	크래커 ku·leh·kuh
cream	크림 ku·leem
cream cheese	크림치즈 ku·leem·chee·ju
cream, whipped	휘핑크림 hwih·peeng·ku·leem
cucumber	오이 oh·ee
custard	커스터드 kuh·su·tuh·du
diced radish kimchi	깍두기 kkahk·ttoo·gee
diced raw fish with mixed vegetables on rice	회덮밥 hweh·duhp·ppahp
doughnut	도넛 doh·nuht
dried persimmon	곶감 kkoht·kkahm
duck	오리고기 oh·lee·goh·gee
dumpling	만두 mahn·doo
dumpling soup	만두국 mahn·doo·kkook
eel	장어 jahng·uh

egg	계란 geh·lahn
eggplant [aubergine]	가지 gah·jee
fish	생선 sehng·suhn
fish cake	오뎅 oh·dehng
five-grain rice	오곡밥 oh·gohk·ppahp
French fries	감자튀김 gahm·jah·twih·geem
fruit	과일 gwah·eel
garlic	마늘 mah·nul
garlic sauce	마늘소스 mah·nul·ssoh·su
giblet	닭내장 dahng·neh·jahng
gin	진 jeen
ginger	생강 sehng·gahng
ginseng chicken soup	삼계탕 sahm·geh·tahng
goldfish cake (pastry filled with sweet red bean paste)	붕어빵 boong·uh·ppahng
grapefruit	자몽 jah·mohng
grapes	포도 poh·doh
grilled breast of chicken	닭가슴살 구이 dahk·kkah·sum·sahl goo·ee
grilled eel	장어 구이 jahng·uh goo·ee
halibut	넙치 nuhp·chee
ham	햄 hehm
hamburger	햄버거 hehm·buh·guh
handmade noodles with soup	칼국수 kahl·gook·ssoo
hazelnut	헤이즐넛 heh·ee·jul·nuht
hen	암탉 ahm·tahk
herb	허브 huh·bu

herring	청어 chuhng·uh
honey	꿀 kkool
honey cake	약과 yahk·kkwah
hot and spicy fish stew	매운탕 meh·oon·tahng
hot chilli pepper paste	고추장 goh·choo·jahng
hot dog	핫도그 haht·doh·gu
ice (cube)	얼음 uh·lum
ice cream	아이스크림 ah·ee·su·ku·leem
jam	잼 tzehm
jelly	젤리 jehl·lee
juice	주스 joo·su
jujube (fruit)	대추 deh·choo
kelp	다시마 dah·see·mah
ketchup	케첩 keh·chuhp
kimchi (pickled vegetables)	김치 geem·chee
kiwi	키위 kee·wih
Korean cake (generic)	떡 ttuhk
Korean melon	참외 chah·mweh
Korean pear	배 beh
Korean radish	무 moo
Korean sausage	순대 soon·deh
Korean traditional sweets (generic)	한과 hahn·gwah
lamb	양고기 yahng·goh·gee
leg	다리 dah·lee
lemon	레몬 leh·mohn
lemonade	레모네이드 leh·moh·neh·ee·du

lettuce (leaf)	상추 sahng·choo
liqueur	술 sool
liver	간 gahn
lobster	바닷가재 bah·daht·kkah·jeh
macaroni	마카로니 mah·kah·loh·nee
mackerel	고등어 goh·dung·uh
mango	망고 mahng·goh
mayonnaise	마요네즈 mah·yo·neh·ju
meat	고기 goh·gee
melon	메론 meh·lohn
milk	우유 oo·yoo
milk shake	밀크 셰이크 meel·ku syeh·ee·ku
mint	박하 bah·kah
mixed seafood stew	해물 잡탕 heh·mool jahp·tahng
monkfish	아구 ah·goo
monkfish stew	아구탕 ah·goo·tahng
mung bean pancake	빈대떡 been·deh·ttuhk
mushroom	버섯 buh·suht
mussel	홍합 hohng·hahp
mustard	겨자 gyuh·jah
noodle	국수 gook·ssoo
noodle cassorole	국수 전골 gook·ssoo juhn·gohl
nuts	견과류 gyuhn·gwah·lyoo
octopus	문어 moo·nuh
olive	올리브 ohl·lee·bu
olive oil	올리브유 ohl·lee·bu·yoo
omelet	오물렛 oh·mool·leht
onion	양파 yahng·pah

orange	오렌지 oh·lehn·jee
organ meat [offal]	내장 neh·jahng
ox	소 soh
oxtail	소꼬리 soh·kkoh·lee
oyster	굴 gool
pancake	팬케이크 pehn·keh·ee·ku
peach	복숭아 bohk·ssoong·ah
peanut	땅콩 ttahng·kohng
peas	완두콩 wahn·doo·kohng
pepper (seasoning/ vegetable)	후추/고추 hoo·choo/goh·choo
perilla (herb)	깻잎 kkehn·neep
persimmon	감 gahm
pickle	피클 pee·kul
pickled crab in soy sauce	간장 게장 gahn·jahng geh·jahng
pie	파이 pah·ee
pineapple	파인애플 pah·ee·neh·pul
pizza	피자 pee·tzah
plum	자두 jah·doo
poached egg	수란 soo·lahn
pollack	명태 myuhng·teh
pomegranate	석류 suhng·nyoo
pork	돼지고기 dweh·jee·goh·gee
porridge	죽 jook
pot stew	찌개 tzee·geh
potato	감자 gahm·jah
potato chips [crisps]	감자칩 gahm·jah·cheep

pufferfish	복어 boh·guh
pufferfish and hot pepper stew	복어 매운탕 boh·guh meh·oon·tahng
pumpkin	늙은 호박 nul·gun hoh·bahk
radish soup	무국 moo·kkook
raisin	건포도 guhn·poh·doh
raspberry	산딸기 sahn·ttahl·gee
red cabbage	빨간 양배추 ppahl·gahn yahng·beh·choo
rib of beef	갈비 gahl·bee
rib of pork	돼지갈비 dweh·jee·gahl·bee
rice (cooked/ uncooked)	밥/쌀 bahp/ssahl
rice with bean sprouts	콩나물밥 kohng·nah·mool·ppahp
rice with nuts and herbs in a hot stone pot	영양 돌솥밥 yuhng·yahng dohl·soht·ppahp
rice with red beans	팥밥 paht·ppahp
rice with vegetables and fried egg, mixed with red pepper sauce	비빔밥 bee·beem·ppahp
rice wrapped in dried seaweed paper	김밥 geem·ppahp
rice wrapped in lettuce	상추쌈 sahng·choo·ssahm
roasted seaweed paper	구운 김 goo·oon geem
roll	롤빵 lohl ppahng
rosemary	로즈메리 loh·ju·meh·lee
salad	샐러드 ssehl·luh·du
salmon	연어 yuh·nuh

salmon, smoked	훈제 연어 hoon·jeh yuh·nuh
salt	소금 soh·gum
sandwich	샌드위치 ssehn·du·wih·chee
sauce	소스 ssoh·su
sausage	소시지 ssoh·seh·jee
scallion [spring onion]	파 pah
scallion pancake	파전 pah·juhn
scallop	가리비 gah·lee·bee
scotch	스카치 su·kah·chee
seafood	해산물 heh·sahn·mool
seasoned soy bean paste with hot pepper paste	쌈장 ssahm·jahng
seasoned steamed pollack	북어찜 boo·guh·tzeem
seasoned, broiled fish	생선 구이 sehng·suhn goo·ee
seasoning	조미료 joh·mee·lyo
seaweed	미역 mee·yuhk
seaweed soup	미역국 mee·yuhk·kkook
sesame cake	깨강정 kkeh·gahng·johng
shellfish	조개류 joh·geh·lyoo
shoulder	어깨 살 uh·kkeh ssahl
shrimp	새우 seh·oo
sirloin	등심 dung·seem
sirloin steak	등심 스테이크 dung·seem su·teh·ee·ku
snack	간식 gahn·seek
soda	탄산음료 tahn·sah·num·nyo
sole	서대기 suh·deh·gee
soup	국 gook

soy bean [soya bean]	콩 kohng
soy bean paste	된장 dwehn·jahng
soy bean paste soup	된장국 dwehn·jahng·kkook
soy milk [soya milk]	두유 doo·yoo
soy sauce	간장 gahn·jahng
spaghetti	스파게티 su·pah·geh·tee
spices	양념 yahng·nyuhm
spinach	시금치 see·gum·chee
spinach soup	시금치국 see·gum·chee·kkook
square rice cake coated with bean flour	인절미 een·juhl·mee
squash	호박 hoh·bahk
squid	오징어 oh·jeeng·uh
steak	스테이크 su·teh·ee·ku
steamed egg, Asian style	계란 찜 gyeh·lahn tzeem
steamed half-moon rice cake, stuffed with chestnuts or sesame seeds	송편 sohng·pyuhn
steamed rice balls with raw fish topping	생선 초밥 sehng·suhn choh·bahp
stew made with tofu and/or vegetables	전골 juhn·gohl
stir-fried anchovy	멸치 볶음 myuhl·chee bohk·kkum
stir-fried rice cake with spicy sauce	떡볶이 ttuhk·ppohk·kkee
stir-fried rice with vegetables	볶음밥 bohk·kkum·bahp

stir-fried vermicelli noodles with vegetables and meat	잡채 jahp·cheh
strawberry	딸기 ttahl·gee
sugar	설탕 suhl·tahng
sweet cinnamon punch	수정과 soo·juhng·gwah
sweet potato	고구마 goh·goo·mah
sweet rice cake dumpling	경단 gyuhng·dahn
sweet rice punch	식혜 seek·keh
sweet, fried rice cake	화전 hwah·juhn
sweet, spiced rice flavored with nuts and raisins	약식 yahk·sseek
sweetener	감미료 gahm·mee·lyo
swordfish	황새치 hwahng·seh·chee
syrup	시럽 see·luhp
tangerine	감귤 gahm·gyool
T-bone steak	티본 스테이크 tee·bohn su·teh·ee·ku
tea	차 chah
tenderloin	안심 ahn·seem
toast	토스트 toh·su·tu
tofu	두부 doo·boo
tofu kimchi	두부 김치 doo·boo geem·chee
tomato	토마토 toh·mah·toh
tongue	혀 hyuh
tonic water	탄산수 tahn·sahn·soo

tripe in a spicy beef broth with noodles and vegetables	곱창 전골 gohp·chahng juhn·gohl
trout	송어 sohng·uh
tuna	참치 chahm·chee
unseasoned pork bacon	삼겹살 sahm·gyuhp·ssahl
vanilla	바닐라 bah·neel·lah
veal	송아지 고기 sohng·ah·jee goh·gee
vegetable	채소 cheh·soh
vinegar	식초 seek·choh
waffle	와플 wah·pul
walnut	호두 hoh·doo
water	물 mool
watermelon	수박 soo·bahk
wheat	밀 meel
wheat noodles with onions, fried soybean curd, red pepper powder and egg	우동 oo·dohng
whisky	위스키 wee·su·kee
white Chinese cabbage kimchi	백김치 behk·geem·chee
whitebait	뱅어 behng·uh
yellow corvina (fish)	조기 joh·gee
yogurt	요구르트 yo·goo·ru·tu
young radish kimchi	총각김치 chohng·gahk·geem·chee

▼ *People*

Talking

Essential

Hello.	안녕하세요. an·nyuhng·hah·seh·yo
How are you?	잘 지내십니까? jahl jee·neh·seem·nee·kkah
Fine, thanks.	네, 좋습니다. neh joht·ssum·nee·dah
Excuse me!	실례합니다! seel·leh·hahm·nee·dah
Do you speak English?	영어 하십니까? yuhng·uh hah·seem·nee·kkah
What's your name?	이름이 어떻게 되십니까? ee·lu·mee uh·ttuh·keh dweh·seem·nee·kkah
My name is...	제 이름은…입니다. jeh ee·lu·mun… eem·nee·dah
Nice to meet you.	만나서 반갑습니다. mahn·nah·suh bahn·gahp·ssum·nee·dah
Where are you from?	어디서 오셨습니까? uh·dee·suh oh·syuht·ssum·nee·kkah
I'm from the *U.S./U.K.*	저는 미국에서/영국에서 왔습니다. juh·nun *mee·goo·geh·suh/yuhng·goo·geh·suh* waht·ssum·nee·dah
What do you do?	무슨 일 하십니까? moo·sun neel hah·seem·nee·kkah
I work for...	저는…에서 일합니다. juh·nun…eh·suh eel·hahm·nee·dah
I'm a student.	저는 학생입니다. juh·nun hahk·ssehng·eem·nee·dah
I'm retired.	저는 은퇴했습니다. juh·nun un·tweh·heht·ssum·nee·dah
Do you like...?	…좋아하십니까? …joh·ah hah·seem·nee·kkah

| Goodbye. (to someone leaving) | 안녕히 가세요. ahn·nyuhng·hee gah·seh·yo |
| See you later. | 나중에 뵙겠습니다. nah·joong·eh bwehp·kkeht·ssum·nee·dah |

> **i**
> In formal Korean, 씨 **ssee** (Mr., Mrs. or Miss) is said after a colleague's or subordinate's full name and 님 **neem** (an honorific form added to a kinship term, a job title or a personal name) is used for one's superiors or distant adults to show respect. Also note that the last name precedes the first name.

▶ For formal and informal forms, see page 156.

Communication Difficulties

Do you speak English?	영어 하십니까? yuhng·uh hah·seem·nee·kkah
Does anyone here speak English?	여기 영어 하시는 분 계십니까? yuh·gee yuhng·uh hah·see·nun boon geh·seem·nee·kkah
I don't speak (much) Korean.	한국어 (잘) 못 합니다. han·goo·guh (jahl) moh tahm·nee·dah
Can you speak more slowly?	더 천천히 말씀해 주시겠습니까? duh chuhn·chuh·nee mahl·ssum·heh joo·see·geht·ssum·nee·kkah
Can you repeat that?	다시 말씀해 주시겠습니까? dah·see mahl·ssum·heh joo·see·geht·ssum·nee·kkah
Excuse me?	뭐라고 하셨습니까? mwuh·lah·goh hah·syuht·ssum·nee·kkah
What was that?	뭐라고요? mwuh·lah·goh·yo
Can you spell it?	철자가 어떻게 됩니까? chuhl·tzah·gah uh·ttuh·keh dwehm·nee·kkah
Please write it down.	좀 써 주십시오. johm ssuh joo·seep·ssee·yo

Can you translate this into English for me?	이거 영어로 번역해 주시겠습니까? ee-guh yuhng-uh-loh byuh-nyuh-keh joo-see-geht-ssum-nee-kkah
What does *this/that* mean?	이거/저거 무슨 뜻입니까? *ee-guh/juh-guh* moo-sun ttu-seem-nee-kkah
I understand.	알겠습니다. ahl-geht-ssum-nee-dah
I don't understand.	모르겠습니다. moh-lu-geht-ssum-nee-dah
Do you understand?	아시겠습니까? ah-see-geht-ssum-nee-kkah

You May Hear...

영어 조금 밖에 못 합니다. yuhng-uh joh-gum bah-kkeh moh tahm-nee-dah

I only speak a little English.

영어 못 합니다. yuhng-uh moh tahm-nee-dah

I don't speak English.

Making Friends

Hello!	안녕하세요! ahn-nyuhng-hah-seh-yo
My name is...	제 이름은…입니다. jeh ee-lu-mun… eem-nee-dah
What's your name?	이름이 어떻게 되십니까? ee-lu-mee uh-ttuh-keh dweh-seem-nee-kkah
I'd like to introduce you to...	…께 소개시켜 드리겠습니다. …kkeh soh-geh see-kyuh du-lee-geht-ssum-nee-dah
Nice to meet you.	만나서 반갑습니다. mahn-nah-suh bahn-gahp-ssum-nee-dah
How are you?	잘 지내십니까? jahl jee-neh-seem-nee-kkah
Fine, thanks. And you?	네, 좋습니다. 잘 지내십니까? neh joh-ssum-nee-dah jahl jee-neh-seem-nee-kkah

i Politeness and etiquette are valued in Korean society. When greeting someone or departing, Koreans nod or bow their heads. Try to use both hands when you hand something (e.g., a business card or gift) to someone, for it shows respect.

Travel Talk

I'm here…	여기…왔습니다. yuh·gee… waht·ssum·nee·dah
– on business	– 일 때문에 eel tteh·moo·neh
– on vacation [holiday]	– 휴가로 hyoo·gah·loh
– studying	– 공부하러 gohng·boo·hah·luh
I'm staying for…	…동안 머물 겁니다. …ttohng·ahn muh·mool kkuhm·nee·dah
I've been here…	여기…동안 있었습니다. yuh·gee… ttohng·ahn eet·ssuht·ssum·nee·dah
– a day	– 하루 hah·loo
– a week	– 일주일 eel·tzoo·eel
– a month	– 한 달 hahn dahl

▶ For numbers, see page 159.

99

| Where are you from? | 어디서 오셨습니까? uh·dee·suh oh·syuht·ssum·nee·kkah |
| I'm from... | …에서 왔습니다. ...eh·suh waht·ssum·nee·dah |

Relationships

Who are you with?	누구하고 같이 오셨습니까? noo·goo·hah·goh gah·chee oh·syuht·ssum·nee·kkah
I'm here alone.	여기 혼자 왔습니다. yuh·gee hohn·jah waht·ssum·nee·dah
I'm with my...	…하고 같이 왔습니다. ...hah·goh gah·chee waht·ssum·nee·dah
– husband/wife	– 남편/아내 nahm·pyuhn/ah·neh
– boyfriend/girlfriend	– 남자친구/여자친구 nahm·jah·cheen·goo/yuh·jah·cheen·goo
– mother/father	– 어머니/아버지 uh·muh·nee/ah·buh·jee
– friend/colleague	– 친구/직장 동료 cheen·goo/jeek·tzahng dohng·nyo
When's your birthday?	생일이 언제입니까? sehng·ee·lee uhn·jeh·eem·nee·kkah
How old are you?	나이가 어떻게 되십니까? nah·ee·gah uh·ttuh·keh dweh·seem·nee·kkah
I'm...	저는… juh·nun...

▶ For numbers, see page 159.

Are you married?	결혼하셨습니까? gyuh·lohn·hah·syuht·ssum·nee·kkah
I'm...	저는… juh·nun...
– single/in a relationship	– 미혼입니다/사귀는 사람이 있습니다 mee·hoh·neem·nee·dah/sah·gwih·nun sah·lah·mee eet·ssum·nee·dah

– engaged/married	– 약혼했습니다/결혼했습니다 yahk·khohn·heht·ssum·nee·dah/ gyuh·lohn·heht·ssum·nee·dah
– divorced/separated	– 이혼했습니다/별거 중입니다 ee·hohn·heht·ssum·nee·dah/byuhl·guh joong·eem·nee·dah
– widowed	– 사별했습니다 sah·byuhl·heht·ssum·nee·dah
Do you have *children/* *grandchildren*?	자녀가/손자가 있으십니까? *jah·nyuh·gah/sohn·jah·gah* eet·ssu·seem·nee·kkah

Work and School

What do you do?	무슨 일하십니까? moo·sun neel·hah·seem·nee·kkah
What are you studying?	무슨 공부하십니까? moo·sun gohng·boo·hah·seem·nee·kkah
I'm studying Korean.	한국어 공부하고 있습니다. hahn·goo·guh gohng·boo·hah·goh eet·ssum·nee·dah
I...	저는… juh·nun...
– work *full-time/* *part-time*	– 풀타임으로/파트타임으로 일합니다 *pool·tah·ee·mu·loh/pah·tu·tah·ee·mu·loh* eel·hahm·nee·dah
– am unemployed	– 직업이 없습니다 jee·guh·bee uhp·ssum·nee·dah
– work at home	– 재택 근무합니다 jeh·tehk kkun·moo·hahm·nee·dah

▶ For business travel, see page 135.

Weather

| What's the forecast? | 일기 예보 들었어요? eel·gee yeh·boh
du·luht·ssuh·yo |

What *beautiful/terrible* weather!	날씨가 참 좋군요/안 좋군요! nahl·ssee·gah chahm joh·koon·nyo/ahn joh·koon·nyo
Will it be... tomorrow?	내일 날씨…까요? neh·eel nahl·ssee… kkah·yo
It's...	…날씨예요. …nahl·ssee·yeh·yo
– cool/warm	– 시원한/따뜻한 see·wuhn·hahn/ttah·ttu·tahn
– cold/hot	– 추운/더운 choo·oon/duh·oon
– rainy/sunny	– 비 오는/화창한 bee oh·nun/ hwah·chahng·hahn
– snowy/icy	– 눈 내리는/아주 추운 noon neh·lee·nun/ ah·joo choo·oon
Do I need *a jacket/an umbrella*?	잠바가/우산이 필요할까요? jahm·bah·gah/oo·sah·nee pee·lyo·hahl·kkah·yo

▶ For temperature, see page 165.

Romance

Essential

Would you like to go out for *a drink/dinner*?	술 한 잔/저녁 같이 하실래요? *sool hahn jahn/juh·nyuhk gah·chee hah·seel·leh·yo*
What are your plans for *tonight/tomorrow*?	오늘/내일 뭐 하세요? *oh·nul/neh·eel mwuh hah·seh·yo*
Can I have your number?	전화번호 주시겠어요? *juhn·hwah·buhn·hoh joo·see·geht·ssuh·yo*
Can I join you?	같이 앉아도 될까요? *gah·chee ahn·jah·doh dwehl·kkah·yo*

Can I get you a drink?	마실 거 갖다 드릴까요? mah·seel kkuh gaht·ttah du·leel·kkah·yo
I *like/love* you.	좋아해요/사랑해요. joh·ah·heh·yo/ sah·lahng·heh·yo

Making Plans

Would you like to go out for…?	…같이 하실래요? …gah·chee hah·seel·leh·yo
– coffee	– 커피 한 잔 kuh·pee hahn jahn
– a drink	– 술 한 잔 sool hahn jahn
– dinner	– 저녁 juh·nyuhk
What are your plans for…?	…무슨 계획 있으세요? …moo·sun geh·hwehk eet·ssu·seh·yo
– today	– 오늘 oh·nul
– tonight	– 오늘밤 oh·nul·ppahm
– tomorrow	– 내일 neh·eel
– this weekend	– 이번 주말 ee·buhn tzoo·mahl
Where would you like to go?	어디 가실래요? uh·dee gah·seel·leh·yo
I'd like to go to…	…가고 싶어요. …gah·goh see·puh·yo
Do you like…?	…좋아하세요? …joh·ah·hah·seh·yo
Can I have your *number/e-mail*?	전화번호/이메일 주소 주시겠어요? *juhn·hwah·buhn·hoh/ee·meh·eel joo·soh* joo·see·geht·ssuh·yo

▶ For e-mail and phone, see page 50.

Pick-up [Chat-up] Lines

Can I join you?	같이 앉아도 될까요? gah·chee ahn·jah·doh dwehl·kkah·yo

| You're very attractive. | 정말 매력적이세요 juhng·mahl meh·lyuhk·tzuh·gee·seh·yo |
| Let's go somewhere quieter. | 더 조용한 곳으로 가요. duh joh·yong·hahn goh·su·loh gah·yo. |

Accepting and Rejecting

I'd love to.	좋아요. joh·ah·yo
Where should we meet?	어디서 만날까요? uh·dee·suh mahn·nahl·kkah·yo
I'll meet you at *the bar/your hotel*.	바에서/호텔에서 뵐게요. *bah·eh·suh/ hoh·teh·leh·suh* bwehl·kkeh·yo
I'll come by at...	…시에 들를게요. …*see·eh* dul·lul·kkeh·yo

▶ For time, see page 161.

I'm busy.	저 바빠요. juh bah·ppah·yo
I'm not interested.	관심 없어요. gwahn·seem uhp·ssuh·yo
Leave me alone.	혼자 있고 싶어요. hohn·jah eet·kkoh see·puh·yo
Stop bothering me!	이제 그만하세요! ee·jeh gu·mahn·hah·seh·yo

Getting Physical

Can I *hug/kiss* you?	안아도/키스해도 될까요? *ah·nah·doh/ kee·ssu*·heh·doh dwehl·kkah·yo
Yes.	네. neh
No.	아니요. ah·nee·yo
Stop!	그만해요! gu·mahn·heh·yo
I *like/love* you.	좋아해요/사랑해요. joh·ah·heh·yo/ sah·lahng·heh·yo

Sexual Preferences

Are you gay?   동성연애자세요?
                 dohng·suhng·yuh·neh·jah·seh·yo

I'm gay.   저는 동성연애자예요. juh·nun
                 dohng·suhng·yuh·neh·jah·yeh·yo

Do you like *men/*   남자/여자 좋아하세요? *nahm·jah/yuh·jah*
women?   joh·ah·hah·seh·yo

▼ Fun

Essential

Where's the tourist information office?	관광 안내소가 어디 있습니까? gwahn·gwahng ahn·neh·soh·gah uh·dee eet·ssum·nee·kkah
What are the main attractions?	주요 볼 거리가 무엇입니까? joo·yo bohl kkuh·lee·gah moo·uh·seem·nee·kkah
Do you have tours in English?	영어 투어 있습니까? yuhng·uh too·uh eet·ssum·nee·kkah
Can I have a *map/ guide*?	지도/안내서 하나 주시겠습니까? *jee·doh/ahn·neh·suh* hah·nah joo·see·geht·ssum·nee·kkah

Tourist Information Office

Do you have information on...?	…에 대한 안내 있습니까? ...eh deh·hahn ahn·neh eet·ssum·nee·kkah
Can you recommend...?	…추천해 주시겠습니까? ...choo·chuhn·heh joo·see·geht·ssum·nee·kkah
– a boat trip	– 보트 관광 하나 boh·tu gwahn·gwahng hah·nah
– an excursion to...	– …로 유람 코스 하나 ...loh yoo·lahm koh·su hah·nah
– a sightseeing tour	– 관광 코스 하나 gwahn·gwahng koh·su hah·nah

i 한국 관광 공사 **hahn·gook gwahn·gwahng gohng·sah** (Korean National Tourism Organization, KNTO) provides a wealth of information for travelers online and at 관광 안내 전시관 **gwahn·gwahng ahn·neh juhn·see·gwahn** (Tourist Information Centers, TIC). Free internet access is also available at KNTO TICs, as are brochures, maps and other details in print. For 24-hour travel information in English, dial 1330 in Seoul; if calling from a cell phone or from outside of the city, dial the region's area code first.

▶ For useful websites, see page 166.

Tours

I'd like to go on the tour to…	…로 투어 가고 싶습니다. …loh too·uh gah·goh seep·ssum·nee·dah
When's the next tour?	다음 투어는 언제입니까? dah·um too·uh·nun uhn·jeh·eem·nee·kkah
Are there tours in English?	영어로 하는 투어 있습니까? yuhng·uh·loh hah·nun too·uh eet·ssum·nee·kkah
Is there an English *guide book/audio guide*?	영어 안내책자/음성안내 있습니까? yuhng·uh *ahn·neh·chehk·tzah/ um·suhng·ahn·neh* eet·ssum·nee·kkah
I'd like to see…	…보고 싶습니다. …boh·goh seep·ssum·nee·dah
Can we stop here…?	…여기 멈출 수 있습니까? …yuh·gee muhm·chool ssoo eet·ssum·nee·kkah
– to take photos	– 사진 찍고 싶은데 sah·jeen tzeek·kkoh see·pun·deh
– for souvenirs	– 기념품 사고 싶은데 gee·nyuhm·poom sah·goh see·pun·deh
– for the restrooms [toilets]	– 화장실 가고 싶은데 hwah·jahng·seel gah·goh see·pun·deh
Can we look around?	둘러봐도 됩니까? dool·luh·bwah·doh dwehm·nee·kkah
Is it handicapped [disabled]-accessible?	장애인도 구경할 수 있습니까? jahng·eh·een·doh goo·gyuhng·hahl ssoo eet·ssum·nee·kkah

▶ For ticketing, see page 21.

Sights

Where's…?	…어디 있습니까? …uh·dee eet·ssum·nee·kkah
– the botanical garden	– 식물원 seeng·moo·lwuhn
– the downtown area	– 중심가 joong·seem·gah
– the fountain	– 분수 boon·soo
– the library	– 도서관 doh·suh·gwahn
– the market	– 시장 see·jahng
– the (war) memorial	– (전쟁) 기념관 (juhn·jehng) gee·nyuhm·gwahn
– the museum	– 박물관 bahng·mool·gwahn
– the opera house	– 오페라하우스 oh·peh·lah hah·oo·su
– the palace	– 궁 goong
– the park	– 공원 gohng·wuhn
– the shopping area	– 상가 sahng·gah
– the theater	– 극장 guk·tzahng

Can you show me on the map?	지도에서 보여 주시겠습니까? jee·doh·eh·suh boh·yuh joo·see·geht·ssum·nee·kkah

▶ For directions, see page 36.

Impressions

It's beautiful.	아름다워요. ah·lum·dahp·wuh·yo
It's interesting.	흥미로워요. hung·mee·loh·wuh·yo
It's romantic.	낭만적이에요. nahng·mahn·juh·gee·eh·yo
It's strange.	이상해요. ee·sahng·heh·yo
It's terrible.	끔찍해요. kkum·tzee·keh·yo
It's ugly.	못생겼어요. moht·ssehng·gyuht·ssuh·yo
I (don't) like it.	마음에 (안) 들어요. mah·u·meh (ahn) du·luh·yo

Religion

Where's...?	…어디 있습니까? ...uh·dee eet·ssum·nee·kkah
– the cathedral	– 성당 suhng·dahng
– the *Catholic/ Protestant* church	– 카톨릭/개신교 교회 *kah·tohl·leek/ geh·seen·gyo* gyo·hweh
– the mosque	– 회교 사원 hweh·gyo sah·wuhn
– the shrine	– 사당 sah·dahng
– the temple	– 절 juhl
What time is *mass/ the service*?	미사는/예배는 언제입니까? *mee·sah·nun/yeh·beh·nun* uhn·jeh·eem·nee·kkah

Essential

Where's the *market/ mall [shopping centre]*?	시장/상가 어디 있습니까? *see·jahng/ sahng·gah* uh·dee eet·ssum·nee·kkah
I'm just looking.	그냥 둘러보는 중입니다. gu·nyahng dool·luh·boh·nun joong·eem·nee·dah
Can you help me?	도와주시겠습니까? doh·wah·joo·see·geht·ssum·nee·kkah
I'm being helped.	다른 분이 도와주고 계십니다. dah·lun boo·nee doh·wah·joo·goh geh·seem·nee·dah
How much?	얼마입니까? uhl·mah·eem·nee·kkah
That one, please.	저거 주세요. juh·guh joo·seh·yo
That's all.	다 됐습니다. dah dweht·ssum·nee·dah
Where can I pay?	어디서 계산합니까? uh·dee·suh geh·sahn·hahm·nee·kkah
I'll pay *in cash/by credit card*.	현금으로/신용카드로 지불하겠습니다. *hyuhn·gu·mu·loh/see·nyong·kah·du·loh* jee·bool·hah·geht·ssum·nee·dah
A receipt, please.	영수증 주세요. yuhng·soo·jung joo·seh·yo

Stores

Where's…?	…어디 있습니까? …uh·dee eet·ssum·nee·kkah
– the antiques store	– 골동품 가게 gohl·ttohng·poom kkah·geh
– the bakery	– 제과점 jeh·gwah·juhm
– the bank	– 은행 un·hehng
– the bookstore	– 서점 suh·juhm

Where's...?	…어디 있습니까? …uh·dee eet·ssum·nee·kkah
– the camera store	– 카메라 가게 kah·meh·lah kkah·geh
– the clothing store	– 옷가게 oht·kkah·kkeh
– the department store	– 백화점 beh·kwah·juhm
– the duty-free shop	– 면세점 myuhn·seh·juhm
– the florist	– 꽃집 kkoht·tzeep
– the gift shop	– 선물 가게 suhn·mool kkah·geh
– the hardware store	– 철물점 chul·mool·juhm
– the health food store	– 건강 식품점 guhn·gahng seek·poom·juhm
– the jeweler	– 보석상 boh·suhk·ssahng
– the liquor store [off-licence]	– 주류 판매점 joo·lyoo pahn·meh·juhm
– the market	– 시장 see·jahng
– the music store	– 음반 가게 um·bahn kkah·geh
– the pharmacy [chemist]	– 약국 yahk·kkook
– the produce [grocery] store	– 식료품점 seeng·nyo·poom·juhm
– the shoe store	– 신발 가게 seen·bahl kkah·geh
– the shopping mall [shopping centre]	– 상가 sahng·gah
– the souvenir store	– 기념품 가게 gee·nyuhm·poom kkah·geh
– the supermarket	– 슈퍼마켓 syoo·puh·mah·keht
– the tobacconist	– 담배 가게 dahm·beh kkah·geh
– the toy store	– 장난감 가게 jahng·nahn·kkahm kkah·geh

Services

Can you recommend…?	…추천해 주시겠습니까? …choo·chuhn·heh joo·see·geht·ssum·nee·kkah
– a barber	– 이발소 ee·bahl·soh
– a dry cleaner	– 세탁소 seh·tahk·ssoh
– a hairstylist	– 미용실 mee·yong·seel
– a laundromat [launderette]	– 빨래방 ppahl·leh·bahng
– a spa	– 사우나 ssah·oo·nah
– a travel agency	– 여행사 yuh·hehng·sah
Can you…this?	이거…주시겠습니까? ee·guh… joo·see·geht·ssum·nee·kkah
– alter	– 수선해 soo·suhn·heh
– clean	– 세탁해 seh·tah·keh
– fix [mend]	– 고쳐 goh·chuh
– press	– 다림질해 dah·leem·jeel·heh
When will it be ready?	언제 다 됩니까? uhn·jeh dah dwehm·nee·kkah

Spa

I'd like…	… 해 주세요. …heh joo·seh·yo
– an eyebrow wax	– 눈썹 제모 noon·ssuhp jeh·moh
– a facial	– 얼굴 마사지 uhl·gool mah·ssah·jee
– a *manicure/ pedicure*	– 매니큐어/페디큐어 meh·nee·kyoo·uh/ peh·dee·kyoo·uh
– a (sports) massage	– (스포츠) 마사지 (su·poh·chu) mah·ssah·jee
Do you do acupuncture?	침 놓아요? cheem noh·ah·yo
Do you have a sauna?	사우나 있어요? ssah·oo·nah eet·ssuh·yo

Hair Salon

I'd like…	… 주세요. …joo·seh·yo
– an appointment for *today/tomorrow*	– 오늘/내일 예약해 *oh·nul/neh·eel* yeh·yah·keh
– some *color/ highlights*	– 염색해/브리지해 yuhm·seh·keh/ bu·leet·tzee·heh
– my hair *styled/ blow-dried*	– 머리 해/드라이해 muh·lee *heh/ du·lah·ee·heh*
– a haircut	– 머리 잘라 muh·lee jahl·lah
– a trim	– 다듬어 dah·du·muh
Not too short.	너무 짧게 말고요. nuh·moo tzahl·kkeh mahl·goh·yo
Shorter here.	여기 더 짧게 해 주세요. yuh·gee duh tzahl·kkeh heh joo·seh·yo

Sales Help

When do you *open/close*?	언제 문 엽니까/닫습니까? uhn·jeh moon yuhm·nee·kkah/daht·ssum·nee·kkah
Where's…?	…어디 있습니까? …uh·dee eet·ssum·nee·kkah
– the cashier	– 계산대 geh·sahn·deh
– the escalator	– 에스컬레이터 eh·su·kuhl·leh·ee·tuh
– the elevator [lift]	– 엘리베이터 ehl·lee·beh·ee·tuh
– the fitting room	– 탈의실 tah·lee·seel
– the store directory	– 상가 안내 sahng·gah ahn·neh
Can you help me?	도와주시겠습니까? doh·wah·joo·see·geht·ssum·nee·kkah
I'm just looking.	그냥 둘러보는 중입니다. gu·nyahng dool·luh·boh·nun joong·eem·nee·dah
I'm being helped.	다른 분이 도와주고 계십니다. dah·lun boo·nee doh·wah·joo·goh gyeh·seem·nee·dah
Do you have…?	…있습니까? …eet·ssum·nee·kkah
Can you show me…?	…보여 주시겠습니까? …boh·yuh joo·see·geht·ssum·nee·kkah
Can you *ship/wrap* it?	배달해/포장해 주시겠습니까? beh·dahl·heh/poh·jahng·heh joo·see·geht·ssum·nee·kkah
How much?	얼마입니까? uhl·mah·eem·nee·kkah
That's all.	다 됐습니다. dah dweht·ssum·nee·dah

▶ For clothing items, see page 122.

▶ For food items, see page 82.

▶ For souvenirs, see page 118.

You May Hear...

뭘 도와드릴까요? mwuhl doh·wah·du·leel·kkah·yo	Can I help you?
무엇을 원하십니까? moo·uh·sul wuhn·hah·seem·nee·kkah	What would you like?
더 필요한 거 없으십니까? duh pee·lyo·hahn guh uhp·ssu·seem·nee·kkah	Anything else?

You May See...

영업 중/영업 끝 yuhng·uhp tzoong/ yuhng·uhp kkut	open/closed
계산대 geh·sahn·deh	cashier
현금만 받습니다 hyuhn·gum·mahn baht·ssum·nee·dah	cash only
신용카드 받습니다 see·nyong·kah·du baht·ssum·nee·dah	credit cards accepted
입구/출구 eep·kkoo/chool·goo	entrance/exit

Preferences

I'd like something...	…거 주세요. ...guh joo·seh·yo
– cheap/expensive	– 싼/비싼 ssahn/bee·ssahn
– larger/smaller	– 더 큰/더 작은 duh kun/duh jah·gun
– nicer	– 더 좋은 duh joh·un
– from this region	– 이 지방 ee jee·bahng
Around...Won.	…원 정도. ...wuhn juhng·doh
Can you show me *this/that*?	이거/저거 보여 주세요? *ee·guh/juh·guh* boh·yuh joo·seh·yo

Decisions

That's not quite what I want.	그건 제가 원하는 게 아니에요. gu·guhn jeh·gah wuhn·hah·nun geh ah·nee·eh·yo
No, I don't like it.	아니요, 마음에 안 들어요. ah·nee·yo mah·u·meh ahn du·luh·yo
It's too expensive.	너무 비싸요. nuh·moo bee·ssah·yo
I have to think about it.	생각해 봐야겠어요. sehng·gah·keh bwah·yah ·geht·ssuh·yo
I'll take it.	이걸로 주세요. ee·guhl·loh joo·seh·yo

Bargaining

That's too much.	너무 비싼데요. nuh·moo bee·ssahn·deh·yo
I'll give you...	…드릴게요. ...du·leel·kkeh·yo
Can you give me a discount?	깎아 주시겠어요? kkah·kkah joo·see·geht·ssuh·yo

▶ For numbers, see page 159.

Paying

How much?	얼마예요? uhl·mah·yeh·yo
I'll pay...	…낼게요. ...nehl·kkeh·yo
– in cash	– 현금으로 hyuhn·gu·mu·loh
– by credit card	– 신용카드로 see·nyong·kah·du·loh
– by traveler's check [cheque]	– 여행자 수표로 yuh·hehng·jah soo·pyo·loh
A receipt, please.	영수증 주세요. yuhng·soo·jung joo·seh·yo

i Credit and debit cards are accepted at a growing number of stores, restaurants and hotels. However, many vendors still take cash only. Though traveler's checks may be an accepted form of payment at large establishments, it's best to have some cash handy.

A sales tax or value-added tax (VAT) of 10% is charged on most products and services purchased. This tax is included in the retail price.

You May Hear...

어떻게 계산하시겠습니까? uh·ttuh·keh geh·sahn·hah·see·geht·ssum·nee·kkah	How are you paying?
신용카드 결제가 안 됐습니다. see·nyong·kah·du gyuhl·tzeh·gah ahn dweht·ssum·nee·dah	Your credit card has been declined.
신분증 보여 주십시오. seen·boon·tzung boh·yuh joo·seep·ssee·oh	ID, please.
현금만 받습니다. hyuhn·gum·mahn baht·ssum·nee·dah	Cash only, please.

Complaints

I'd like...	...주세요. ...joo·seh·yo
– to exchange this	– 이거 교환해 ee·guh gyo·hwahn·heh
– a refund	– 환불해 hwahn·bool·heh
– to see the manager	– 매니저 불러 meh·nee·juh bool·luh

Souvenirs

hanbok (traditional Korean clothing)	한복 hahn·bohk
handicrafts	수공예품 soo·gohng·yeh·poom
doll	인형 een·hyuhng
electronics	전자제품 juhn·jah·jeh·poom
embroidery	자수품 jah·soo·poom
key ring	열쇠고리 yuhl·ssweh·goh·lee

jar of kimchi	김치 한 병 geem·chee hahn byuhng
postcard	엽서 yuhp·ssuh
pottery	도자기 doh·jah·gee
T-shirt	티셔츠 tee·syuh·chu
Can I see *this/that*?	이거/저거 볼 수 있습니까? *ee·guh/ juh·guh* bohl ssoo eet·ssum·nee·kkah
It's in the *window/ display case.*	진열창에/진열장에 있습니다. *jee·nyuhl·chahng·eh/jee·nyuhl·tzahng·eh* eet·ssum·nee·dah
I'd like...	…주세요. ...joo·seh·yo
– a battery	– 건전지 guhn·juhn·jee
– a bracelet	– 팔찌 pahl·tzee
– a brooch	– 브로치 bu·loh·chee
– a clock	– 시계 see·geh
– earrings	– 귀걸이 gwih·guh·lee
– a necklace	– 목걸이 mohk·kkuh·lee
– a ring	– 반지 bahn·jee
– a watch	– 손목시계 sohn·mohk·ssee·geh

I'd like...	···주세요. ...joo·seh·yo
– crystal	– 수정 soo·juhng
– cut glass	– 세공 유리 seh·gohng yoo·lee
– diamonds	– 다이아몬드 dah·ee·ah·mohn·du
– *white/yellow* gold	– 백금/ 황금 behk·kkum/hwahng·gum
– pearls	– 진주 jeen·joo
– pewter	– 백랍 behng·nahp
– platinum	– 백금 behk·kkum
– sterling silver	– 순은 soo·nun
Is this real?	이거 진품입니까? ee·guh jeen·poo·meem·nee·kkah
Is there a certificate for it?	보증서가 있습니까? boh·jung·suh·gah eet·ssum·nee·kkah
Can you engrave it?	새길 수 있습니까? seh·geel ssoo eet·ssum·nee·kkah

 인사동 **een·sah·dohng** (Insa-dong) is a favorite outdoor shopping area in Seoul, featuring all kinds of souvenirs, arts and crafts and antiques. Most of the Insa-dong shops sell traditional products, such as pottery, calligraphy, jewelry, books, woodcrafts and papercrafts. Be sure items are labeled "Made in Korea" if you want to purchase a locally made product. Insa-dong also offers the largest collection of antiques in South Korea. For tourists who would like to bring a taste of Korea home, kimchi and ginseng tea are popular food items that travel well.

Shopping malls and department stores are fixtures of most Korean cities. Clothing, jewelry, sports, toy and other retailers sell imported goods as well as local products. Some shopping malls and large stores feature food courts, playgrounds and other leisure facilities.

Antiques

How old is it?	이거 얼마나 됐습니까? ee·guh uhl·mah·nah dweht·ssum·nee·kkah
Do I have to fill out any forms?	작성해야 될 서류가 있습니까? jahk·ssuhng·heh·yah dwehl suh·lyoo·gah eet·ssum·nee·kkah
Is there a certificate of authenticity?	감정서 있습니까? gahm·juhng·suh eet·ssum·nee·kkah

Clothing

I'd like…	…주세요. …joo·seh·yo
Can I try this on?	입어봐도 되요? ee·buh·bwah·doh dweh·yo
It doesn't fit.	맞지 않아요. maht·tzee ah·nah·yo
It's too…	너무… nuh·moo…
– big/small	– 커요/작아요 kuh·yo/jah·gah·yo
– short/long	– 짧아요/길어요 tzal·bah·yo/gee·luh·yo
– tight/loose	– 껴요/헐렁해요 kkyuh·yo/huhl·luhng·heh·yo
Do you have this in size…?	이거…사이즈 있어요? ee·guh…ssah·ee·ju eet·ssuh·yo
Do you have this in a *bigger/smaller* size?	이거 더 큰/작은 사이즈 어요? ee·guh duh kun/jah·gun ssah·ee·ju eet·ssuh·yo

▶ For numbers, see page 159.

You May See…

신사복 seen·sah·bohk	men's
숙녀복 soong·nyuh·bohk	women's
아동복 ah·dohng·bohk	children's

Color

I'd like something…	…색으로 주세요. …seh·gu·loh joo·seh·yo
– beige	– 베이지 beh·ee·jee
– black	– 검은 guh·mun
– blue	– 파란 pah·lahn
– brown	– 갈 gahl
– green	– 초록 choh·rohk
– gray	– 회 hweh
– orange	– 오렌지 oh·lehn·jee
– pink	– 분홍 boon·hohng
– purple	– 보라 boh·lah
– red	– 빨간 ppahl·gahn
– white	– 흰 heen
– yellow	– 노란 noh·lahn

Clothes and Accessories

backpack	배낭 beh·nahng
belt	벨트 behl·tu
bikini	비키니 bee·kee·nee
blouse	블라우스 bu·lah·oo·su
bra	브래지어 bu·leh·jee·uh
briefs [underpants]	팬티 pehn·tee
coat	코트 koh·tu
dress	드레스 du·leh·su
dress shirt	와이셔츠 wah·ee·syuh·chu
hat	모자 moh·jah
jacket	재킷 jeh·keet
jeans	청바지 chuhng·bah·jee

pajamas [pyjamas]	잠옷 jah·moht
pants [trousers]	바지 bah·jee
pantyhose [tights]	팬티스타킹 pehn·tee·su·tah·keeng
purse [handbag]	핸드백 hehn·du·behk
raincoat	비옷 bee·oht
scarf	스카프 su·kah·pu
shirt	셔츠 syuh·chu
shorts	반바지 bahn·bah·jee
skirt	치마 chee·mah
socks	양말 yahng·mahl
suit	양복 yahng·bohk
sunglasses	선글라스 ssuhn·gul·lah·su
sweater	스웨터 su·weh·tuh
sweatshirt	추리닝 choo·lee·neeng
swimsuit	수영복 soo·yuhng·bohk
T-shirt	티셔츠 tee·syuh·chu
tie	넥타이 nehk·tah·ee
underwear	속옷 soh·goht

Fabric

I'd like…	…주세요. …joo·seh·yo
– cotton	– 면 myuhn
– denim	– 데님 deh·neem
– lace	– 레이스 leh·ee·su
– leather	– 가죽 gah·jook
– linen	– 마 mah
– silk	– 실크 sseel·ku
– wool	– 모 moh

Is it machine washable?	세탁기로 빨 수 있나요? seh·tahk·kkee·loh ppahl ssoo een·nah·yo

Shoes

I'd like...	…주세요. ...joo·seh·yo
– high-heels/flats	– 하이힐/낮은 구두 hah·ee·heel/nah·jun goo·doo
– boots	– 부츠 boo·chu
– flip-flops	– 쪼리 tzoh·lee
– hiking boots	– 등산화 dung·sahn·hwah
– loafers	– 끈 없는 편한 구두 kkun uhm·nun pyuhn·hahn goo·doo
– sandals	– 샌들 ssehn·dul
– shoes	– 신발 seen·bahl
– slippers	– 슬리퍼 sul·lee·puh
– sneakers	– 운동화 oon·dohng·hwah
Size...	…사이즈. ...ssah·ee·ju

▶ For numbers, see page 159.

Sizes

woman's/man's	여자/남자 yuh·jah/nahm·jah
small	소, 55♀/90♂ soh oh·oh♀/goo·seep♂
medium	중, 66♀/95♂ joong yoong·nyook♀/ goo·see·boh♂
large	대, 77♀/100♂ deh cheel·cheel♀/behk♂
extra large	특대, 88♀/105♂ tuk·tteh pahl·pahl♀/ beh·goh♂
extra extra large	특특대, 110♂ tuk·tuk·tteh behk seep♂

Newsstand and Tobacconist

Do you sell English-language newspapers?	영어 신문 파세요? yuhng·uh seen·moon pah·seh·yo
I'd like…	…주세요. …joo·seh·yo
– candy [sweets]	– 사탕 sah·tahng
– chewing gum	– 껌 kkuhm
– a *pack/carton* of cigarettes	– 담배 한 갑/보루 dahm·beh hahn *gahp/boh·loo*
– a lighter	– 라이터 lah·ee·tuh
– a magazine	– 잡지 jahp·tzee
– matches	– 성냥 suhng·nyahng
– a newspaper	– 신문 seen·moon
– a postcard	– 엽서 yuhp·ssuh
– a *road/town* map of…	– …도로/시내 지도 …*doh·roh/see·neh* jee·doh

Photography

I'd like *digital/disposable* camera.	디지털/일회용 카메라 주세요. *dee·jee·tuhl/eel·hweh·yong* kah·meh·lah joo·seh·yo
I'd like…	…주세요. …joo·seh·yo
– a battery	– 건전지 guhn·juhn·jee
– digital prints	– 디지털 프린트 dee·jee·tuhl pu·leen·tu
– a memory card	– 메모리카드 meh·moh·lee·kah·du
Can I print digital photos here?	여기서 디지털 사진 뽑을 수 있어요? yuh·gee·suh dee·gee·tuhl sah·jeen ppoh·bul ssoo eet·ssuh·yo

Sports and Leisure

Essential

When's the game?	경기 언제 합니까? gyuhng·gee uhn·jeh hahm·nee·kkah
Where's…?	…어디 있습니까? …uh·dee eet·ssum·nee·kkah
– the beach	– 해변 heh·byuhn
– the park	– 공원 kohng·wuhn
– the pool	– 수영장 soo·yuhng·jahng
Is it safe to swim here?	여기 수영하기에 안전합니까? yuh·gee soo·yuhng·hah·gee·eh ahn·juhn·hahm·nee·kkah
Can I rent [hire] golf clubs?	골프채 빌릴 수 있습니까? gohl·pu·cheh beel·leel ssoo eet·ssum·nee·kkah
How much per hour?	시간당 얼마입니까? see·gahn·dahng uhl·mah·eem·nee·kkah
How far is it to…?	…까지 얼마나 멉니까? …kkah·jee uhl·mah·nah muhm·nee·kkah
Show me on the map, please.	지도에서 보여 주십시오. jee·doh·eh·suh boh·yuh joo·seep·ssee·yo

Spectator Sports ——————

When's…*game/match*?	…경기 언제 합니까? …gyuhng·gee uhn·jeh·hahm·nee·kkah
– the baseball	– 야구 yah·goo
– the basketball	– 농구 nohng·goo
– the boxing	– 권투 gwuhn·too
– the golf	– 골프 gohl·pu
– the Korean wrestling	– 씨름 ssee·lum

– the hockey	– 하키 hah·kee
– the soccer [football]	– 축구 chook·kkoo
– the tennis	– 테니스 teh·nee·su
– the volleyball	– 배구 beh·goo
Who's playing?	어느 팀이 경기합니까? uh·nu tee·mee gyuhng·gee hahm·nee·kkah
Where's the *racetrack/stadium*?	경마장/경기장 어디 있습니까? *gyuhng·mah·jahng/gyuhng·gee·jahng* uh·dee eet·ssum·nee·kkah
Where can I place a bet?	어디서 돈을 걸 수 있습니까? uh·dee·suh doh·nul guhl ssoo eet·ssum·nee·kkah

▶ For ticketing, see page 21.

i In addition to the traditional martial arts of 태권도 **teh·kkwuhn·doh** (taekwondo) and 태견 **teh·kkyuhn** (taekkyeon), practically every classic sport is played in Korea. 씨름 **ssee·lum** (traditional Korean wrestling) can be seen at tournaments held all over the country and is often accompanied by traditional folk music and dance.

Participating

Where *is/are*…?	…어디 있습니까? …uh·dee eet·ssum·nee·kkah
– the golf course	– 골프장 gohl·pu·jahng
– the gym	– 헬스클럽 hehl·ssu·kul·luhp
– the park	– 공원 gohng·wuhn
– the tennis courts	– 테니스장 teh·nee·su·jahng
How much per…?	…에 얼마입니까? …eh uhl·mah eem·nee·kkah
– day	– 하루 hah·loo

How much per…?	…에 얼마입니까? …eh uhl·mah eem·nee·kkah
– hour	– 시간 see·gahn
– game	– 경기 gyuhng·gee
– round	– 라운드 lah·oon·du
Can I rent [hire]…?	…빌릴 수 있습니까? …beel·leel ssoo eet·ssum·nee·kkah
– clubs	– 골프채 gohl·pu·cheh
– equipment	– 장비 jahng·bee
– a racket	– 라켓 lah·keht

At the Beach/Pool

Where's the *beach/ pool*?	해변/수영장 어디 있습니까? *heh·byuhn/soo·yuhng·jahng* uh·dee eet·ssum·nee·kkah
Is there…?	…있습니까? …eet·ssum·nee·kkah
– a kiddie [paddling] pool	– 어린이 수영장 uh·lee·nee soo·yuhng·jahng
– an *indoor/outdoor* pool	– 실내/실외 수영장 *seel·neh/seel·weh* soo·yuhng·jahng
– a lifeguard	– 구조원 goo·joh·wuhn
Is it safe…?	…에 안전합니까? …eh ahn·juhn·hahm·nee·kkah
– to swim	– 수영하기 soo·yuhng·hah·gee
– to dive	– 다이빙하기 dah·ee·beeng·hah·gee
– for children	– 아이들 놀기 ah·ee·dul nohl·gee
I'd like to rent [hire]…	…빌리고 싶습니다. …beel·lee·goh seep·ssum·nee·dah
– a deck chair	– 접는 의자 juhm·nun u·jah
– diving equipment	– 스쿠버다이빙 장비 su·koo·buh·dah·ee·beeng jahng·bee

– a jet ski	– 제트스키 jeh·tu·su·kee
– a motorboat	– 모터보트 moh·tuh·boh·tu
– a rowboat	– 노 젓는 배 noh juhn·nun beh
– snorkeling equipment	– 잠수 장비 jahm·soo jahng·bee
– a towel	– 수건 soo·guhn
– an umbrella	– 비치 파라솔 bee·chee pah·lah·sohl
– water skis	– 수상스키 soo·sahng·su·kee
For…hours.	…시간 동안. …see·gahn ttohng·ahn

Winter Sports

A lift pass for a day, please.	하루 리프트 사용권 주세요. hah·loo lee·pu·tu sah·yong·kkwuhn joo·seh·yo
I'd like to rent [hire]…	…빌리고 싶어요. …beel·lee·goh see·puh·yo
– boots	– 부츠 boo·chu
– a helmet	– 헬멧 hehl·meht
– poles	– 폴대 pohl·tteh
– skis	– 스키 su·kee
– a snowboard	– 스노우보드 su·noh·oo·boh·du
– snowshoes	– 스노슈즈 su·noh·syoo·ju
These are too *big/ small*.	이건 너무 커요/작아요. ee·guhn nuh·moo *kuh·yo/jah·gah·yo*
Are there lessons?	강습 있어요? gahng·sup eet·ssuh·yo

In the Countryside

A map of…, please.	…지도 하나 주십시오. …jee·doh hah·nah joo·seep·ssee·yo
– this region	– 이 지역 ee jee·yuhk
– the walking routes	– 산책로 sahn·chehng·noh

A map of…, please.	…지도 하나 주십시오. …jee·doh hah·nah joo·seep·ssee·yo
– the bike routes	– 자전거 도로 jah·juhn·guh doh·loh
– the trails	– 등산로 dung·sahn·noh
Is it *easy/difficult*?	쉽습니까/어렵습니까? swihp·ssum·nee·kkah/uh·lyuhp·ssum·nee·kkah
Is it *far/steep*?	멉니까/가파릅니까? muhm·nee·kkah/gah·pah·lum·nee·kkah
How far is it to…?	…까지 얼마나 멉니까? …kkah·jee uhl·mah·nah muhm·nee·kkah
Show me on the map, please.	지도에서 보여주십시오. jee·doh·eh·suh boh·yuh·joo·seep·ssee·yo
I'm lost.	길을 잃어버렸습니다. gee·lul ee·luh·buh·lyuht·ssum·nee·dah
Where's…?	…어디 있습니까? …uh·dee eet·ssum·nee·kkah
– the bridge	– 다리 dah·lee
– the cave	– 동굴 dohng·gool
– the forest	– 숲 soop
– the hill	– 언덕 uhn·duhk
– the lake	– 호수 hoh·soo
– the mountain	– 산 sahn
– the nature preserve	– 자연 보호 지역 jah·yuhn boh·hoh jee·yuhk
– the overlook [viewpoint]	– 전망대 juhn·mahng·deh
– the park	– 공원 gohng·wuhn
– the path	– 산책로 sahn·chehng·noh
– the picnic area	– 피크닉 구역 pee·ku·neek kkoo·yuhk
– the river	– 강 gahng
– the sea	– 바다 bah·dah

– the spring	– 샘 sehm
– the waterfall	– 폭포 pohk·poh

Culture and Nightlife

Essential

What's there to do at night?	밤에 할 거 뭐 있습니까? bah·meh hahl kkuh mwuh eet·ssum·nee·kkah
Do you have a program of events?	행사 프로그램 있습니까? hehng·sah pu·loh·gu·lehm eet·ssum·nee·kkah
What's playing tonight?	오늘 밤에 뭐 있습니까? oh·nul bah·meh mwuh eet·ssum·nee·kkah
Where's…?	…어디 있습니까? …uh·dee eet·ssum·nee·kkah
– the downtown area	– 시내 see·neh
– the bar	– 바 bah
– the dance club	– 클럽 kul·luhp
Is there a cover charge?	입장료 있습니까? eep·tzahng·nyo eet·ssum·nee·kkah

Entertainment

Can you recommend…?	…추천해 주시겠습니까? …choo·chuhn·heh joo·see·geht·ssum·nee·kkah
– a traditional dance event	– 전통 춤 juhn·tohng choom
– a traditional music event	– 국악 공연 goo·gahk kkohng·yuhn
– an opera	– 오페라 oh·peh·lah

131

Can you recommend…?	…추천해 주시겠습니까? …choo·chuhn·heh joo·see·geht·ssum·nee·kkah
– a play	– 연극 yuhn·guk
When does it *start/end*?	언제 시작합니까? / 끝납니까? uhn·jeh see·jah·kahm·nee·kkah/kkun·nahm·nee·kkah
Where's…?	…어디 있습니까? …uh·dee eet·ssum·nee·kkah
– the concert hall	– 연주회장 yuhn·joo·hweh·jahng
– the opera house	– 오페라 하우스 oh·peh·lah hah·oo·su
– the theater	– 극장 guk·tzahng
What's the dress code?	옷은 어떻게 입어야 됩니까? oh·sun uh·ttuh·keh ee·buh·yah dwehm·nee·kkah
What's playing tonight?	오늘 밤에 뭐 있습니까? oh·nul bah·meh mwuh eet·ssum·nee·kkah

▶ For ticketing, see page 21.

Information on upcoming events can be found in two English-language newspapers, *The Korea Times* and *The Korea Herald*; your hotel concierge, the local tourist information office and the Korean National Tourism Organization (KNTO) and Korean Broadcasting Commission (KBS) websites can also provide entertainment details.

▶ For useful websites, see page 166.

You May Hear…

| 휴대폰 꺼 주시기 바랍니다. hyoo·deh·pohn kkuh joo·see·gee bah·lahm·nee·dah | Turn off your cell [mobile] phones, please. |

Nightlife ─────────────

What's there to do at night?	밤에 할 거 뭐 있습니까? bah·meh hahl kkuh mwuh eet·ssum·nee·kkah
Can you recommend…?	…추천해 주시겠습니까? …choo·chuhn·heh joo·see·geht·ssum·nee·kkah
– a bar	– 바 bah
– a casino	– 카지노 kah·jee·noh
– a dance club	– 클럽 kul·luhp
– a jazz club	– 재즈 클럽 tzeh·ju kul·luhp
– club with Korean music	– 한국 음악 나오는 클럽 hahn·goo gu·mahk nah·oh·nun kul·luhp
Is there live music?	생음악 있습니까? sehng·u·mahk eet·ssum·nee·kkah
How do I get there?	거기 어떻게 갑니까? guh·gee uh·ttuh·keh gahm·nee·kkah
Is there a cover charge?	입장료 있습니까? eep·tzahng·nyo eet·ssum·nee·kkah
Let's go dancing.	춤추러 갑시다. choom·choo·luh gahp·ssee·dah

▼ *Special Needs*

Business Travel

Essential

I'm here on business.	여기 일 때문에 왔습니다. yuh·gee eel tteh·moo·neh waht·ssum·nee·dah
Here's my business card.	여기 제 명함 있습니다. yuh·gee jeh myuhng·hahm eet·ssum·nee·dah
Can I have your card?	명함 하나 주시겠습니까? myuhng·hahm hah·nah joo·see·geht·ssum·nee·kkah
I have a meeting with...	…하고 약속이 있습니다. …hah·goh yahk·ssoh·gee eet·ssum·nee·dah
Where's...?	…어디 있습니까? …uh·dee eet·ssum·nee·kkah
– the business center	– 비즈니스 센터 bee·jee·nee·su sehn·tuh
– the convention hall	– 회의장 hweh·ee·jahng
– the meeting room	– 회의실 hweh·ee·seel

Business Communication

I'm here...	여기…왔습니다. yuh·gee…waht·ssum·nee·dah
– on business	– 일 때문에 eel tteh·moo·neh
– for a seminar	– 세미나 때문에 sseh·mee·nah tteh·moo·neh
– for a conference	– 컨퍼런스 때문에 kuhn·puh·luhn·su tteh·moo·neh
– for a meeting	– 회의 때문에 hweh·ee tteh·moo·neh
My name is...	제 이름은…입니다. jeh ee·lu·mun… eem·nee·dah
I have *a meeting/an appointment* with...	…하고 회의가/약속이 있습니다. …hah·goh *hweh·ee·gah/yahk·ssoh·gee* eet·ssum·nee·dah

I need an interpreter.	통역 불러 주십시오. tohng·yuhk bool·luh joo·seep·ssee·yo
You can reach me at the...Hotel.	···호텔로 연락 주십시오. ...hoh·tehl·loh yuhl·lahk joo·seep·ssee·yo
I'm here until...	···까지 있을 겁니다. ...kkah·jee eet·ssul·kkuhm·nee·dah
I need to...	···겠습니다. ...geht·ssum·nee·dah
– make a call	– 전화해야 juhn·hwah·heh·yah
– make a photocopy	– 복사해야 bohk·ssah·heh·yah
– send an e-mail	– 이메일을 보내야 ee·meh·ee·lul boh·neh·yah
– send a fax	– 팩스를 보내야 pehk·su·lul boh·neh·yah
– send a package (overnight)	– 소포를 (익일) 보내야 soh·poh·lul (ee·geel) boh·neh·yah
It was a pleasure to meet you.	만나서 반가웠습니다. mahn·nah·suh bahn·gah·wuht·ssum·nee·dah

▶ For internet and communications, see page 50.

> **i** When meeting and departing, it is customary for business
> people to shake hands, and bow to each other while
> shaking hands. Verbal communication is also important; it
> is customary to use the official business title of the person,
> instead of 씨 **ssee** (the equivalent of Mr., Mrs. or Miss). This
> is said following the person's surname. For example, one
> would address Mr. Smith, the CEO of a company, as 스미스
> 사장님 **su·mee·su sah·jahng·neem** (Smith CEO).

You May Hear...

예약하셨습니까? yeh·yah·kah·syuht·ssum·nee·kah	Do you have an appointment?
어느 분하고요? uh·nu boon·hah·goh·yo	With whom?
잠깐 기다려 주십시오. jahm·kkahn gee·dah·lyuh joo·seep·ssee·yo	One moment, please.

Travel with Children

Essential

Is there a discount for kids?	어린이 할인됩니까? uh·lee·nee hah·leen dwehm·nee·kkah
Can you recommend a babysitter?	애 봐줄 사람 하나 추천해 주시겠습니까? eh bwah·jool ssah·lahm hah·nah choo·chuhn·heh joo·see·geht·ssum·nee·kkah
Do you have a *child's seat*/*highchair*?	어린이용/높은 의자 있습니까? *uh·lee·nee·yong/noh·pun u·jah* eet·ssum·nee·kkah
Where can I change the baby?	기저귀 어디서 갈 수 있습니까? gee·juh·gwih uh·dee·suh gahl ssoo eet·ssum·nee·kkah

Fun with Kids

Can you recommend something for kids?	애들 위한 거 추천해 주시겠습니까? eh·dul wih·hahn guh choo·chuhn·heh joo·see·geht·ssum·nee·kkah
Where's…?	…어디 있습니까? …uh·dee eet·ssum·nee·kkah
– the amusement park	– 놀이 공원 noh·lee gohng·wuhn
– the arcade	– 오락실 oh·lahk·sseel
– the kiddie [paddling] pool	– 어린이 수영장 uh·lee·nee soo·yuhng·jahng
– the park	– 공원 gohng·wuhn
– the playground	– 놀이터 noh·lee·tuh
– the zoo	– 동물원 dohng·moo·lwuhn
Are kids allowed?	아이들도 들어갈 수 있습니까? ah·ee·dul·doh du·luh·gahl ssoo eet·ssum·nee·kkah
Is it safe for kids?	아이들에게 안전합니까? ah·ee·dul·eh·geh ahn·juhn·hahm·nee·kkah
Is it suitable for… year olds?	…살 짜리 아이에게 적절합니까? …sahl tzah·lee ah·ee·eh·geh juhk·tzuhl·hahm·nee·kkah

▶ For numbers, see page 159.

You May Hear…

귀여워라! gwih·yuh·wuh·lah	How cute!
얘 이름이 뭐예요? yeh ee·lu·mee mwuh·eh·yo	What's his/her name?
얘 몇 살이에요? yeh myuht ssah·lee·eh·yo	How old is he/she?

Basic Needs for Kids

Do you have …?	…있습니까? …eet·ssum·nee·kkah
– a baby bottle	– 젖병 juht·ppyuhng
– baby food	– 이유식 ee·yoo·seek
– baby wipes	– 아기용 물휴지 ah·gee·yong mool·hyoo·jee
– a car seat	– 카시트 kah·ssee·tu
– a children's menu	– 어린이 메뉴 uh·lee·nee·yong meh·nyoo

▶ For dining with kids, see page 64.

– a *child's seat/ highchair*	– 어린이용/높은 의자 *uh·lee·nee·yong/ noh·pun* u·jah
– a crib [child's cot]	– 아기용 침대 ah·gee·yong cheem·deh
– diapers [nappies]	– 기저귀 gee·juh·gwih
– formula [baby food]	– 이유식 ee·yoo·seek
– a pacifier [soother]	– 고무 젖꼭지 goh·moo juht·kkohk·tzee
– a stroller [pushchair]	– 유모차 yoo·moh·chah
Where can I *breastfeed/change* the baby?	어디서 수유할/기저귀 갈 수 있습니까? uh·dee·suh *soo·yoo·hahl/gee·juh·gwih gahl* ssoo eet·ssum·nee·kkah

Babysitting

Can you recommend a babysitter?	애 봐줄 사람 하나 추천해 주시겠습니까? eh bwah·jool ssah·lahm hah·nah choo·chuhn·heh joo·see·geht·ssum·nee·kkah
What's the charge?	비용이 어떻게 됩니까? bee·yong·ee uh·ttuh·keh dwehm·nee·kkah
I'll be back by...	…까지 돌아오겠습니다. ...kkah·jee doh·lah·oh·geht·ssum·nee·dah
I can be reached at...	… (으)로 연락 주십시오.* ...(u·)loh yuhl·lahk joo·seep·ssee·oh

Health and Emergency

Can you recommend a pediatrician?	소아과 의사 하나 추천해 주시겠습니까? soh·ah·kkwah u·sah hah·nah choo·chuhn·heh joo·see·geht·ssum·nee·kkah
My child is allergic to...	제 애는…알레르기가 있습니다. jeh eh·nun...ahl·leh·lu·gee·gah eet·ssum·nee·dah
My child is missing.	제 아이가 없어졌습니다. jeh ah·ee·gah uhp·ssuh·juht·ssum·nee·dah
Have you seen a *boy/girl*?	남자애/ 여자애 보셨습니까? *nahm·jah·eh/yuh·jah·eh* boh·syuht·ssum·nee·kkah

▶ For food items, see page 82.

▶ For health, see page 147.

▶ For police, see page 144.

---

* When the word ends in a consonant, use 으로 u·loh; when the word ends in a vowel, use 로 loh.

For the Disabled

Essential

Is there…?	…있습니까? …eet·ssum·nee·kkah
– access for the disabled	– 장애인이 이용할 수 jahng·eh·ee·nee ee·yong·hahl ssoo
– a wheelchair ramp	– 휠체어 진입로 wihl·cheh·uh jee·neem·noh
– a handicapped- [disabled-] accessible toilet	– 장애인용 화장실 jahng·eh·een·nyong hwah·jahng·seel
I need…	…필요합니다. …pee·lyo·hahm·nee·dah
– assistance	– 도움이 doh·oo·mee
– an elevator [a lift]	– 엘리베이터가 ehl·lee·beh·ee·tuh·gah
– a ground-floor room	– 일층방이 eel·chung·bahng·ee

Getting Help

I'm…	저는… juh·nun…
– disabled	– 장애인입니다 jahng·eh·ee·neem·nee·dah
– visually impaired	– 시각 장애인입니다 see·gahk jahng·eh·ee·neem·nee·dah
– hearing impaired	– 청각 장애인입니다 chuhng·gahk jahng·eh·ee·neem·nee·dah
– unable to walk far	– 멀리 걸을 수 없습니다 muhl·lee guh·lul ssoo uhp·ssum·nee·dah
– unable to use the stairs	– 계단을 이용할 수 없습니다 geh·dah·nul ee·yong·hahl ssoo uhp·ssum·nee·dah
Please speak louder.	더 크게 말씀해 주십시오. duh ku·geh mahl·ssum·heh joo·seep·ssee·oh

Can I bring my wheelchair?	제 휠체어를 가져 와도 됩니까? jeh wihl·cheh·uh·lul gah·juh wah·doh dwehm·nee·kkah
Are guide dogs permitted?	맹도견이 들어갈 수 있습니까? mehng·doh·gyuh·nee du·luh·gahl ssoo eet·ssum·nee·kkah
Can you help me?	도와주시겠습니까? doh·wah·joo·see·geht·ssum·nee·kkah
Please *open/hold* the door.	문 좀 열어/잡아 주십시오. moon johm *yuh·luh/jah·bah* joo·seep·ssee·oh

▼ Resources

Emergencies

Help!	도와주세요! doh·wah·joo·seh·yo
Go away!	저리 가세요! juh·lee gah·seh·yo
Stop, thief!	거기서. 도둑이야! guh·gee·suh doh·doo·gee·yah
Get a doctor!	의사 불러 주세요! u·sah bool·luh joo·seh·yo
Fire!	불이야! boo·lee·yah
I'm lost.	길을 잃어버렸어요. gee·lul ee·luh·buh·lyuht·ssuh·yo
Can you help me?	도와주시겠어요? doh·wah·joo·see·geht·ssuh·yo

Police

Call the police!	경찰 불러주세요! gyung·chahl bool·luh·joo·seh·yo
Where's the police station?	경찰서가 어디 있습니까? gyuhng·chahl·ssuh·gah uh·dee eet·ssum·nee·kkah
There was an accident.	사고 났습니다. sah·goh naht·ssum·nee·dah
There was an attack.	폭행 당했습니다. poh·kehng dahng·heht·ssum·nee·dah
My child is missing.	제 아이가 없어졌습니다. jeh ah·ee·gah uhp·ssuh·juht·ssum·nee·dah
I need an interpreter.	통역을 불러 주십시오. tohng·yuh·gul bool·luh joo·seep·ssee·yo

I need...	…해야겠습니다. …heh·yah·geht·ssum·nee·dah
– to contact my lawyer	– 제 변호사에게 연락 jeh byuhn·hoh·sah·eh·geh yuhl·lahk
– to make a phone call	– 전화 통화 juhn·hwah tohng·hwah
– to contact my consulate	– 영사관에 연락 yuhng·sah·gwah·neh yuhl·lahk
I'm innocent.	전 죄가 없습니다. juhn jweh·gah uhp·ssum·nee·dah

You May Hear...

신분증 좀 보여 주십시오. seen·boon·tzung johm boh·yuh joo·seep·ssee·oh	Your identification, please.
언제/어디서 일어난 일입니까? uhn·jeh/uh·dee·suh ee·luh·nahn nee·leem·nee·kkah	*When/Where* did it happen?
어떻게 생겼습니까? uh·ttuh·keh sehng·gyuht·ssum·nee·kkah	What does he/she look like?

Contact your consulate, ask the concierge at your hotel or ask the tourist information office for telephone numbers of the local ambulance, emergency services and police. For 24-hour non-emergency assistance in English, dial Korea Travel Phone: 1330 in Seoul; if calling from a cell phone or from outside of the city, dial the region's area code first.

Lost Property and Theft

I'd like to report...	…신고하고 싶습니다. …seen·goh·hah·goh seep·ssum·nee·dah
– a mugging	– 노상강도 noh·sahng·gahng·doh
– a rape	– 강간 gahng·gahn

I'd like to report...	···신고하고 싶습니다. ...seen·goh·hah·goh seep·ssum·nee·dah
– a theft	– 도난 doh·nahn
I was *mugged/ robbed*.	노상강도/도난 당했습니다. *noh·sahng·gahng·doh/doh·nahn* dahng·heht·ssum·nee·dahh
I lost my...	···잃어버렸습니다. ...ee·luh·buh·lyuht·ssum·nee·dah
My...*was/were* stolen.	제···도둑 맞았습니다.. je...doh·doong mah·jaht·ssum·nee·dah
– backpack	– 배낭 beh·nahng
– bicycle	– 자전거 jah·juhn·guh
– camera	– 카메라 kah·meh·lah
– (rental [hire]) car	– (렌터)카 (lehn·tuh) kah
– computer	– 컴퓨터 kuhm·pyoo·tuh
– credit card	– 신용카드 see·nyong·kah·du
– jewelry	– 보석 boh·suhk
– money	– 돈 dohn
– passport	– 여권 yuh·kkwuhn
– purse [handbag]	– 핸드백 hehn·du·behk
– traveler's checks [cheques]	– 여행자 수표 yuh·hehng·jah soo·pyo
– wallet	– 지갑 jee·gahp
I need a police report.	경찰 조서가 필요합니다. gyuhng·chahl joh·suh·gah pee·lyo·hahm·nee·dah

Health

Essential

I'm sick [ill].	제가 아픕니다. jeh·gah ah·pum·nee·dah
I need an English-speaking doctor.	영어 하는 의사가 필요합니다. yuhng·yuh hah·nun u·sah·gah pee·lyo·hahm·nee·dah
It hurts here.	여기가 아픕니다. yuh·gee·gah ah·pum·nee·dah
I have a stomachache.	배가 아픕니다. beh·gah ah·pum·nee·dah

Finding a Doctor

Can you recommend a *doctor/dentist*?	의사/치과의사 하나 추천해 주시겠습니까? u·sah/chee·kkwah·u·sah hah·nah choo·chuhn·heh joo·see·geht·ssum·nee·kkah
Can the doctor come here?	의사 선생님이 여기로 오실 수 있습니까? u·sah suhn·sehng·nee·mee yuh·gee·loh oh·seel ssoo eet·ssum·nee·kkah
I need an English-speaking doctor.	영어 하는 의사가 필요합니다. yuhng·yuh hah·nun u·sah·gah pee·lyo·hahm·nee·dah
What are the office hours?	진료 시간이 언제입니까? jeel·lyo see·gah·nee uhn·jeh·eem·nee·kkah
I'd like an appointment for…	…예약하고 싶습니다. …yeh·yah·kah·goh seep·ssum·nee·dah
– today	– 오늘 oh·nul
– tomorrow	– 내일 neh·eel
– as soon as possible	– 가능한 한 빨리 gah·nung·hahn hahn ppahl·lee
It's urgent.	급합니다. gu·pahm·nee·dah

Symptoms

I'm bleeding.	피가 납니다. pee·gah nahm·nee·dah
I'm constipated.	변비 걸렸습니다. byuhn·bee gyuhl·lyuht·ssum·nee·dah
I'm dizzy.	어지럽습니다 uh·jee·ruhp·sum·nee·dah
I'm nauseous.	토할 거 같습니다. toh·hahl kkuh gaht·ssum·nee·dah
I'm vomiting.	자꾸 토합니다. jah·kkoo toh·hahm·nee·dah
It hurts here.	여기가 아픕니다. yuh·gee·gah ah·pum·nee·dah
I sprained my *ankle/ wrist*.	발목을/손목을 삐었습니다. *bahl·moh·gul/ sohn·moh·gul* ppee·uht·ssum·nee·dah
I have...	…있습니다. …eet·ssum·nee·dah
– an allergic reaction	– 알레르기 반응 ahl·leh·lu·gee bah·nung
– chest pain	– 가슴에 통증 gah·su·meh tohng·tzung
– congestion	– 충혈 choong·hyuhl
– cramps	– 복통 bohk·tohng
– diarrhea	– 설사 suhl·ssah
– an earache	– 귀에 통증 gwih·eh tohng·tzung
– a fever	– 열 yuhl
– pain	– 통증 tohng·tzung
– a rash	– 두드러기 doo·du·luh·gee
– some swelling	– 좀 부어 johm boo·uh
– a sore throat	– 목에 통증 moh·geh tohng·tzung
– a stomachache	– 복통 bohk·tohng
– sunstroke	– 일사병 eel·ssah·ppyuhng

| I've been sick [ill] for...days. | …일 동안 아팠습니다. ...eel ttohng·ahn ah·paht·ssum·nee·dah |

▶For numbers, see page 159.

Health Conditions

I'm...	저는…이 있습니다. juh·nun...ee eet·ssum·nee·dah
– anemic	– 빈혈 been·hyuhl
– asthmatic	– 천식 chuhn·seek
– diabetic	– 당뇨병 dahng·nyo·ppyuhng
I'm allergic to *antibiotics/penicillin*.	항생제에/페니실린에 알레르기가 있습니다. *hahng·sehng·jeh·eh/ peh·nee·seel·lee·neh* ahl·leh·lu·gee·gah eet·ssum·nee·dah

▶For food items, see page 82.

I have...	…이 있습니다. ...ee eet·ssum·nee·dah
– arthritis	– 관절염 gwahn·juhl·lyuhm
– a heart condition	– 심장 질환 seem·jahng jee·lwahn
– *high/low* blood pressure	– 고혈압/저혈압 goh·hyuh·lahp/ juh·hyuh·lahp
I'm on medication.	약을 복용 중입니다. yah·gul boh·gyong joong·eem·nee·dah
I'm on...	…복용 중입니다. ...boh·gyong joong·eem·nee·dah

You May Hear...

| 어디가 안 좋으세요? uh·dee·gah ahn joh·u·seh·yo | What's wrong? |
| 어디가 아프세요? uh·dee·gah ah·pu·seh·yo | Where does it hurt? |

여기가 아프세요? yuh·gee·gah ah·pu·seh·yo	Does it hurt here?
약 드시는 거 있으세요? yahk du·see·nun guh eet·ssu·seh·yo	Are you on medication?
알레르기 있으세요? ahl·leh·lu·gee eet·ssu·seh·yo	Are you allergic to anything?
입 벌리세요. eep buhl·lee·seh·yo	Open your mouth.
숨 깊이 들이쉬세요. soom gee·pee du·lee·swih·seh·yo	Breathe deeply.
병원에 가세요. byuhng·wuh·neh gah·seh·yo	Go to the hospital.

Treatment

| Do I need a prescription/ medicine? | 처방전/약 필요합니까?
chuh·bahng·juhn/yahk pee·lyo·hahm·nee·kkah |
| Where can I get it? | 어디서 구할 수 있습니까? uh·dee·suh
goo·hahl ssoo eet·ssum·nee·kkah |

▶ For dosage instructions, see page 153.

Hospital

Notify my family, please.	제 가족에게 연락해 주십시오. jeh gah·joh·geh·geh yuhl·lah·keh joo·seep·ssee·oh
I'm in pain.	저 지금 아픕니다. juh jee·gum ah·pum·nee·dah
I need a *doctor/ nurse*.	의사/간호사 불러 주십시오. *u·sah/ gahn·hoh·sah* bool·luh joo·seep·ssee·oh
When are visiting hours?	방문 시간이 언제입니까? bahng·moon see·gah·nee uhn·jeh·eem·nee·kkah
I'm visiting...	...문병왔습니다. ...moon·byuhng·waht·ssum·nee·dah

Dentist

I have a broken tooth.	이빨이 부러졌습니다. ee·ppah·lee boo·luh·jyuht·ssum·nee·dah
I've lost a filling.	이빨 때운 게 빠졌습니다. ee·ppahl tteh·oon geh ppah·juht·ssum·nee·dah
I have a toothache.	이빨이 아픕니다. ee·ppah·lee ah·pum·nee·dah
Can you fix this denture?	이 틀니를 고쳐 주시겠습니까? ee tul·lee·lul goh·chyuh joo·see·geht·ssum·nee·kkah

Gynecologist

I have *cramps/a vaginal infection*.	복통이/질염이 있습니다. *bok·tohng·ee/ jeel·lyuh·mee* eet·ssum·nee·dah
I missed my period.	생리 안 했습니다. sehng·nee ahn heht·ssum·nee·dah
I'm on the Pill.	피임약 먹고 있습니다. pee·eem·nyahk muh·kkoh eet·ssum·nee·dah
I'm (…months) pregnant.	저는 임신 (…개월)입니다. juh·nun eem·seen (…geh·wuhl) eem·nee·dah
I'm not pregnant.	저는 임신하지 않았습니다. juh·nun eem·seen·hah·jee ah·naht·ssum·nee·dah
My last period was…	마지막으로…에 생리했습니다. mah·jee·mah·gu·loh…eh sehng·nee·heht·ssum·nee·dah

Optician

I lost…	…잃어버렸습니다. …ee·luh·buh·ryuht·ssum·nee·dah
– a contact lens	– 콘택트 렌즈 kohn·tehk·tu lehn·ju
– my glasses	– 안경 ahn·gyuhng
– a lens	– 안경알 ahn·gyuhng·ahl

Payment and Insurance

How much?	얼마입니까? uhl·mah·eem·nee·kkah
Can I pay by credit card?	신용카드로 계산할 수 있습니까? see·nyong·kah·du·loh geh·sahn·hahl ssoo eet·ssum·nee·kkah
I have insurance.	보험이 있습니다. boh·huh·mee eet·ssum·nee·dah
I need a receipt for my insurance.	보험용 영수증이 필요합니다. boh·huhm·nyong yuhng·soo·jung·ee pee·lyo·hahm·nee·dah

Pharmacy [Chemist]

Essential

Where's the pharmacy [chemist]?	약국 어디 있습니까? yahk·kkook uh·dee eet·ssum·nee·kkah
What time does it *open/close*?	몇 시에 문 엽니까/닫습니까? myuh·ssee·eh moon *yuhm·nee·kkah/ daht·ssum·nee·kkah*
What would you recommend for…?	…에 좋은 약 있습니까? …eh joh·un yahk eet·ssum·nee·kkah
How much do I take?	얼마큼 먹어야 합니까? uhl·mah·kum muh·guh·yah hahm·nee·kkah
Can you fill [make up] this prescription?	이 처방대로 약 주시겠습니까? ee chuh·bahng·deh·loh yahk joo·see·geht·ssum·nee·kkah
I'm allergic to…	…알레르기가 있습니다. …ahl·leh·lu·gee·gah eet·ssum·nee·dah

There are many pharmacies in South Korea, and most Western drugs are available. Some pharmacies sell toiletries and non-prescription medication, as well as traditional remedies. Opening hours are 9 a.m. to 9 p.m., but this can vary.

Dosage Instructions

How much do I take?	얼마큼 먹어야 합니까?	uhl·mah·kum muh·guh·yah hahm·nee·kkah
How often?	얼마 간격으로 먹습니까?	uhl·mah gahn·gyuh·gu·loh muhk·ssum·nee·kkah
Is it safe for children?	어린이가 먹어도 됩니까?	uh·lee·nee·gah muh·guh·doh dwehm·nee·kkah
I'm taking…	…복용 중입니다.	…boh·gyong joong·eem·nee·dah
Are there side effects?	부작용 있습니까?	boo·jah·gyong eet·ssum·nee·kkah

You May See...

하루 일회/삼회 복용 hah·loo *eel·hweh/ sahm·hweh* boh·gyong	*once/three* times a day
식후/식전/식사와 함께 *see·koo/seek·tzuhn/ seek·ssa·wah* hahm·kkeh	*after/before/with* meals

공복에 먹을것 gohng·boh·geh muh·gul·guht	take on an empty stomach
졸음을 유발할 수 있음 joh·lu·mul yoo·bahl·hahl ssoo eet·ssum	may cause drowsiness

Health Problems

I need something for...	...약 주세요. ...yahk tzoo·seh·yo
– a cold	– 감기 gahm·gee
– a cough	– 기침 gee·cheem
– diarrhea	– 설사 suhl·ssah
– insect bites	– 벌레 물린데 buhl·leh mool·leen·deh
– motion [travel] sickness	– 멀미 muhl·mee
– a sore throat	– 목 아픈 데 moh gah·pun deh
– sunburn	– 일광 화상 eel·gwahng hwah·sahng
– an upset stomach	– 복통 bohk·tohng

Basic Needs

I'd like...	...주세요. ...joo·seh·yo
– acetaminophen [paracetamol]	– 아세트아미노펜 ah·seh·tu·ah·mee·noh·pehn
– antiseptic cream	– 살균 크림 sahl·gyoon ku·leem
– aspirin	– 아스피린 ah·su·pee·leen
– bandages	– 붕대 boong·deh
– a comb	– 빗 beet
– condoms	– 콘돔 kohn·dohm
– contact lens solution	– 콘텍트 렌즈 용액 kohn·tehk·tu lehn·ju yong·ehk
– a hairbrush	– 헤어 브러시 heh·uh bu·luh·see

– ibuprofen	– 이부프로펜 ee·boo·pu·loh·pehn
– insect repellent	– 제충제 jeh·choong·jeh
– lotion	– 로션 loh·syuhn
– a nail file	– 손톱줄 sohn·tohp·tzool
– a (disposable) razor	– (일회용) 면도기 (eel·hweh·yong) myuhn·doh·gee
– razor blades	– 면도날 myuhn·doh·nahl
– sanitary napkins [pads]	– 생리대 sehng·nee·deh
– shampoo/ conditioner	– 샴푸/컨디셔너 syahm·poo/ kuhn·dee·syuh·nuh
– soap	– 비누 bee·noo
– sunscreen	– 자외선 차단 크림 jah·weh·suhn chah·dahn ku·leem
– tampons	– 탐폰 tahm·pohn
– tissues	– 화장지 hwah·jahng·jee
– toilet paper	– 화장실 휴지 hwah·jahng·seel hyoo·jee
– a toothbrush	– 칫솔 cheet·ssohl
– toothpaste	– 치약 chee·yahk

▶For baby products, see page 139.

Reference

Grammar

Verbs

Korean verbs are conjugated to indicate tense, formality, mood and other aspects. There are three types of speech styles in Korean: formal polite, informal polite and casual.

Formal Polite Style

(used in the media, business meetings, speeches, formal interviews, etc., and used more frequently by men than women)

with verb stems ending in a vowel: add ㅂ니다 (m·nee·dah)

with verb stems ending in a consonant: add 습니다 (ssum·need·dah)

Informal Polite Style

(used in daily conversation where formality is not necessary, and used more frequently by women than men, even in some formal situations)

When the final vowel of verb stem is ㅏ or ㅗ : add 아요 (ah·yo)

with other stems: add 어요 (uh·yo)

Casual Style

(used with children and close friends)

drop 요 from informal polite style

There are also honorific ending, which indicate high-level respect and politeness: 으십니다 u·seem·nee·dah/으세요 u·seh·yo and 십니다 seem·nee·dah/세요 seh·yo. The former is used when the verb stem ends in a consonant and the latter is used when the verb stem ends in a vowel.

The Past Tense

When the final vowel of the verb stem is ㅏ ah or ㅗ oh, add 았 aht, and when the final vowel of the verb stem is other than ㅏ ah or ㅗ oh, add 었 uht. When the verb ends with 하다 hah·dah, add 였 yuht after 하 hah and final form is 했 heht.

The Future Tense

For the simple future, add ㄹ 것/거 guht/guh when the verb stem ends in a vowel, and add 을 것/거 ul·guht/guh when the verb stem ends in a consonant (for the causal form, add 야 at the end). For the intentional future, which is used to express the speaker's strong will or intention, add 겠 geht at the end of the verb stem.

Irregular Verbs

There are many irregular verbs in Korean that do not follow a pattern. Following are few examples of irregular verbs.

	Formal Form	Polite Form	Casual Form
to help	돕습니다 dohp·ssum·nee·dah	도와요 doh·wah·yo	도와 doh·wah
to walk	걷습니다 guh·ssum·nee·dah	걸어요 guh·luh·yo	걸어 guh·luh
to call	부릅니다 boo·lum·nee·dah	불러요 bool·luh·yo	불러 bool·luh

Imperatives

Unlike English, in which the infinitive form of a verb indicates a command, Korean uses verb endings to form an imperative expression. An example of the formal polite imperative is the verb ending - 십시오 -seep·ssee·yo; the informal polite is the verb ending - 세요 seh·yo.

Word Order

Basic word order in Korean is generally subject-object-verb. When there is additional information, word order can be flexible as long as the predicate is placed at the end.

Simple Questions

To form simple questions, change the 다 dah ending of the statement into the 까 kkah question ending and add rising intonation.

피터가 시내에 갑니다. pee·tuh·gah see·neh·eh gahm·nee·dah
(Peter is going to town.)

피터가 시내에 갑니까? pee·tuh·gah see·neh·eh gahm·nee·kkah
(Is Peter going to town?)

Negation

안 ahn (no/not) is added in front of verbs and adjectives to indicate negation.

시내에 갑니다. see·neh·eh gahm·nee·dah (I'm going to town.)

시내에 안 갑니다. see·neh·eh ahn gahm·nee·dah (I'm not going to town.)

Nouns

Nouns in Korean include particles (see below). Plural forms are not often used in Korean. Whether the noun is singular or plural is judged from the context, or by a number modifying the noun:

표 pyo (ticket)

표 세 장 pyo seh jahng (three tickets)

Pronouns

Pronouns are rarely used; names and titles are used instead. Pronouns have no gender nor case markings (subject, object, etc.). Instead, particles are used to indicate case; these appear after the noun to which they refer.

When the subject of the sentence is a pronoun and the subject is understood through context, then the subject pronoun is often omitted.

Particles

Korean has various particles. For example, subject particles 이/가 ee/gah are attached to a noun to indicate the subject of the sentence. The topic particles 은/는 un/nun are attached to a noun and are used to introduce someone or something, to compare or contrast and for emphasis. The object particles 을/를 ul/lul are attached to a noun to indicate the object of the sentence. When honorific subject particle 께서 kkeh·suh is used, it shows special respect towards the subject of the sentence.

Adjectives

An adjective usually precedes the noun to which it refers, as in English: 차 chah (car); 좋은 차 joh·un chah (nice car).

Comparative and Superlative

To form a comparative, 더 duh is added in front of an adjective.

좋은 차 joh·un chah (nice car), 더 좋은 차 duh joh·un chah (nicer car)

To form a superlative, 제일 jeh·eel is added in front of an adjective.

제일 좋은 차 jeh·eel joh·un chah (nicest car)

Adverbs and Adverbial Expressions

Adverbs are placed in front of a verb or an adjective. Commonly used adverbs include:

아주 ah·joo (very)

또 ttoh (again)

가끔 gah·kkum (sometimes)

자주 jah·joo (often)

빨리 ppahl·lee (quickly)

많이 mah·nee (a lot)

너무 nuh·moo (too)

항상 hang·sahng (always)

Numbers

Essential

	Sino-Korean*	Korean*
0	영/공 yuhn/gohng	
1	일 eel	하나 hah·nah
2	이 ee	둘 dool
3	삼 sahm	셋 seht
4	사 sah	넷 neht
5	오 oh	다섯 dah·suht
6	육 yook	여섯 yuh·suht
7	칠 cheel	일곱 eel·gohp
8	팔 pahl	여덟 yuh·duhl
9	구 goo	아홉 ah·hohp
10	십 seep	열 yuhl
11	십일 see·beel	열하나 yuhl·hah·nah
12	십이 see·bee	열둘 yuhl·ttool
13	십삼 seep·ssahm	열셋 yuhl·seht

*Sino-Korean numbers are used for years, months, days or money. Korean numbers are used with particles or counters.

14	십사 seep·ssah	열넷 yuhl·neht
15	십오 see·boh	열다섯 yuhl·ttah·shut
16	십육 seem·nyook	열여섯 yuhl·yuh·suht
17	십칠 seep·cheel	열일곱 yuhl·eel·ghop
18	십팔 seep·pahl	열여덟 yuhl·yuh·duhl
19	십구 seep·kkoo	열아홉 yuhl·ah·hohp
20	이십 ee·seep	스물 su·mool
21	이십일 ee·see·beel	스물하나 su·mool·hah·nah
22	이십이 ee·see·bee	스물둘 su·mool·dool
30	삼십 sahm·seep	서른 suh·lun
31	삼십일 sahm·see·beel	서른하나 suh·lun·hah·nah
40	사십 sah·seep	마흔 mah·hun
50	오십 oh·seep	쉰 swihn
60	육십 yook·sseep	예순 yeh·soon
70	칠십 cheel·sseep	일흔 eel·hun
80	팔십 pahl·sseep	여든 yuh·dun
90	구십 goo·seep	아흔 ah·hun
100	백 behk	
101	백일 beh·geel	
200	이백 ee·behk	
500	오백 oh·behk	
1,000	천 chuhn	
10,000	만 mahn	
100,000	십만 seem·mahn	
1,000,000	백만 behng·mahn	

There are two numbering systems in Korean: Sino-Korean numbers and pure Korean numbers. Sino-Korean numbers are used to count years, months, days, minutes and currency; Korean numbers are used mostly for counting people or things. For 100 and greater, only one counting system is used. Arabic numbers are usually used for written forms.

Ordinal Numbers

first	첫째	chuht·tzeh
second	둘째	dool·tzeh
third	셋째	seht·tzeh
fourth	넷째	neht·tzeh
fifth	다섯째	dah·suht·tzeh
once	한 번	hahn buh
twice	두 번	doo buh
three times	세 번	seh buh

Time

Essential

What time is it?	몇 시입니까? myuht ssee·eem·nee·kkah
It's noon [midday].	정오입니다. juhng·oh·eem·nee·dah
At midnight.	자정에요. jah·juhng·eh·yo
From one o'clock to two o'clock.	한 시부터 두 시까지요. hahn see·boo·tuh doo see·kkah·jee·yo
Five after [past] three.	세 시 오 분요. seh see oh boon·nyo
A quarter to four.	네 시 십오 분 전요. neh see see·boh boon juhn·nyo
5:30 *a.m./p.m.*	오전/오후 다섯 시 삼십 분요. *oh·juhn/ oh·hoo* dah·suht ssee sahm·see ppoon·nyo

161

Days ―――――――――――――――――――――――――――――

Monday	월요일 wuh·lyo·eel
Tuesday	화요일 hwah·yo·eel
Wednesday	수요일 soo·yo·eel
Thursday	목요일 moh·gyo·eel
Friday	금요일 gu·myo·eel
Saturday	토요일 toh·yo·eel
Sunday	일요일 ee·lyo·eel

Dates ―――――――――――――――――――――

| yesterday | 어제 uh·jeh |
| today | 오늘 oh·nul |

tomorrow	내일 neh·eel
day	일 eel
week	주 joo
month	월 wuhl
year	년 nyuhn

Months

January	일월 ee·lwuhl
February	이월 ee·wuhl
March	삼월 sah·mwuhl
April	사월 sah·wuhl
May	오월 oh·wuhl
June	유월 yoo·wuhl
July	칠월 chee·lwuhl
August	팔월 pah·lwuhl
September	구월 goo·wuhl
October	시월 see·wuhl
November	십일월 see·bee·lwuhl
December	십이월 see·bee·wuhl

Seasons

spring	봄 bohm
summer	여름 yuh·lum
fall [autumn]	가을 gah·ul
winter	겨울 gyuh·ool

Holidays

South Korea

January 1, New Year's Day	신정 seen·johng

March 1, Independence Movement Day	삼일절 sah·meel·tzuhl
May 5, Children's Day	어린이날 uh·lee·nee nahl
June 6, Memorial Day	현충일 hyuhn·choong·eel
August 15, Liberation Day	광복절 gwahng·bohk·tzuhl
October 3, National Foundation Day	개천절 geh·chuhn·juhl
December 25, Christmas	성탄절 suhng·than·juhl

In addition to the holidays listed above, there are also three public holidays in South Korea that are based on the lunar calendar and, so, fall on different days every year: 구정 **goo·juhng** (Lunar New Year, in January or February), 석가 탄신일 **suhk·kkah tahn·see·neel** (Buddha's Birthday, in May) and the 추석 **choo suhk** (Harvest Moon Festival, in September or October).

Conversion Tables

When you know	Multiply by	To find
ounces	28.3	grams
pounds	0.45	kilograms
inches	2.54	centimeters
feet	0.3	meters
miles	1.61	kilometers
square inches	6.45	sq. centimeters
square feet	0.09	sq. meters

square miles	2.59	sq. kilometers
pints (U.S./Brit.)	0.47/0.56	liters
gallons (U.S./Brit.)	3.8/4.5	liters
Fahrenheit	5/9, after −32	Centigrade
Centigrade	9/5, then +32	Fahrenheit

Mileage

1 km − 0.62 miles
5 km − 3.1 miles
10 km − 6.2 miles
50 km − 31 miles
100 km − 62 miles

Measurement

1 gram	그램 gu·lehm	0.035 oz.
1 kilogram (kg)	킬로 그램 keel·loh gu·lehm	2.2 lb
1 liter (l)	리터 lee·tuh	1.06 U.S/0.88 Brit. quarts
1 centimeter (cm)	센티 미터 sehn·tee mee·tuh	0.4 inch
1 meter (m)	미터 mee·tuh	3.28 ft.
1 kilometer (km)	킬로 미터 keep·loh mee·tuh	0.62 mile

Temperature

-40° C − -40° F	-1° C − 30° F	20° C − 68° F
-30° C − -22° F	0° C − 32° F	25° C − 77° F
-20° C − -4° F	5° C − 41° F	30° C − 86° F
-10° C − 14° F	10° C − 50° F	35° C − 95° F
-5° C − 23° F	15° C − 59° F	

Oven Temperature

100° C – 212° F	177° C – 350° F
121° C – 250° F	204° C – 400° F
149° C – 300° F	260° C – 500° F

Useful Websites

english.tour2korea.com
Korean National Tourism Organization (KNTO) website

english.visitseoul.net
Official Seoul city tourism board website

www.korail.com
Korail (Korean National Railroad) website

www.kobus.co.kr
Kobus (express bus service) website

www.smrt.co.kr
Seoul subway website

www.koreapost.go.kr
Korea Post website

english.knps.or.kr
Korea National Park Service website

world.kbs.co.kr/english
Korean Broadcasting Commission (KBS) website

www.tsa.gov
U.S. Transportation Security Administration (TSA)

www.caa.co.uk
U.K. Civil Aviation Authority (CAA)

www.hihostels.com
Hostelling International website

www.berlitzpublishing.com
Berlitz phrase books and travel guides

English–Korean Dictionary

A

accept 받다 baht·ttah

access 접근 juhp·kkun

accident 사고 sah·goh

accidentally 실수로 seel·ssoo·loh

accommodations 숙박 시설 sook·ppahk see·suhl

accompany 같이 가다 gah·chee gah·dah

acetaminophen 아세트아미노펜 ah·seh·tu·ah·mee·noh·pehn

acupuncture 침 cheem

adapter 어댑터 uh·dehp·tuh

address 주소 joo·soh

after 지나서 jee·nah·suh

aftershave 애프터셰이브 로션 eh·pu·tuh·syeh·ee·bu loh·syuhn

afternoon 오후 oh·hoo

air conditioning 냉방 nehng·bahng

airline 항공사 hahng·gohng·sah

airmail 항공우편 hahng·gohng·oo·pyuhn

airport 공항 gohng·hahng

airsickness 비행기 멀미 bee·hehng·gee muhl·mee

aisle 통로 tohng·noh

alarm clock 자명종 jah·myuhng·johng

allergic 알레르기가 있다 ahl·leh·lu·gee·gah eet·ttah

allergy 알레르기 ahl·leh·lu·gee

allow 허락하다 huh·lah·kah·dah

allowance 허용 한도 huh·yong hahn·doh

alone 혼자 hohn·jah

already 이미 ee·mee

also 또한 ttoh·hahn

alter 바꾸다 bah·kkoo·dah

alternate 다른 dah·lun

aluminum foil 쿠킹 호일 koo·keeng hoh·eel

always 항상 hahng·sahng

amazing 놀라운 nohl·lah·oon

ambassador 대사 deh·sah

ambulance 구급차 goo·gup·chah

American 미국인 mee·goo·geen

amount 금액 gu·mehk

amusement park 놀이 공원 noh·lee gohng·wuhn

anesthetic 마취제 mah·chwih·jeh

and 그리고 gu·lee·goh

animal 동물 dohng·mool

another 다른 dah·lun

antacid 제산제 jeh·sahn·jeh

antibiotics 항생제 hahng·sehng·jeh

antifreeze 부동액 boo·dohng·ehk

antique 골동품 gohl·ttohng·poom

antiseptic 소독약 soh·dohng·nyahk

any 어떤 uh·ttuhn

anyone 누군가 noo·goon·gah

anything 무언가 moo·uhn·gah

apartment 아파트 ah·pah·tu

apologize 사과하다 sah·gwah·hah·dah

appendix 부록 boo·lohk

appetite 식욕 see·gyok

adj	adjective	adv	adverb	**BE**	British English
n	noun	v	verb		

appointment (meeting) 약속
yahk·ssohk; (doctor, hair, etc.) 예약
yeh·yahk

approve 허락하다 huh·lah·kah·dah

area 구역 goo·yuhk

area code 지역 번호 jee·yuhk
ppuhn·hoh

arm 팔 pahl

aromatherapy 아로마테라피
ah·loh·mah·teh·lah·pee

around (time) 쯤 tzum

arrivals 도착 doh·chahk

arrive 도착하다 doh·chah·kah·dah

art gallery 미술관 mee·sool·gwahn

arthritis 관절염 gwahn·juhl·lyuhm

ashtray 재떨이 jeh·ttuh·lee

ask 묻다 moot·ttah

aspirin 아스피린 ah·su·pee·leen

assistance 도움 doh·oom

asthma 천식 chuhn·seek

at 에 eh

ATM 현금 인출기 hyuhn·gum
een·chool·gee

attack 폭행 poh·kehng

attractive 매력적인
meh·lyuhk·tzuh·geen

audio guide 음성 안내 um·suhng
ahn·meh

authentic 진짜 jeen·tzah

automatic 자동 jah·dohng

available 이용할 수 있는 ee·yong·hahl
ssoo een·nun

away 떨어져 ttuh·luh·jyuh

B

baby 아기 ah·gee

baby bottle 젖병 juht·ppyuhng

baby food 이유식 ee·yoo·seek

baby wipe 아기용 물휴지 ah·gee·yong
mool·hyoo·jee

babysitter 애 봐주는 사람 eh
bwah·joo·nun sah·lahm

back 등 dung

backpack 배낭 beh·nahng

bad 나쁜 nah·ppun

bag 가방 gah·bahng

baggage [BE] 짐 jeem

baggage claim 수하물 찾는 곳
soo·hah·mool chan·nun goht

bakery 제과점 jeh·gwah·juhm

ball 공 gohng

ballet 발레 bahl·leh

band 악단 ahk·ttahn

bandage 붕대 boong·deh

bank 은행 un·hehng

bar 바 bah

barber 이발소 ee·bahl·soh

bargain 흥정 hung·juhng

baseball 야구 yah·goo

basement 지하실 jee·hah·seel

basket 바구니 bah·goo·nee

basketball 농구 nohng·goo

bath 목욕 moh·gyohk

bathroom 화장실 hwah·jahng·seel

battery 건전지 guhn·juhn·jee

battlesite 전적지 juhn·juhk·tzee

be 이다 ee·dah

beach 해변 heh·byuhn

beautiful 아름다운 ah·lum·dah·oon

because 때문에 tteh·moo·neh

bed 침대 cheem·deh

bedding 침구 cheem·goo

bedroom 침실 cheem·seel

before 전에 juh·neh**

begin 시작하다 see·jah·kah·dah

behind 뒤에 dwih·eh

belong 속하다 soh·kah·dah

belt 벨트 bel·tu

bet 내기 neh·gee

between 사이에 sah·ee·eh

beware 조심하다 joh·seem·hah·dah

bib 턱받이 tuhk·ppah·jee

bicycle 자전거 jah·juhn·guh

big 큰 kun

bike path 자전거 도로 jah·juhn·guh doh·loh

bikini 비키니 bee·kee·nee

bill 계산서 geh·sahn·suh

binoculars 쌍안경 ssahng·ahn·gyuhng

bird 새 seh

birthday 생일 sehng·eel

bite 벌레 물린데 buhl·leh mool·leen·deh

bitter 쓴 ssun

blanket 담요 dahm·nyo

bleach 표백제 pyo·behk·tzeh

bleed 피가 나다 pee·gah nah·dah

blister 물집 mool·tzeep

blood 혈액 hyuh·lehk

blood pressure 혈압 hyuh·lahp

blouse 블라우스 bu·lah·oo·su

board 탑승하다 tahp·ssung·hah·dah

boarding card 탑승 카드 tahp·ssung kah·du

boat trip 보트 관광 boh·tu gwahn·gwahng

bone 뼈 ppyuh

book 책 chehk

bookstore 서점 suh·juhm

boots 부츠 boo·chu

boring 따분한 ttah·boon·hahn

born 태어난 teh·uh·nahn

borrow 빌리다 beel·lee·dah

botanical garden 식물원 seeng·moo·lwuhn

bother 귀찮게 하다 gwih·chahn·keh hah·dah

bottle 병 byuhng

bottle opener 병따개 byuhng·ttah·geh

bowl 사발 sah·bahl

box 상자 sahng·jah

boxing 권투 gwuhn·too

boy 남자애 nahm·jah·eh

boyfriend 애인 eh·een

bra 브래지어 bu·leh·jee·uh

bracelet 팔찌 pahl·tzee

brake 브레이크 bu·leh·ee·ku

break 부수다 boo·soo·dah

break down 고장 goh·jang

breakfast 아침 식사 ah·cheem seek·ssah

breast 가슴 gah·sum

breastfeed 수유하다 soo·yoo·hah·dah

breathe 숨쉬다 soom·swih·dah

bridge 다리 dah·lee

bring 가져오다 gah·jyuh·oh·dah

British 영국인 yuhng·goo·geen

brochure 팸플릿 pahm·pul·leht

broken 고장난 goh·jahng·nahn

broom 빗자루 beet·tzah·loo

browse 둘러보다 dool·luh·boh·dah

bruise 멍 muhng

bucket 양동이 yahng·dohng·ee

bug 벌레 buhl·leh

building 건물 guhn·mool

build 짓다 jeet·ttah

burn 화상 hwah·sahng

bus 버스 buh·su

bus station 버스 터미널 buh·su
 tuh·mee·nuhl

bus stop 버스 정류장 buh·su
 juhng·nyoo·jang

bus ticket 버스표 buh·su·pyo

business 사업 sah·uhp

business card 명함 myuhng·hahm

business center 비즈니스 센터
 bee·jee·nee·su ssehn·tuh

business class 비즈니스석
 bee·jee·nee·su·suhk

business district 상업 지구 sahng·uhp
 tzee·goo

busy 바쁜 bah·ppun

but 그러나 gu·luh·nah

butane gas 부탄가스 boo·tahn·kkah·su

button 단추 dahn·choo

buy 사다 sah·dah

by (means) 으로 u·loh; (place) 옆에
 yuh·peh; (time) 까지 kkah·jee

bye (to someone leaving) 안녕히
 가세요 ahn·nyuhng·hee gah·seh·yo; (to
 someone staying) 안녕히
 계세요 ahn·nyuhng·hee geh·seh·yo

C

cabin 오두막집 oh·doo·mahk·tzeep

calendar 달력 dahl·lyuhk

call 부르다 boo·lu·dah

calorie 칼로리 kahl·loh·lee

camera 카메라 kah·meh·lah

camp 캠핑하다 kehm·peeng·hah·dah

campsite 캠핑장 kehm·peeng·jahng

can 깡통 kkahng·tohng

can opener 통조림 따개
 tohng·joh·leem ttah·geh

Canada 캐나다 keh·nah·dah

canal 운하 oon·hah

cancel 취소하다 chwih·soh·hah·dah

cancer 암 ahm

candle 양초 yahng·choh

candy store 사탕 가게 sah·tahng
 kkah·geh

canoe 카누 kah·noo

car 자동차 jah·dohng·chah

car hire [BE] 렌터카 lehn·tuh·kah

car park [BE] 주차장 joo·chah·jahng

car rental 렌터카 lehn·tuh·kah

car seat 카시트 kah·ssee·tu

card 카드 kah·du

carpet 카페트 kah·peh·tu

carry-on luggage 기내 휴대 수하물
 gee·neh hyoo·deh soo·hah·mool

cart 카트 kah·tu

carton (cigarettes) 보루 boh·loo

cash 현금 hyuhn·gum

cash register 계산대 geh·sahn·deh

cashier 계산원 geh·sah·nwuhn

casino 카지노 kah·jee·noh

castle 성 suhng

catch 잡다 jahp·ttah

caution 조심 joh·seem

cave 동굴 dohng·gool

CD 시디 ssee·dee

CD player 시디플레이어
 ssee·dee·pul·leh·ee·uh

cell phone 휴대폰 hyoo·deh·pohn

cemetery 공동 묘지 gohng·dohng
 myo·jee

ceramics 도자기 doh·jah·gee

certificate 보증서 boh·jung·suh

chain 사슬 sah·sul

change n 잔돈 jahn·dohn; v 바꾸다
 bah·kkoo·dah

charge 요금 yo·gum

cheap 싼 ssahn

check 확인하다 hwah·geen·hah·dah

check in 탑승 수속 tahp·ssung
soo·sohk

check out 체크 아웃 cheh·ku ah·oot

cheers 건배 guhn·beh

chemical toilet 휴대 변기 hyoo·deh
byuhn·gee

chemist [BE] 약국 yahk·kkook

cheque [BE] 수표 soo·pyo

chest 가슴 gah·sum

child 어린이 uh·lee·nee

child seat 어린이용 의자
uh·lee·nee·yong u·jah

children's menu 어린이용 메뉴
uh·lee·nee·yong meh·nyoo

children's portion 어린이용 메뉴
uh·lee·nee·yong meh·nyoo

choose 고르다 goh·lu·dah

chopsticks 젓가락 juht·kkah·lahk

church 교회 gyo·hweh

cigarette 담배 dahm·beh

cigar 시가 ssee·gah

cinema [BE] 영화관
yuhng·hwah·gwahn

class 등급 dung·gup

clean 깨끗한 kkeh·kku·tahn

clearance 재고 정리 jeh·goh juhng·nee

cliff 절벽 juhl·byuhk

cling film [BE] 랩 lehp

clinic 병원 byuhng·wuhn

clock 시계 see·geh

close 닫다 daht·ttah

clothes shop [BE] 옷가게 oht·kkah·geh

clothing store 옷가게 oht·kkah·geh

club (golf) 골프채 gohl·pu·cheh

coast 해안 heh·ahn

coat 코트 koh·tu

coat check 휴대품 보관소
hyoo·deh·poom boh·gwahn·soh

code 지역 번호 jee·yuhk ppuhn·hoh

coin 동전 dohng·juhn

cold adj 차가운 chah·gah·oon;
n 감기 gahm·gee

collapse 쓰러지다 ssu·luh·jee·dah

colleague 동료 dohng·nyo

collect 모으다 moh·u·dah

collection 수집 soo·jeep

color 색 sehk

comb 빗 beet

come 오다 oh·dah

commission 수수료 soo·soo·lyo

company 회사 hweh·sah

compartment 객실 gehk·sseel

computer 컴퓨터 kuhm·pyoo·tuh

concert 음악회 u·mah·kweh

concert hall 연주회장
yuhn·joo·hweh·jahng

concession 양보 yahng·boh

concussion 뇌진탕 nweh·jeen·tahng

conditioner 컨디셔너
kuhn·dee·syuh·nuh

condom 콘돔 kohn·dohm

conductor 지휘자 jee·hwih·jah

conference 회의 hweh·ee

confirm 확인하다 hwah·geen·hah·dah

congratulations 축하합니다
choo·kah·ham·nee·dah

connect 연결하다 yuhn·gyuhl·hah·dah

connection 연결 yuhn·gyuhl

conscious 의식하는 u·see·kah·nun

conservation area 보호 구역 boh·hoh
goo·yuhk

constant 일정한 eel·tzuhng·hahn

constipation 변비 byun·bee

consulate 영사관 yuhng·sah·gwahn

consult 상담하다 sahng·dahm·hah·dah

contact 연락하다 yuhl·lah·kah·dah

contact lens 콘텍트 렌즈 kohn·tehk·tu lehn·ju

contact lens solution 콘텍트 렌즈 용액 kohn·tehk·tu lehn·ju yong·ehk

contagious 전염성의 juh·nyuhm·ssuhng·eh

contain 포함하다 poh·hahm·hah·dah

contemporary 현대 hyuhn·deh

contest n 대회 deh·hwee

continuous 끊임없는 kku·neem·uhm·nun

contraceptive 피임약 pee·eem·nyahk

contribution 기부 gee·boo

control n 관리 gwahl·lee

convention 회의 hwee·ee

convention hall 회의장 hwee·ee·jahng

cook v 요리하다 yo·lee·hah·dah

cooking facilities 주방 시설 joo·bahng see·suhl

cool 시원한 see·wuhn·hahn

copper 구리 goo·lee

copy 복사하다 bohk·ssah·hah·dah

corkscrew 코르크 마개뽑이 koh·lu·ku mah·geh·ppoh·bee

corner 모퉁이 moh·toong·ee

correct 맞는 mahn·nun

cosmetic 화장품 hwah·jahng·poom

cost n 비용 bee·yong; v 들다 dul·dah

cot [BE] 아기용 침대 ah·gee·yong cheem·deh

cottage 별장 byuhl·tzang

cotton 면 myuhn

cough n 기침 gee·cheem; v 기침하다 gee·cheem·hah·dah

counter 카운터 kah·oon·tuh

country 나라 nah·lah

country code 국가 번호 gook·kkah buhn·hoh

cover charge 입장료 eep·tzahng·nyo

cramp 경련 gyuhng·nyuhn

credit card 신용카드 see·nyong·kah·du

crib 아기용 침대 ah·gee·yong cheem·deh

crowd 군중 goon·joong

cruise 유람선 여행 yoo·lahm·suhn yuh·hehng

crutches 목발 mohk·ppahl

crystal 수정 soo·juhng

cup 컵 kuhp

currency 돈 dohn

currency exchange office 환전소 hwan·juhn·soh

curtain 커튼 kuh·tun

curve 커브 kuh·bu

custom made 맞춤 maht·choom

customer service 고객 서비스 goh·gehk ssuh·bee·su

customs 세관 seh·gwahn

customs declaration form 세관 신고서 seh·gwahn seen·goh·suh

cut n 절단 juhl·ttahn

cute 귀여운 gwih·yuh·oon

D

daily 매일 meh·eel

dairy 유제품의 yoo·jeh·poo·meh

damage 손상 sohn·sahng

damp 습한 su·pahn

dance 춤추다 choom·choo·dah

dance club 클럽 kul·luhp

dangerous 위험한 wih·huhm·hahn

dark 어두운 uh·doo·oon

day 일 eel

day trip 당일치기 여행
dahng·eel·chee·gee yuh·hehng

dead (battery) 떨어진 ttuh·luh·jeen

deaf 귀머거리 gwih·muh·guh·lee

deck chair 접는 의자 juhm·nun u·jah

declare 신고하다 seen·goh·hah·dah

decorative 장식 jahng·seek

deep 깊은 gee·pun

defrost 녹이다 noh·gee·dah

degree 도 doh

delay 지연 jee·yuhn

delete 삭제하다 sahk·tzeh·hah·dah

delicious 맛있는 mah·seen·nun

deliver 배달하다 beh·dahl·hah·dah

delivery 배달 beh·dahl

dental floss 치실 chee·seel

dentist 치과 의사 chee·kkwah u·sah

denture 틀니 tul·lee

deodorant 방취제 bahng·chwih·jeh

depart 출발하다 chool·bahl·hah·dah

department store 백화점
beh·kwah·juhm

departures 출발 chool·bahl

deposit 입금 eep·kkum

describe 묘사하다 myo·sah·hah·dah

destination 목적지 mohk·juhk·tzee

detergent 세제 seh·jeh

develop 현상하다 hyuhn·sahng·hah·dah

diabetes 당뇨병 dahng·nyo·ppyuhng

diabetic 당뇨병 환자
dahng·nyo·ppyuhng hwahn·jah

dial 전화 걸다 juhn·hwah guhl·dah

diamond 다이아몬드
dah·ee·ah·mohn·du

diaper 기저귀 gee·juh·gwih

diarrhea 설사 suhl·ssah

dictionary 사전 sah·juhn

diesel 디젤 dee·jehl

diet 다이어트 dah·ee·uh·tu

difficult 어려운 uh·lyuh·oon

digital 디지털 dee·jee·tuhl

dine 식사하다 seek·ssah·hah·dah

dining car 식당차 seek·ttahng·chah

dining room 식당 seek·ttahng

dinner 저녁 식사 juh·nyuhk seek·ssah

direct *adj* 직행 jee·kehng

direction 방향 bahng·hyahng

director 이사 ee·sah

directory (phone) 전화 번호부
juhn·hwah buhn·hoh·boo

dirty 더러운 duh·luh·oon

disabled 장애인 jahng·eh·een

disconnect 접속을 끊다 juhp·soh·gul
kkun·tah

discount 할인 hah·leen

dish (food) 음식 um·seek; **(plate)** 접
시 juhp·ssee

dishwasher 식기 세척기 seek·kkee
seh·chuhk·kkee

dishwashing liquid 주방용 세제
joo·bahng·nyong seh·jeh

dislocate 삐다 ppee·dah

display case 진열장 jee·nyuhl·tzahng

disposable (camera) 일회용
(카메라) eel·hweh·nyong (kah·meh·lah)

dissolve 녹이다 noh·gee·dah

distance 거리 guh·lee

disturb 방해하다 bahng·heh·hah·dah

dive 다이빙하다 dah·ee·beeng·hah·dah

diving equipment 스쿠버 다이빙
장비 su·koo·buh dah·ee·beeng
jahng·bee

divorce 이혼 ee·hohn

dizzy 어지러운 uh·jee·luh·oon

do 하다 hah·dah

dock 부두 boo·doo

doctor 의사 u·sah

dog 개 geh

doll 인형 een·hyuhng

dollar 달러 dahl·luh

domestic 국내 goong·neh

donation 기부 gee·boo

door 문 moon

dosage 복용량 boh·gyong·nyahng

double 이인용 ee·een·nyong

double room 이인용 방 ee·een·nyong bahng

downstairs 아래층 ah·leh·chung

downtown 중심가 joong·seem·gah

dozen 다스 dah·su

dress 드레스 du·leh·su

dress code 복장 규정 bohk·tzang gyoo·juhng

drink *n* 음료수 um·nyo·soo; *n* **(alcoholic)** 술 sool; *v* 마시다 mah·see·dah

drip 뚝뚝 떨어지다 ttook·ttook ttuh·luh·jee·dah

drive 운전하다 oon·juhn·hah·dah

driver 운전사 oon·juhn·sah

driver's license 운전 면허증 oon·juhn myuhn·huh·tzung

drop 떨어뜨리다 ttuh·luh·ttu·lee·dah

drown 물에 빠지다 moo·leh ppah·jee·dah

drowsy 졸린 johl·leen

drowsiness 졸음 joh·lum

drugstore 약국 yahk·kkook

dry 말리다 mahl·lee·dah

dry clean 드라이 클리닝하다 du·lah·ee kul·lee·neeng·hah·dah

dry cleaner 세탁소 seh·tahk·ssoh

dubbed 더빙된 duh·beeng·dwehn

dummy [BE] 고무 젖꼭지 goh·moo juht·kkohk·tzee

during 동안 dohng·ahn

duty (tax) 세금 seh·gum

duty-free 면세 myuhn·seh

E

ear 귀 gwih

ear drops 귀약 gwih·yahk

earache 귀통증 gwih·tohng·tzung

early 일찍 eel·tzeek

earrings 귀걸이 gwih·guh·lee

east 동쪽 dohng·tzohk

easy 쉬운 swih·oon

eat 먹다 muhk·ttah

economy class 이코노미석 ee·koh·noh·mee·suhk

electrical outlet 전기 콘센트 juhn·gee kohn·sehn·tu

elevator 엘리베이터 ehl·lee·beh·ee·tuh

e-mail 이메일 ee·meh·eel

e-mail address 이메일 주소 ee·meh·eel joo·soh

embassy 대사관 deh·sah·gwahn

emerald 에메랄드 eh·meh·lahl·du

emergency 비상 bee·sahng

emergency brake 비상 브레이크 bee·sahng bu·leh·ee·ku

emergency exit 비상구 bee·sahng·goo

emergency service 긴급 서비스 geen·gup ssuh·bee·su

empty 텅 빈 tuhng been

end 끝 kkut

engaged 약혼한 yah·kohn·hahn

England 영국 yuhng·gook

English 영어 yuhng-uh
engrave 새기다 seh-gee-dah
enjoy 즐기다 jul-gee-dah
enlarge 확대하다 hwahk-tteh-hah-dah
enough 충분한 choong-boon-hahn
entertainment guide 오락 안내 oh-lah
gahn-neh
entrance 입구 eep-kkoo
entrance fee 입장료 eep-tzang-nyo
entrance ramp 입구 진입로 eep-kkoo
jee-neem-noh
entry 입장 eep-tzahng
entry visa 입국 비자 eep-kkook bee-jah
envelope 편지 봉투 pyuhn-jee bohng-too
equipment 장비 jahng-bee
error 오류 oh-lyoo
escalator 에스컬레이터
eh-su-kuhl-leh-ee-tuh
essential 필수적인 peel-ssoo-juh-geen
e-ticket 전자티켓 juhn-jah-tee-keht
euro 유로 yoo-loh
Eurocheque 유로체크 yoo-loh-cheh-ku
evening 저녁 juh-nyuhk
event 행사 hehng-sah
every 모든 moh-dun
exact 정확한 juhng-hwah-kahn
examination 검사 guhm-sah
example 예 yeh
except 외에 weh-eh
exchange 바꾸다 bah-kkoo-dah
exchange rate 환율 hwahn-nyool
excursion 짧은 여행 tzahl-bun
yuh-hehng
exhausted 지친 jee-cheen
exit 출구 chool-goo
expensive 비싼 bee-ssahn
experience 경험 gyuhng-huhm

expose 드러내다 du-luh-neh-dah
express mail 특급 우편 tuk-kku
boo-pyuhn
extension (phone) 내선 번호 neh-suhn
buhn-hoh
extra 여분 yuh-boon
extract 뽑아내다 ppoh-bah-neh-dah
eye 눈 noon
eyebrow 눈썹 noon-ssuhp

F

fabric 천 chuhn
face 얼굴 uhl-gool
facial 얼굴 마사지 uhl-gool
mah-ssah-jee
facility 시설 see-suhl
factor 요인 yo-een
faint v 기절하다 gee-juhl-hah-dah
family 가족 gah-johk
famous 유명한 yoo-myuhng-hahn
fan 선풍기 suhn-poong-gee
far 먼 muhn
far-sighted 원시 wuhn-see
farm 농장 nohng-jahng
fast 빠른 ppah-lun
fast food 패스트 푸드 peh-su-tu
poo-du
faucet 수도꼭지 soo-doh-kkohk-tzee
favorite 좋아하는 joh-ah-hah-nun
fax 팩스 pehk-su
fax machine 팩스기 pehk-su-gee
fax number 팩스 번호 pehk-su
buhn-hoh
feature 특징 tuk-tzeeng
feed 먹이다 muh-gee-dah
feel 느끼다 nu-kkee-dah
female 여자 yuh-jah

ferry 보트 boh·tu

fever 열 yuhl

few 조금 joh·gum

field 들판 dul·pahn

fight 싸움 ssah·oom

fill 채우다 cheh·oo·dah

filling 속 sohk

film 영화 yuhng·hwah

filter 필터 peel·tuh

find 찾다 chaht·ttah

fine *n* 벌금 buhl·gum; *adj* 좋은 joh·un

finger 손가락 sohn·kkah·lahk

fire 불 bool

fire alarm 화재 경보 hwah·jeh gyuhng·boh

fire door 방화문 bahng·hwah·moon

fire escape 화재 비상 계단 hwah·jeh bee·sahng geh·dahn

fire exit 화재 비상구 hwah·jeh bee·sahng·goo

fire extinguisher 소화기 soh·hwah·gee

first 첫 chuht

first class 일등석 eel·ttung·suhk

fishing 낚시 nahk·ssee

fit 맞다 maht·ttah

fitting room 탈의실 tah·lee·seel

fix 고치다 goh·chee·dah

flash 번쩍이다 buhn·tzuh·gee·dah

flat 평평한 pyuhng·pyuhng·hahn

flavor 맛 maht

flea market 벼룩시장 byuh·look·ssee·jahng

flight 비행기 bee·hehng·gee

flight attendant 승무원 sung·moo·wuhn

flight number 항공기 편명 hahng·gohng·gee pyuhn·myuhng

floor (level) 층 chung

flower 꽃 kkoht

flush 물 내리다 mool neh·lee·dah

fog 안개 ahn·geh

follow 따라가다 ttah·lah·gah·dah

food 음식 um·seek

food poisoning 식중독 seek·tzoong·dohk

foot 발 bahl

football [BE] 축구 chook·kkoo

for 동안 dohng·ahn

for sale 판매용 pahn·meh·yong

foreign 외국의 weh·goo·geh

forest 숲 soop

forget 잊다 eet·ttah

fork 포크 poh·ku

form 양식 yahng·seek

formal dress 정장 juhng·jahng

formula (baby) 분유 boo·nyoo

fountain 분수 boon·soo

fracture 골절상 gohl·tzuhl·sahng

free (available) 시간 있는 see·gahn een·nun

free of charge 공짜 gohng·tzah

freeze 얼리다 uhl·lee·dah

freezer 냉동고 nehng·dohng·goh

frequent 잦은 jah·jun

fresh 신선한 seen·suhn·hahn

friend 친구 cheen·goo

from 부터 boo·tuh

front 앞 ahp

frying pan 후라이팬 hoo·lah·ee·pen

fuel 연료 yuhl·lyo

full 가득 찬 gah·duk chahn

fun 재미 jeh·mee

funny 웃기는 oot·kkee·nun

furniture 가구 gah·goo

G

gallery 화랑 hwah·lahng

game 경기 gyuhng·gee

garage (parking) 차고 cha·goh; (repair) 정비 공장 juhng·bee gohng·jahng

garbage bag 쓰레기 봉투 ssu·leh·gee bohng·too

garden 정원 juhng·wuhn

gas 기름 gee·lum

gas station 주유소 joo·yoo·soh

gate (airport) 탑승구 tahp·ssung·goo

gauze 거즈 guh·ju

gear 기어 gee·uh

genuine 진짜 jeen·tzah

get (find) 구하다 goo·hah·dah

get off (bus) 내리다 neh·lee·dah

gift 선물 suhn·mool

gift store 선물 가게 suhn·mool kkah·geh

girl 여자애 yuh·jah·eh

girlfriend 여자 친구 yuh·jah cheen·goo

give 주다 joo·dah

glass (for drinking) 유리잔 yoo·lee·jahn

glasses (optical) 안경 ahn·gyuhng

gloves 장갑 jahng·gahp

go 가다 gah·dah

goggles 물안경 moo·lahn·gyuhng

gold 금 gum

golf 골프 gohl·pu

golf club 골프채 gohl·pu·cheh

golf course 골프장 gohl·pu·jahng

good 좋은 joh·un

goodbye (to someone leaving) 안녕히 가세요 ahn·nyuhng·hee gah·seh·yo; (to someone staying) 안녕히 계세요 ahn·nyuhng·hee geh·seh·yo

gram 그램 gu·lehm

grass 잔디 jahn·dee

great 근사한 gun·sah·hahn

Great Britain 영국 yuhng·gook

grocer [BE] 식료품점 seeng·nyo·poom·juhm

grocery store 식료품점 seeng·nyo·poom·juhm

group 단체 dahn·cheh

guarantee 보증 boh·jung

guesthouse 숙소 sook·ssoh

guide (tour) 안내원 ahn·neh·wuhn

guide book 안내 책자 ahn·neh chehk·tzah

guide dog 맹도견 mehng·doh·gyuhn

guided tour 가이드 투어 gah·ee·du too·uh

guitar 기타 gee·tah

gym 헬스클럽 hehl·ssu·kul·luhp

gynecologist 부인과 boo·een·kkwah

H

hair 머리 muh·lee

hairbrush 헤어 브러시 heh·uh bu·luh·see

hairdresser 미용사 mee·yong·sah

halal 이슬람교 식용육 ee·sul·lahm·gyo see·gyong·nyook

half 반 bahn

hammer 망치 mahng·chee

hand 손 sohn

hand luggage 손가방 sohn·kkah·bahng

handbag [BE] 핸드백 hehn·du·behk

handicapped 장애인 jahng·eh·een

handicrafts 수공예품 soo·gohng·yeh·poom

hanger 옷걸이 oht·kkuh·lee

hangover 숙취 sook·chwih

happy 행복한 hehng·boh·kahn

harbor 항구 hahng·goo

hard 딱딱한 ttahk·ttah·kahn

hardware store 철물점
chuhl·mool·juhm

hat 모자 moh·jah

have 갖다 gaht·ttah

hay fever 꽃가루 알레르기
kkoht·kkah·loo ahl·leh·lu·gee

head 머리 muh·lee

headache 두통 doo·tohng

headlight 헤드라이트 heh·du·lah·ee·tu

health 건강 guhn·gahng

health food store 건강 식품점
guhn·gahng seek·poom·juhm

health insurance 의료 보험 u·lyo
boh·huhm

hear 듣다 dut·ttah

hearing aid 보청기 boh·chuhng·gee

hearing impaired 청각 장애인
chuhng·gahk jahng·eh·een

heart 심장 seem·jahng

heart attack 심장마비
seem·jahng·mah·bee

heart condition 심장 질환 seem·jahng
jeel·hwahn

heat 난방 nahn·bahng

heating [BE] 난방 nahn·bahng

heavy 무거운 moo·guh·oon

heels 하이힐 hah·ee·heel

height (person) 키 kee

hello 안녕하세요
ahn·nyuhng·hah·seh·yo

helmet 헬멧 hehl·meht

help n 도움 doh·oom; v 돕다 dohp·ttah

here 여기 yuh·gee

hi 안녕하세요 ahn·nyuhng·hah·seh·yo

high 높은 noh·pun

highchair 높은 의자 noh·pun u·jah

highway 고속도로 goh·sohk·ttoh·loh

hike 하이킹 hah·ee·keeng

hill 언덕 uhn·duhk

hire 빌리다 beel·lee·dah

historical 역사적인 yuhk·ssah·juh·geen

hobby 취미 chwih·mee

hold 붙들다 boot·ttul·dah

hole 구멍 goo·muhng

holiday [BE] 휴가 hyoo·gah

home 집 jeep

homemade 직접 만든 jeek·tzuhp
mahn·dun

honeymoon 신혼여행
seen·hohn·yuh·hehng

horn 뿔 ppool

horse 말 mahl

horseback riding 승마 sung·mah

horse racing 경마 gyuhng·mah

horsetrack 경마장 gyuhng·mah·jahng

hospital 병원 byuhng·wuhn

hot 뜨거운 ttu·guh·oon

hotel 호텔 hoh·tehl

hour 시간 see·gahn

house 집 jeep

how 어떻게 uh·ttuh·keh

how many 몇 개 myuht kkeh

how much 얼마나 ul·mah·nah

hug 안다 ahn·ttah

hunger 배고픔 beh·goh·pum

hungry 배고픈 beh·goh·pun

hunt 사냥하다 sah·nyahng·hah·dah

hurry 서두르다 suh·doo·lu·dah

hurt 아프다 ah·pu·dah

husband 남편 nahm·pyuhn

I

ibuprofen 이부프로펜
ee·boo·pu·loh·pehn

ice hockey 아이스 하키 ah·ee·su
hah·kee

ice skating 아이스 스케이트 ah·ee·su
su·keh·ee·tu

ice skating rink 아이스 스케이트장
ah·ee·su su·keh·ee·tuh·jahng

identification 신분증 seen·boon·tzung

ill [BE] 아픈 ah·pun

illegal 불법 bool·ppuhp

imitation 모조품 moh·joh·poom

important 중요한 joong·yo·hahn

improve 나아지다 nah·ah·jee·dah

in 에 eh

include 포함하다 poh·hahm·hah·dah

indigestion 소화불량
soh·hwah·bool·lyahng

indoor pool 실내 수영장 seel·leh
soo·yuhng·jahng

inexpensive 저렴한 juh·lyuhm·hahn

infect 감염시키다
gah·myuhm·see·kee·dah

infection 감염 gah·myuhm

inflammation 염증 yuhm·tzung

information 안내 ahn·neh

information desk 안내 데스크 ahn·neh
deh·su·ku

injection 주사 joo·sah

injure 다치게 하다 dah·chee·geh
hah·dah

innocent 결백한 gyuhl·beh·kahn

insect 벌레 buhl·leh

insect bite 벌레 물린 데 buhl·leh
mool·leen deh

insect repellent 제충제 jeh·choong·jeh

insert 삽입하다 sah·bee·pah·dah

inside 안에 ah·neh

insist 우기다 oo·gee·dah

insomnia 불면증 bool·myuhn·tzung

instant messenger 메신저
meh·sseen·juh

instead 대신에 deh·see·neh

instructions 설명서 suhl·myuhng·suh

instructor 강사 gahng·sah

insulin 인슐린 een·syool·leen

insurance 보험 boh·huhm

insurance card 보험 카드 boh·huhm
kah·du

insurance claim 보험금 청구
boh·huhm·gum chuhng·goo

interest (hobby) 취미 chwih·mee

interference 방해 bahng·heh

intermission 막간 mahk·kkahn

international 국제 gook·tzeh

International Student Card
국제 학생증 gook·tzeh
hahk·ssehng·tzung

internet 인터넷 een·tuh·neht

internet cafe 피시방 pee·ssee·bahng

interpreter 통역 tohng·yuhk

intersection 교차로 gyo·chah·loh

introduce 소개하다 soh·geh·hah·dah

invite 초대하다 choh·deh·hah·dah

Ireland 아일랜드 ah·eel·lehn·du

iron 다리미 dah·lee·mee

itch 가려움 gah·lyuh·oom

item 품목 poom·mohk

itemized 명세 myuhng·seh

J

jacket 재킷 jeh·keet

jar 병 byuhng

jaw 턱 tuhk

jeans 청바지 chuhng·bah·jee

jet lag 시차 see·chah

jeweler 보석상 boh·suhk·ssahng

jewelry 보석 boh·suhk

job 직업 jee·guhp

join 참가하다 chahm·gah·hah·dh

joint 관절 gwahn·juhl

joke 농담 nohng·dahm

journey 여행 yuh·hehng

K

keep 보유하다 boh·yoo·hah·dah

keep out 들어가지 않다 du·luh·gah·jee ahn·tah

key 열쇠 yuhl·ssweh

key card 키카드 kee·kah·du

key ring 열쇠고리 yuhl·ssweh·goh·lee

kiddie pool 어린이 수영장 uh·lee·nee soo·yuhng·jahng

kind 친절한 cheen·juhl·hahn

kiss 키스하다 kee·ssu·hah·dah

kitchen 부엌 boo·uhk

knee 무릎 moo·lup

knife 칼 kahl

knock 두드리다 doo·du·lee·dah

know 알다 ahl·dah

Korean wrestling 씨름 ssee·lum

kosher 유대교 음식 yoo·deh·gyo um·seek

L

label 상표 sahng·pyo

lace 레이스 leh·ee·su

lactose intolerant 유당 불내증 yoo·dahng bool·leh·tzung

ladder 사다리 sah·dah·lee

lake 호수 hoh·soo

lamp 전등 juhn·dung

land n 땅 ttahng; v 착륙하다 chahng·nyoo·kah·dah

lane 차선 chah·suhn

large 큰 kun

last adj 마지막 mah·jee·mahk; v 지속하다 jee·soh·kah·dah

late 늦다 nut·ttah

later 나중에 nah·joong·eh

launderette [BE] 빨래방 ppahl·leh·bahng

laundromat 빨래방 ppahl·leh·bahng

laundry service 세탁 서비스 seh·tahk ssuh·bee·su

laundry facilities 세탁 시설 seh·tahk see·suhl

lawyer 변호사 byuhn·hoh·sah

laxative 관장약 gwahn·jahng·yahk

lead n 납 nahp; v 인도하다 een·doh·hah·dah

leader (group) 지도자 jee·doh·jah

leak n 누출 noo·chool; v 새다 seh·dah

learn 배우다 beh·oo·dah

leather 가죽 gah·jook

leave 떠나다 ttuh·nah·dah

left 왼쪽 wehn·tzohk

leg 다리 dah·lee

legal 합법적 hahp·ppuhp·tzuhk

lend 빌려주다 beel·lyuh·joo·dah

length 길이 gee·lee

lens 렌즈 lehn·ju

less 더 적은 duh juh·gun

lesson 수업 soo·uhp

let 하게 하다 hah·geh hah·dah

letter 편지 pyuhn·jee

level 단계 dahn·geh

library 도서관 doh·suh·gwahn

life 생명 sehng·myuhng

life boat 구명 보트 goo·myuhng boh·tu

life guard 구조원 goo·joh·wuhn

life jacket 구명 조끼 goo·myuhng joh·kkee

lift [BE] 엘리베이터 ehl·lee·beh·ee·tuh

light 전등 juhn·dung

lightbulb 전구 juhn·goo

lighthouse 등대 dung·deh

lighter 라이터 lah·ee·tuh

like 좋아하다 joh·ah·hah·dah

line 노선 noh·suhn

linen 마 mah

lip 입술 eep·ssool

lipstick 립스틱 leep·ssu·teek

liquor store 주류 판매점 joo·lyoo pahn·meh·juhm

liter 리터 lee·tuh

little 작은 jah·gun

live 살다 sahl·dah

lobby (theater, hotel) 로비 loh·bee

local 지방 jee·bahng

lock *n* 자물쇠 jah·mool·ssweh; *v* 잠그다 jahm·gu·dah

log on 접속하다 juhp·ssoh·kah·dah

log off 접속을 끊다 juhp·ssoh·gul kkun·tah

long 긴 geen

long-distance bus 장거리 버스 jahng·guh·lee buh·su

long-sighted [BE] 원시 wuhn·see

look 보다 boh·dah

loose 헐렁한 huhl·luhng·hahn

lose 잃어버리다 ee·luh·buh·lee·dah

lost 잃어버린 ee·luh·buh·leen

lost-and-found 분실물 센터 boon·seel·mool ssehn·tuh

lost property office [BE] 분실물 센터 boon·seel·mool ssehn·tuh

lottery 복권 boh·kkwuhn

loud 시끄러운 see·kku·luh·oon

love *v* 사랑하다 sah·lahng·hah·dah

low 낮은 nah·jun

luggage 수하물 soo·hah·mool

luggage cart 수하물 카트 soo·hah·mool kah·tu

luggage trolley [BE] 수하물 카트 soo·hah·mool kah·tu

lunch 점심 juhm·seem

M

magazine 잡지 jahp·tzee

magnificent 웅장한 oong·jahng·hahn

mail *n* 편지 pyuhn·jee; *v* 편지 보내다 pyuhn·jee boh·neh·dah

mailbox 우체통 oo·cheh·tohng

main 주요한 joo·yo·hahn

make-up 화장 hwah·jahng

male 남자 nahm·jah

mall 쇼핑센터 syo·peeng·ssehn·tuh

man 남자 nahm·jah

manager 매니저 meh·nee·juh

mandatory 의무적인 u·moo·juh·geen

manicure 매니큐어 meh·nee·kyoo·uh

many 많이 mah·nee

map 지도 jee·doh

market 시장 see·jahng

marry 결혼하다 gyuhl·hohn·hah·dah

mass 미사 mee·sah

massage 마사지 mah·ssah·jee

matches 성냥 suhng·nyahng

matinée 마티네 mah·tee·neh

mattress 매트리스 meh·tu·lee·su

maybe 아마 ah·mah

meal 식사 seek·ssah

mean v 뜻하다 ttu·tah·dah

measure 재다 jeh·dah

measurement 치수 chee·soo

mechanic 자동차 수리공 jah·dohng·chah soo·lee·gohng

medication 약물 yahng·mool

medicine 약 yahk

medium 중간 joong·gahn

meet 만나다 mahn·nah·dah

meeting 회의 hweh·ee

meeting room 회의실 hweh·ee·seel

meeting place 회의 장소 hweh·ee jahng·soh

member 회원 hweh·wuhn

memorial n 기념관 gee·nyuhm·gwahn

memory card 메모리 카드 meh·moh·lee kah·du

mend (clothes) 수선하다 soo·suhn·hah·dah

menstrual cramps 생리통 sehng·nee·tohng

menu 메뉴 meh·nyoo

merge 합치다 hahp·chee·dah

message 메시지 meh·ssee·jee

metal 금속 gum·sohk

microwave (oven) 전자레인지 juhn·jah·leh·een·jee

midday [BE] 정오 juhng·oh

midnight 자정 jah·juhng

migraine 편두통 pyuhn·doo·tohng

mini 소형 soh·hyuhng

miniature 축소 모형 chook·ssoh moh·hyuhng

mini-bar 미니바 mee·nee·bah

minute 분 boon

mirror 거울 guh·ool

missing 없어진 uhp·ssuh·jeen

mistake 실수 seel·ssoo

mobile home 이동식 주택 ee·dohng·seek joo·tehk

mobile phone [BE] 휴대폰 hyoo·deh·pohn

moisturizer (cream) 보습 크림 boh·sup ku·leem

money 돈 dohn

money order 우편환 oo·pyuhn·hwahn

month 달 dahl

mop 대걸레 deh·guhl·leh

more 더 많이 duh mah·nee

morning 아침 ah·cheem

mosque 회교 사원 hweh·gyo sah·wuhn

motion sickness 멀미 muhl·mee

motor 모터 moh·tuh

motor boat 모터 보트 moh·tuh boh·tu

motorcycle 오토바이 oh·toh·bah·ee

motorway [BE] 고속도로 goh·sohk·ttoh·loh

mountain 산 sahn

mouth 입 eep

move 옮기다 ohm·gee·dah

movie 영화 yuhng·hwah

movie theater 영화관 yuhng·hwah·gwahn

much 훨씬 hwuhl·sseen

mugging 노상 강도 noh·sahng gahng·doh

muscle 근육 gu·nyook

museum 박물관 bahng·mool·gwahn

music 음악 u·mahk

must 해야 하다 heh·yah hah·dah

N

nail 손톱 sohn·tohp

nail salon 미용실 mee·yong·seel

name 이름 ee·lum

napkin 냅킨 nehp·keen

nappy [BE] 기저귀 gee·juh·gwih

narrow 좁은 joh·bun

national 국가의 gook·kkah·eh

nationality 국적 gook·tzuhk

native 토박이 toh·bah·gee

nature 자연 jah·yuhn

nature reserve 자연 보호 지역 jah·yuhn boh·hoh jee·yuhk

nature trail 산책로 sahn·chehng·noh

nausea 메스꺼움 meh·su·kkuh·oom

nauseous 토할 거 같은 toh·hahl kkuh gah·tun

near 가까이 gah·kkah·ee

nearby 근처에 gun·chuh·eh

near-sighted 근시 gun·see

necessary 필요한 pee·lyo·hahn

neck 목 mohk

necklace 목걸이 mohk·kkuh·lee

need 필요하다 pee·lyo·hah·dah

network 네트워크 neh·tu·wuh·ku

never 단 한번도 dahn hahn·buhn·doh

new 새로운 seh·loh·oon

New Zealand 뉴질랜드 nyoo·jeel·lehn·du

news 뉴스 nyoo·su

news agent [BE] 신문 가판대 seen·moon gah·pahn·deh

newspaper 신문 seen·moon

newsstand 신문 가판대 seen·moon gah·pahn·deh

next 다음 dah·um

nice 좋은 joh·un

night 밤 bahm

no 아니요 ah·nee·yo

noisy 시끄러운 see·kku·luh·oon

non-smoking 금연 gu·myuhn

non-stop 직행 jee·kehng

noon 정오 juhng·oh

normal 정상 juhng·sahng

north 북쪽 book·tzohk

nose 코 koh

not 아니다 ah·nee·dah

nothing 아무 것도 아님 ah·moo guht·ttoh ah·neem

notify 통보하다 tohng·boh·hah·dah

now 지금 jee·gum

number 번호 buhn·hoh

nurse 간호사 gahn·hoh·sah

O

office 사무실 sah·moo·seel

office hours 영업 시간 yuhng·uhp ssee·gahn

off-lisence [BE] 주류 판매점 joo·lyoo pahn·meh·juhm

off-peak (ticket) 비수기 bee·soo·gee

often 종종 johng·johng

oil 기름 gee·lum

OK 좋다 joh·tah

old (elderly) 늙은 nul·gun; (object) 오래된 oh·leh·dwehn

on 에 eh

once 한 번 hahn buhn

one-way ticket 편도표 pyuhn·doh·pyo

only 오직 oh·jeek

open 열다 yuhl·dah

opening hours [BE] 영업 시간 yuhng·uhp ssee·gahn

opera 오페라 oh·peh·lah

operation 수술 soo·sool

opposite 맞은편 mah·jun·pyuhn

optician 안경점 ahn·gyuhng·juhm

or 또는 ttoh·nun

orchestra 오케스트라 oh·keh·su·tu·lah

order v 주문하다 joo·moon·hah·dah

organize 조직하다 joh·jee·kah·dah

original 원조 wuhn·joh

out 밖 bahk

outdoor 실외 seel·weh

outdoor pool 실외 수영장 seel·weh soo·yuhng·jahng

outside 밖에 bah·kkeh

oven 오븐 oh·bun

over (more than) 이상 ee·sahng

overcharged 바가지 쓴 bah·gah·jee ssun

overheat 과열 gwah·yuhl

overnight 밤새 bahm·seh

owe 빚지다 beet·tzee·dah

own v 소유하다 soh·yoo·hah·dah

owner 주인 joo·een

oxygen 산소 sahn·soh

P

pacifier 고무 젖꼭지 goh·moo juht·kkohk·tzee

pack 싸다 ssah·dah

package 소포 soh·poh

padlock 자물쇠 jah·mool·ssweh

pail 양동이 yahng·dohng·ee

pain 고통 goh·tohng

paint 그리다 gu·lee·dah

painting 그림 gu·leem

pair 한 쌍 hahn ssahng

pajamas 잠옷 jah·moht

palace 궁 goong

panorama 전경 juhn·gyuhng

pants 바지 bah·jee

panty hose 팬티스타킹 pehn·tee·su·tah·keeng

paper towel 종이 타월 johng·ee tah·wuhl

parcel [BE] 소포 soh·poh

parents 부모님 boo·moh·neem

park 공 원 gohng·wuhn

parking attendant 주차 요원 joo·chah yo·wuhn

parking garage 주차장 joo·chah·jahng

parking lot 주차장 joo·chah·jahng

parking meter 주차 미터기 joo·chah mee·tuh·gee

parking ticket 주차 위반 딱지 joo·chah wih·bahn ttahk·jee

partner 상대 sahng·deh

party 파티 pah·tee

pass v 지나다 jee·nah·dah

passenger 승객 sung·gehk

passport 여권 yuh·kkwuhn

password 비밀번호 bee·meel·buhn·hoh

patient n 환자 hwahn·jah

pavement [BE] 보도 boh·doh

pay 계산하다 geh·sahn·hah·dah

pay phone 공중 전화 gohng·joong juhn·hwah

payment 지불 jee·bool

pearl 진주 jeen·joo

pedestrian n 보행자 boh·hehng·jah

pedestrian crossing 횡단보도 hwehng·dahn·boh·doh

pediatrician 소아과 의사 soh·ah·kkwah u·sah

pedicure 페디큐어 peh·dee·kyoo·uh

peg 나무 못 nah·moo moht

pen 펜 pehn

penicillin 페니실린 peh·nee·seel·leen

per 에 eh

performance 공연 gohng·yuhn

perhaps 아마 ah·mah

period (historical) 시대 see·deh;
(menstrual) 생리 sehng·nee

person 사람 sah·lahm

petite 아주 작은 ah·joo jah·gun;
(clothing) 특소 tuk·ssoh

petrol [BE] 기름 gee·lum

petrol station [BE] 주유소 joo·yoo·soh

pharmacy 약국 yahk·kkook

phone n 전화 juhn·hwah

phone call 전화 juhn·hwah

phone card 전화 카드 juhn·hwah
kah·du

phone directory 전화 번호부
juhn·hwah buhn·hoh·boo

phone number 전화 번호 juhn·hwah
buhn·hoh

photocopy v 복사하다
bohk·ssah·hah·dah

photograph 사진 sah·jeen

phrase 구절 goo·juhl

phrase book 기본 회화집 gee·bohn
hweh·hwah·jeep

picnic 피크닉 pee·ku·neek

picnic area 피크닉 구역 pee·ku·neek
goo·yuhk

piece 개 geh

pill 알약 ahl·lyahk

pillow 베개 beh·geh

PIN (personal identification number) 비
밀 번호 bee·meel buhn·hoh

place 자리 jah·lee

plan 계획 geh·hwehk

plane 비행기 bee·hehng·gee

plaster [BE] 반창고 bahn·chahng·goh

plastic 플라스틱 pul·lah·su·teek

plastic wrap 랩 lehp

plate 접시 juhp·ssee

platform 승강장 sung·gahng·jahng

platinum 백금 behk·kkum

play n 연극 yuhn·guk; v (sports)
시합하다 see·hah·pah·dah; v (music)
연주하다 yuhn·joo·hah·dah

playground 놀이터 noh·lee·tuh

playpen 아기 놀이울 ah·gee
noh·lee·ool

pleasant 즐거운 jul·guh·oon

please 좀 johm

plug 플러그 pul·luh·gu

plunger 변기 뚫는 것 byuhn·gee
ttool·nun guht

poison 독 dohk

police 경찰 gyuhng·chahl

police station 경찰서
gyuhng·chahl·ssuh

pollen count 꽃가루 지수
kkoht·kkah·loo jee·soo

pond 연못 yuhn·moht

pool 수영장 soo·yuhng·jahng

popular 인기있는 een·kkee·een·nun

porcelain 자기 jah·gee

port 항구 hahng·goo

porter 짐꾼 jeem·kkoon

portion 분량 bool·lyahng

post office 우체국 oo·cheh·gook

postage 우편 요금 oo·pyuhn nyo·gum

postbox [BE] 우체통 oo·cheh·tohng

postcard 엽서 yuhp·ssuh

pot 냄비 nehm·bee

pottery 도자기 doh·jah·gee

pound 파운드 pah·oon·du

pound sterling 파운드 pah·oon·du

power 힘 heem

practice v 연습하다 yuhn·su·pah·dah

185

pregnant 임신한 eem·seen·hahn

prepaid phone card 선불 전화 카드
suhn·bool juhn·hwah kah·du

prescription 처방 chuh·bahng

present *n* 선물 suhn·mool

press 다림질하다
dah·leem·jeel·hah·dah

pretty 예쁜 yeh·ppun

price 가격 gah·gyuhk

print *v* 프린트하다 pu·leen·tu·hah·dah

prison 감옥 gah·mohk

private 사적인 sah·tzuh·geen

profession 직업 jee·guhp

problem 문제 moon·jeh

prohibited 금지된 gum·jee·dwehn

program 프로그램 pu·loh·gu·lehm

pronounce 발음하다 bah·lum·hah·dah

pub 술집 sool·tzeep

public 공공 gohng·gohng

pull 당기다 dahng·gee·dah

pure 순수한 soon·soo·hahn

purpose 목적 mohk·tzuhk

purse 핸드백 hehn·du·behk

push 밀다 meel·dah

push-chair [BE] 유모차 yoo·moh·chah

put 넣다 nuh·tah

Q

quality 질 jeel

quarter 사분의 일 sah·boo·neh eel

quick 빠른 ppah·lun

quiet 조용한 joh·yong·hahn

R

race course [BE] 경마장
gyuhng·mah·jahng

racetrack 경마장 gyuhng·mah·jahng

racket (tennis) 라켓 lah·keht

railway station [BE] 기차역
gee·chah·yuhk

rain *n* 비 bee; *v* 비 내리다 bee
neh·lee·dah

raincoat 비옷 bee·oht

rape 강간 gahng·gahn

rapids 급류 gum·nyoo

rash 두드러기 doo·du·luh·gee

razor 면도칼 myuhn·doh·kahl

razor blade 면도날 myuhn·doh·nahl

reach 연락하다 yuhl·lah·kah·dah

reaction 반응 bah·nung

read 읽다 eek·ttah

ready 준비된 joon·bee·dwehn

real (genuine) 진짜 jeen·tzah

receipt 영수증 yuhng·soo·jung

receive 받다 baht·ttah

reception (desk) 접수 juhp·ssoo

receptionist 접수원 juhp·ssoo·wuhn

recommend 추천하다
choo·chuhn·hah·dah

reduce 줄이다 joo·lee·dah

reduction 감소 gahm·soh

refrigerator 냉장고 nehng·jahng·goh

refund 환불 hwahn·bool

region 지역 jee·yuhk

registered mail 등기 우편 dung·kkee
oo·pyuhn

registration form 등록 용지 dung·noh
gyong·jee

regular 보통 boh·tohng

relationship 관계 gwahn·geh

reliable 믿을 만한 mee·dul mahn·hahn

religion 종교 johng·gyo

remember 기억하다 gee·uh·kah·dah

remove 제거하다 jeh·guh·hah·dah

renovation 개조 geh·joh

rent v 빌리다 beel·lee·dah

rental car 렌터카 lehn·tuh·kah

repair 수선하다 soo·suhn·hah·dah

repeat 되풀이하다
dweh·poo·lee·hah·dah

replace 바꾸다 bah·kkoo·dah

report v 신고하다 seen·goh·hah·dah

required 필수 peel·ssoo

reservation 예약 yeh·yahk

reservation desk 예약 접수처
yeh·yahk juhp·ssoo·chuh

reserve 예약하다 yeh·yah·kah·dah

reservoir 저수지 juh·soo·jee

responsibility 책임 cheh·geem

rest 쉬다 swih·dah

rest area 휴게소 hyoo·geh·soh

restaurant 음식점 um·seek·tzuhm

restroom 화장실 hwah·jahng·seel

retired 은퇴한 un·tweh·hahn

return v 돌아가다 doh·lah·gah·dah

return ticket [BE] 왕복표 wahng·bohk·pyo

rice bowl 밥그릇 bahp·kku·lut

rice cooker 밥솥 bahp·ssoht

right 오른쪽 oh·lun·tzohk

ring 반지 bahn·jee

river 강 gahng

road 도로 doh·loh

rob 빼앗다 ppeh·aht·ttah

robbery 강도 gahng·doh

rock 록 lohk

romantic 낭만적인
nahng·mahn·juh·geen

roof 지붕 jee·boong

room 방 bahng

room service 룸 서비스 loom
ssuh·bee·su

room temperature 상온 sahng·ohn

rope 밧줄 baht·tzool

rose 장미 jahng·mee

round (of golf) 라운드 lah·oon·du

round-trip ticket 왕복표
wahng·bohk·pyo

route 길 geel

row n 노 noh

rowboat 노 젓는 배 noh juhn·nun beh

rubbish [BE] 쓰레기 ssu·leh·gee

rude 무례한 moo·leh·hahn

rush 서두르다 suh·doo·lu·dah

S

safe adj 안전한 ahn·juhn·hahn;
n 금고 gum·goh

safety 안전 ahn·juhn

safety pin 안전핀 ahn·juhn·peen

sale [BE] 영업 yuhng·uhp

sales tax 판매세 pahn·meh·seh

same 같은 gah·tun

sand 모래 moh·leh

sandals 샌들 sehn·dul

sanitary napkin 생리대 sehng·nee·deh

sanitary pad [BE] 생리대
sehng·nee·deh

satin 공단 gohng·dahn

saucepan 냄비 nehm·bee

sauna 사우나 ssah·oo·nah

save 저장하다 juh·jahng·hah·dah

savings account 보통 예금 계좌
boh·tohng yeh·gum geh·jwah

say 말하다 mahl·hah·dah

scarf 스카프 su·kah·pu

scale 저울 juh·ool

schedule 시간표 see·gahn·pyo

scissors 가위 gah·wih

Scotland 스코틀랜드 su·koh·tul·lehn·du

screwdriver 드라이버 du·lah·ee·buh

sea 바다 bah·dah

sea level 해발 heh·bahl

seasick 뱃멀미 behn·muhl·mee

seat (on train, etc.) 좌석 jwah·suhk

seat belt 안전벨트 ahn·juhn·behl·tu

secondhand 중고 joong·goh

sedative 진정제 jeen·juhng·jeh

see 보다 boh·dah

self-service 셀프서비스
ssehl·pu·ssuh·bee·su

sell 팔다 pahl·dah

seminar 세미나 sseh·mee·nah

send 보내다 boh·neh·dah

senior citizen 노인 noh·een

separate 따로 ttah·loh

separated 별거한 byuhl·guh·hahn

serious 심각한 seem·gah·kahn

serve 봉사하다 bohng·sah·hah·dah

service (religious) 예배 yeh·beh

service charge 봉사료 bohng·sah·lyo

sew 꿰매다 kkweh·meh·dah

sex 성 suhng

shadow 그림자 gu·leem·jah

shallow 얕은 yah·tun

shampoo 샴푸 syahm·poo

shape 모양 moh·yahng

share v 같이 쓰다 gah·chee ssu·dah

sharp 날카로운 nahl·kah·loh·oon

shave 면도하다 myuhn·doh·hah·dah

sheet (bed) 시트 see·tu

ship 배 beh

shock 충격 choong·gyuhk

shoe 신발 seen·bahl

shoe repair 신발 수선 seen·bahl
soo·suhn

shoe store 신발 가게 seen·bahl
kkah·geh

shop assistant 점원 juh·mwuhn

shopping 쇼핑 syo·peeng

shopping area 상가 sahng·gah

shopping basket 바구니 bah·goo·nee

shopping centre [BE] 상가 sahng·gah

shopping mall 상가 sahng·gah

shopping cart 쇼핑 카트 syo·peeng
kah·tu

shopping trolley [BE] 쇼핑 카트
syo·peeng kah·tu

short 짧은 tzahl·bun

short-sighted [BE] 근시 gun·see

shorts 반바지 bahn·bah·jee

shoulder 어깨 uh·kkeh

shovel 삽 sahp

show 보여주다 boh·yuh·joo·dah

shower 샤워 syah·wuh

shut adj 닫힌 dah·cheen; n 닫다
daht·ttah

sick 아픈 ah·pun

side effect 부작용 boo·jah·gyong

sidewalk 보도 boh·doh

sight (attraction) 구경거리
goo·gyuhng·kkuh·lee

sightseeing tour 관광 코스
gwahn·gwahng koh·su

sign n 표지 pyo·jee; v 서명하다
suh·myuhng·hah·dah

silk 실크 seel·ku

silver 은 un

single (individual) 일인용
ee·leen·yong; (marital status)
미혼 mee·hohn

single room 일인용 방 ee·leen·yong
bahng

sink 세면대 seh·myuhn·deh

sit 앉다 ahn·ttah

site 장소 jahng·soh

size 사이즈 ssah·ee·ju

ski slope 스키장 su·kee·jahng

skin 피부 pee·boo

skirt 치마 chee·mah

sleep 자다 jah·dah

sleeper car (train) 침대차
cheem·deh·chah

sleeping bag 침낭 cheem·nahng

sleeping pill 수면제 soo·myuhn·jeh

sleeve 소매 soh·meh

slice 조각 joh·gahk

slippers 슬리퍼 sul·lee·puh

slow 느린 nu·leen

small 작은 jah·gun

smell 냄새 맡다 nehm·seh maht·ttah

smoke 담배를 피우다 dahm·beh·lul
pee·oo·dah

smoking area 흡연석 hu·byuhn·suhk

snack 간식 gahn·seek

snack bar 간이 식당 gah·nee
seek·ttahng

sneakers 운동화 oon·dohng·hwah

snorkle 잠수용 튜브 jahm·soo·yong
tyoo·bu

snow 눈 noon

soap 비누 bee·noo

soccer 축구 chook·kkoo

socket 소켓 soh·keht

socks 양말 yahng·mahl

sold out 매진 meh·jeen

some 다소 dah·soh

someone 누군가 noo·goon·gah

something 무언가 moo·uhn·gah

sometimes 가끔 gah·kkum

somewhere 어딘가 uh·deen·gah

soon 곧 goht

soother [BE] 고무 젖꼭지 goh·moo
juht·kkohk·jee

sore 쑤시는 ssoo·see·nun

sore throat 목 아픈 데 moh gah·pun
deh

sorry 미안하다 mee·ahn·hah·dah

sour 시큼한 see·kum·hahn

south 남쪽 nahm·tzohk

souvenir 기념품 gee·nyuhm·poom

souvenir guide 기념품 안내
gee·nyuhm·poom ahn·neh

souvenir store 기념품 가게
gee·nyuhm·poom kkah·geh

spa 스파 su·pah

space 자리 jah·lee

spare 여분 yuh·boon

speak 얘기하다 yeh·gee·hah·dah

special 특별한 tuk·ppyuhl·hahn

specialist 전문의 juhn·moo·nee

specimen 표본 pyo·bohn

speed *n* 속도 sohk·ttoh;
v 과속하다 gwah·soh·kah·dah

speed limit 제한 속도 jeh·hahn
sohk·ttoh

spell 철자하다 chuhl·tzah·hah·dah

spend 쓰다 ssu·dah

sponge 스폰지 su·pohn·jee

spoon 숟가락 soot·kkah·lahk

sport 운동 oon·dohng

sporting goods store 스포츠
용품점 su·poh·chu yong·poom·juhm

sports club 스포츠 클럽 su·poh·chu
kul·luhp

spot (place, site) 장소 jahng·soh

spouse 배우자 beh·oo·jah

sprain 삐다 ppee·dah

square 광장 gwahng·jahng

stadium 경기장 gyuhng·gee·jahng

staff 직원 jee·gwuhn

stainless steel 스테인레스 su·teh·een·leh·su

stairs 계단 geh·dahn

stamp 우표 oo·pyo

stand *n* 정류장 juhng·nyoo·jahng; *v* 일어서다 ee·luh·suh·dah

standard 표준 pyo·joon

standby ticket 대기표 deh·gee·pyo

start (begin) 시작하다 see·jah·kah·dah

stationery 문구류 moon·goo·lyoo

statue 동상 dohng·sahng

stay 묵다 mook·ttah

steal 훔치다 hoom·chee·dah

steel 철 chuhl

steep 가파른 gah·pah·lun

sterilizing solution 소독액 soh·doh·gehk

sterling silver 순은 soo·nun

stolen 도난 당한 doh·nahn dahng·hahn

stomach 위 wih

stomachache 복통 bohk·tohng

stop *n* 정거장 juhng·guh·jahng; *v* 세우다 seh·oo·dah

store 가게 gah·geh

store directory 상가 안내 sahng·gah ahn·neh

stove 가스 레인지 gah·su leh·een·jee

straight 똑바른 ttohk·bah·lun

stream 개울 geh·ool

street 길 geel

stroller 유모차 yoo·moh·chah

strong 강한 gahng·hahn

student 학생 hahk·ssehng

study 공부하다 gohng·boo·hah·dah

style 스타일 su·tah·eel

subtitled 자막 나오는 jah·mahng nah·oh·nun

suburb 교외 gyo·weh

subway 지하철 jee·hah·chuhl

subway map 지하철 노선도 jee·hah·chuhl noh·suhn·doh

subway station 지하철역 jee·hah·chuhl·lyuhk

suggest 제안하다 jeh·ahn·hah·dah

suit 양복 yahng·bohk

suitable 적당한 juhk·ttahng·hahn

suitcase 여행 가방 yuh·hehng kkah·bahng

sun 해 heh

sunbathe 일광욕하다 eel·gwahng·nyo·kah·dah

sunburn 일광 화상 eel·gwahng hwah·sahng

sunglasses 선글라스 ssuhn·gul·lah·su

sunscreen 자외선 차단 크림 jah·weh·suhn chah·dahn ku·leem

sunstroke 일사병 eel·ssah·ppyuhng

suntan lotion 선탠 크림 ssuhn·tehn ku·leem

superb 최고 chweh·goh

supermarket 슈퍼마켓 syoo·puh·mah·keht

supervision 감독 gahm·dohk

supplement 추가 choo·gah

suppository 좌약 jwah·yahk

sure 확실한 hwahk·sseel·hahn

surfboard 서핑보드 ssuh·peeng·boh·du

swallow 삼키다 sahm·kee·dah

sweater 스웨터 su·weh·tuh

sweep 쓸다 ssul·dah

sweet (taste) 달콤한 dahl·kohm·hahn

swelling 부은 데 boo·un deh

swim 수영하다 soo·yuhng·hah·dah

swimsuit 수영복 soo·yuhng·bohk

swimming pool 수영장 soo·yuhng·jahng

swimming trunks 수영복
soo·yuhng·bohk

swollen 부은 boo·un

symbol 기호 gee·hoh

symptom 증상 jung·sahng

synagogue 유대교 회당 yoo·deh·gyo
hweh·dahng

synthetic 합성 hahp·ssuhng

T

T-shirt 티셔츠 tee·syuh·chu

table 테이블 teh·ee·bul

tablet 알약 ahl·lyahk

take (things) 가지다 gah·jee·dah

taken 임자 있는 eem·jah een·nun

take away [BE] 싸가다 ssah·gah·dah

take off (clothing) 벗다 buht·ttah;
(plane) 이륙하다 ee·lyoo·kah·dah

talk 얘기하다 yeh·gee·hah·dah

tall 키 큰 kee kun

tampon 탐폰 tahm·pohn

tan 태우다 teh·oo·dah

tap [BE] 수도꼭지 soo·doh·kkohk·jee

taste 맛보다 maht·ppoh·dah

taxi 택시 tehk·ssee

taxi stand 택시 승차장 tehk·ssee
sung·chah·jahng

teaspoon 티스푼 tee·su·poon

team 팀 teem

tear 찢다 tzeet·ttah

telephone 전화 juhn·hwah

telephone number 전화 번호
juhn·hwah buhn·hoh

television 텔레비전 tehl·leh·bee·juhn

tell 말하다 mahl·hah·dah

temperature 온도 ohn·doh

tennis 테니스 teh·nee·su

tennis court 테니스 코트 teh·nee·su
koh·tu

tent 텐트 tehn·tu

terminal 터미널 tuh·mee·nuhl

terrible 끔찍한 kkum·tzee·kahn

terrific 굉장한 gwehng·jahng·hahn

text 문자 moon·tzah

thank 감사하다 gahm·sah·hah·dah

that 그것 gu·guht

theater 극장 guk·tzahng

theft 도난 doh·nahn

then (time) 그때 gu·tteh

there 거기 guh·gee

thermometer 온도계 ohn·doh·geh

thick 두꺼운 doo·kkuh·oon

thief 도둑 doh·dook

thigh 넓적다리 nuhp·tzuhk·ttah·lee

thin 가는 gah·nun

thing 물건 mool·guhn

think 생각하다 sehng·gah·kah·dah

thirsty 목마르다 mohng·mah·lu·dah

throat 목구멍 mohk·kkoo·muhng

through 통해서 tohng·heh·suh

thumb 엄지손가락
uhm·jee·sohn·kkah·lahk

ticket 표 pyo

ticket inspector 검표원 guhm·pyo·wuhn

ticket office 매표소 meh·pyo·soh

tie 넥타이 nehk·tah·ee

tight 끼는 kkee·nun

tile 타일 tah·eel

time 시간 see·gahn

timetable [BE] 시간표 see·gahn·pyo

tin opener [BE] 통조림 따개
tohng·joh·leem ttah·geh

tint 빛깔 beet·kkahl

tip 팁 teep

tire 타이어 tah·ee·uh

tired 피곤한 pee·gohn·hahn

tissue 화장지 hwah·jahng·jee

to (place) 으로 u·loh

tobacco 담배 dahm·beh

tobacconist 담배 가게 dahm·beh kkah·geh

today 오늘 oh·nul

toe 발가락 bahl·kkah·lahk

toilet [BE] 화장실 hwah·jahng·seel

toilet paper 화장실 휴지 hwah·jahng·seel hyoo·jee

tomorrow 내일 neh·eel

tongue 혀 hyuh

tonight 오늘밤 oh·nul·ppahm

too 너무 nuh·moo

tooth 이빨 ee·ppahl

toothache 치통 chee·tohng

toothbrush 칫솔 cheet·ssohl

toothpaste 치약 chee·yahk

top 위 wih

torn 찢어진 tzee·juh·jeen

tough 질긴 jeel·geen

tour 여행 yuh·hehng

tour guide 여행 가이드 yuh·hehng gah·ee·du

tourist 관광객 gwahn·gwahng·gehk

tourist office 여행 안내소 yuh·hehng ahn·neh·soh

tournament 대회 deh·hweh

tow truck 견인차 gyuh·neen·chah

towel 수건 soo·guhn

tower 탑 tahp

town 시내 see·neh

town map 시내 지도 see·neh jee·doh

toy 장난감 jahng·nahn·kkahm

toy store 장난감 가게 jahng·nahn·kkahm gah·geh

traditional 전통 juhn·tohng

traditional dance 전통춤 juhn·tohng·choom

traditional music 국악 goo·gahk

traffic 교통 gyo·tohng

trail 등산로 dung·sahn·noh

trailer 트레일러 tu·leh·eel·luh

train 기차 gee·chah

train station 기차역 gee·chah·yuhk

tram 전차 juhn·chah

transfer 갈아타다 gah·lah·tah·dah

transport 수송 soo·sohng

translate 번역하다 buh·nyuh·kah·dah

translation 번역 buh·nyuhk

translator 번역사 buh·nyuhk·ssah

trash 쓰레기 ssu·leh·gee

trash can 쓰레기통 ssu·leh·gee·tohng

travel *n* 여행 yuh·hehng

travel agency 여행사 yuh·hehng·sah

travel sickness 멀미 muhl·mee

traveler's check 여행자 수표 yuh·hehng·jah soo·pyo

traveler's cheque [BE] 여행자 수표 yuh·hehng·jah soo·pyo

tray 쟁반 jehng·bahn

treatment 치료 chee·lyo

tree 나무 nah·moo

trim 다듬다 dah·dum·ttah

trip 여행 yuh·hehng

trolley 카트 kah·tu

trousers [BE] 바지 bah·jee

truck 트럭 tu·luhk

true 사실 sah·seel

try on (clothes) 입어 보다 ee·buh boh·dah; (shoes) 신어 보다 see·nuh boh·dah

tumor 종양 johng·yahng

tunnel 터널 tuh·nuhl

turn 돌다 dohl·dah

tweezers 족집게 johk·tzeep·geh

twist 비틀다 bee·tul·dah

type 종류 johng·nyoo

typical 전형적인 juhn·hyuhng·juh·geen

U

ugly 못생긴 moht·ssehng·geen

umbrella 우산 oo·sahn

unconscious 의식을 잃은 u·see·gul ee·lun

under 아래 ah·leh

underground [BE] 지하철 jee·hah·chuhl

underground station [BE] 지하철 역 jee·hah·chuhl lyuhk

understand 알다 ahl·dah

unemployed 실업자 see·luhp·tzah

United Kingdom 영국 yuhng·gook

United States 미국 mee·gook

until 까지 kkah·jee

upstairs 위층 wih·chung

urgent 급한 gu·pahn

use 사용하다 sah·yong·hah·dah

username 사용자명 sah·yong·jah·myuhng

V

vacant 빈 been

vacation 휴가 hyoo·gah

vacuum cleaner 진공 청소기 jeen·gohng chuhng·soh·gee

vagina 질 jeel

valet service 주차 서비스 joo·chah ssuh·bee·su

valid 유효한 yoo·hyo·hahn

validate 확인하다 hwah·geen·hah·dah

valuable 귀중한 gwih·joong·hahn

value 가격 gah·gyuhk

valve 밸브 behl·bu

van taxi 콜 밴 kohl·behn

VAT [BE] 부가가치세 boo·gah·gah·chee·seh

vegetarian 채식주의자 cheh·seek·jtzoo·ee·jah

vehicle 자동차 jah·dohng·chah

vein 정맥 juhng·mehk

version 버전 buh·juhn

very 매우 meh·oo

view 전망 juhn·mahng

viewpoint 전망대 juhn·mahng·deh

village 마을 mah·ul

vineyard 포도밭 poh·doh·baht

visa 비자 bee·jah

visit *n* 방문 bahng·moon; *v* 방문하다 bahng·moon·hah·dah

visiting hours 방문 시간 bahng·moon see·gahn

visually impaired 시각 장애인 see·gahk jahng·eh·een

volleyball 배구 beh·goo

vomit 토하다 toh·hah·dah

W

wait 기다리다 gee·dah·lee·dah

waiter 남자 종업원 nahm·jah johng·uh·bwuhn

waiting room 대기실 deh·gee·seel

waitress 여자 종업원 yuh·jah johng·uh·bwuhn

wake 깨우다 kkeh·oo·dah

wake-up call 모닝콜 moh·neeng·kohl

walk 걷다 guht·ttah

wall 벽 byuhk

wallet 지갑 jee·gahp

ward (hospital) 병동 byuhng·dohng

warm 따뜻한 ttah·ttu·tahn

war memorial 전쟁 기념관 juhn·jehng gee·nyuhm·gwahn

warning 경고 gyuhng·goh

washing machine 세탁기 seh·tahk·kkee

watch 시계 see·geh

water 물 mool

water skis 수상 스키 soo·sahng su·kee

waterfall 폭포 pohk·poh

waterproof 방수 bahng·soo

wave 파도 pah·doh

way 길 geel

wear 입다 eep·ttah

weather 날씨 nahl·ssee

weather forecast 일기 예보 eel·gee yeh·boh

wedding 결혼식 gyuhl·hohn·seek

week 주일 joo·eel

weekday 평일 pyuhng·eel

weekend 주말 joo·mahl

weekend rate 주말 요금 joo·mahl lyo·gum

weekly 매주 meh·joo

weigh 무게를 달다 moo·geh·lul dahl·dah

weight 무게 moo·geh

welcome 환영 hwah·nyuhng

west 서쪽 suh·tzohk

wetsuit 잠수복 jahm·soo·bohk

what 무엇 moo·uht

wheelchair 휠체어 wihl·cheh·uh

wheelchair ramp 휠체어 진입로 wihl·cheh·uh jee·neem·noh

when 언제 uhn·jeh

where 어디 uh·dee

who 누구 noo·goo

why 왜 weh

wide 넓은 nuhl·bun

wife 아내 ah·neh

wildlife 야생 yah·sehng

wind 바람 bah·lahm

windbreaker 윈드브레이커 wihn·du·bu·leh·ee·kuh

windscreen 차 앞유리 chah ahm·nyoo·lee

windsurfing 윈드서핑 wihn·du·ssuh·peeng

window 창문 chahng·moon

window seat 창문석 chahng·moon·suhk

wipe 닦다 dahk·ttah

wireless 무선 moo·suhn

wish 바라다 bah·lah·dah

with 하고 같이 hah·goh gah·chee

withdraw 출금하다 chool·gum·hah·dah

withdrawal 출금 chool·gum

within 안에 ah·neh

without 없이 uhp·ssee

witness 목격자 mohk·kkyuhk·tzah

Won (Korean currency) 원 wuhn

wool 양모 yahng·moh

work *n* 일 eel; *v* 일하다 eel·hah·dah

wrap *n* 랩 leph; *v* 싸다 ssah·dah

write 쓰다 ssu·dah

writing paper 필기 용지 peel·gee yong·jee

wrong 잘못된 jahl·moht·ttwehn

X

x-ray 엑스레이 ehk·ssu·leh·ee

Y

yacht 요트 yo·tu
year 년 nyuhn
yes 네 neh
yesterday 어제 uh·jeh
yield 양보하다 yahng·boh·hah·dah
young 젊은 juhl·mun

youth 젊음 juhl·mum
youth hostel 유스호스텔
  yoo·su·hoh·su·tehl

Z

zipper 지퍼 jee·puh
zoo 동물원 dohng·moo·lwuhn

Korean–English Dictionary

ㄱ

가게 **gah·geh** store

가격 **gah·gyuhk** price, value

가구 **gah·goo** furniture

가까이 **gah·kkah·ee** near

가끔 **gah·kkum** sometimes

가는 **gah·nun** thin

가다 **gah·dah** go, take (road)

가득 찬 **gah·duk chahn** full

가득 채우다 **gah·duk cheh·oo·dah** fill
up

가려움 **gah·lyuh·oom** itch

가로질러 **gah·loh·jeel·luh** across

가방 **gah·bahng** bag

가스 레인지 **kkah·su leh·een·jee** stove

가슴 **gah·sum** breast, chest

가위 **gah·wih** scissors

가이드 투어 **gah·ee·du too·uh** guided
tour

가져오다 **gah·jyuh·oh·dah** bring

가족 **gah·johk** family

가죽 **gah·jook** leather

가지다 **gah·jee·dah** take

가파른 **gah·pah·lun** steep

간식 **gahn·seek** snack

간이 식당 **gah·nee seek·ttahng** snack
bar

간호사 **gahn·hoh·sah** nurse

갈아타다 **gah·lah·tah·dah** transfer

감기 **gahm·gee** *n* cold

감독 **gahm·dohk** supervision

감사하다 **gahm·sah·hah·dah** thank

감소 **gahm·soh** reduction

감염 **gah·myuhm** infection

감염시키다 **gah·myuhm·see·kee·dah**
infect

감옥 **gah·mohk** prison

강 **gahng** river

강간 **gahng·gahn** rape

강도 **gahng·doh** robbery

강사 **gahng·sah** instructor

강한 **gahng·hahn** strong

갖다 **gaht·ttah** have

같은 **gah·tun** same

같이 가다 **gah·chee gah·dah**
accompany

같이 쓰다 **gah·chee ssu·dah** *v* share

개 **geh** dog; piece

개울 **geh·ool** stream

개조 **geh·joh** renovation

객실 **gehk·sseel** compartment

거기 **guh·gee** there

거리 **guh·lee** distance

거실 **guh·seel** living room

거울 **guh·ool** mirror

거즈 **guh·ju** gauze

건강 **guhn·gahng** health

건강 식품점 **guhn·gahng
seek·poom·juhm** health food store

건물 **guhn·mool** building

건배 **guhn·beh** cheers (toast)

건전지 **guhn·juhn·jee** battery

걷다 **guht·ttah** walk

검사 **guhm·sah** examination

검표원 **guhm·pyo·wuhn** ticket inspector

견인차 **gyuh·neen·chah** tow truck

결백한 **gyuhl·beh·kahn** innocent

결혼식 **gyuhl·hohn·seek** wedding

결혼하다 **gyuhl·hohn·hah·dah** marry

경고 **gyuhng·goh** warning

경기 **gyuhng·gee** game

경기장 **gyuhng·gee·jahng** stadium

경련 **gyuhng·nyuhn** cramp

경마 **gyuhng·mah** horse racing

경마장 **gyugng·mah·jahng** horsetrack [race course BE]

경사 **gyuhng·sah** n incline

경찰 **gyuhng·chahl** police

경찰서 **gyuhng·chahl·ssuh** police station

경찰 조서 **gyuhng·chahl joh·suh** police report

경험 **gyuhng·huhm** experience

계단 **geh·dahn** stairs

계량스푼 **geh·lyahng·su·poon** measuring spoon

계량컵 **geh·lyahng·kuhp** measuring cup

계산대 **geh·sahn·deh** cash register

계산서 **geh·sahn·suh** bill

계산원 **geh·sah·nwuhn** cashier

계산하다 **geh·sahn·hah·dah** pay

계획 **geh·hwehk** plan

고객 서비스 **goh·gehk ssuh·bee·su** customer service

고르다 **goh·lu·dah** choose

고무 젖꼭지 **goh·moo juht·kkohk·tzee** pacifier [soother BE]

고속도로 **goh·sohk·ttoh·loh** highway [motorway BE]

고장난 **goh·jahng·nahn** break down, broken

고전적인 **goh·juhn·juh·geen** classical

고치다 **goh·chee·dah** fix, repair

고통 **goh·tohng** pain

곧 **goht** soon

골동품 **gohl·ttohng·poom** antique

골절상 **gohl·tzuhl·sahng** fracture

골프 **gohl·pu** golf

골프장 **gohl·pu·jahng** golf course

골프채 **gohl·pu·cheh** golf club

공 **gohng** ball, zero

공공 **gohng·gohng** public

공단 **gohng·dahn** satin

공동묘지 **gohng·dohng·myo·jee** cemetery

공부하다 **gohng·boo·hah·dah** study

공연 **gohng·yuhn** performance

공예점 **gohng·yeh·juhm** craft shop

공원 **gohng·wuhn** park

공중전화 **gohng·joong·juhn·hwa** pay phone

공짜 **gohng·tzah** free of charge

공항 **gohng·hahng** airport

과속하다 **gwah·soh·khah·dah** v speed

과열 **gwah·yuhl** overheat

관계 **gwahn·geh** relationship

관광 코스 **gwahn·gwahng koh·su** sightseeing tour

관광객 **gwahn·gwahng·gehk** tourist

관리 **gwahl·lee** n control

관장약 **gwahn·jahng·yahk** laxative

관절 **gwahn·juhl** joint

관절염 **gwahn·juhl·lyuhm** arthritis

광장 **gwahng·jahng** square

굉장한 **gwehng·jahng·hahn** terrific

교외 **gyo·weh** suburb

교차로 **gyo·chah·loh** intersection

교통 **gyo·tohng** traffic

교통 정체 **gyo·tohng juhng·cheh** traffic jam

교회 **gyo·hweh** church

구경거리 **goo·gyuhng·kkuh·lee** sight (attraction)

구급차 **goo·gup·chah** ambulance

구리 **goo·lee** copper

구멍 **goo·muhng** hole

구명 보트 **goo·myuhng boh·tu** life boat

구명 조끼 **goo·myuhng joh·kkee** life jacket

구역 **goo·yuhk** area

구절 **goo·juhl** phrase

구조원 **goo·joh·wuhn** life guard

구하다 **goo·hah·dah** get (find)

국가 번호 **gook·kkah buhn·hoh** country code

국가의 **gook·kkah·eh** national

국내 **goong·neh** domestic

국악 **goo·gahk** traditional music

국적 **gook·tzuhk** nationality

국제 **gook·tzeh** international

국제 학생증 **gook·tzeh hahk·ssehng·tzung** International Student Card

군중 **goon·joong** crowd

궁 **goong** palace

권투 **gwuhn·too** boxing

귀 **gwih** ear

귀걸이 **gwih·guh·lee** earrings

귀머거리 **gwih·muh·guh·lee** deaf

귀약 **gwih·yahk** ear drops

귀여운 **gwih·yuh·oon** cute

귀중한 **gwih·joong·hahn** valuable

귀찮게 하다 **gwih·chahn·keh hah·dah** bother

귀통증 **gwih·tohng·tzung** earache

그것 **gu·guht** that

그것들 **gu·guht·ttul** those

그때 **gu·tteh** then (time)

그램 **gu·lehm** gram

그러나 **gu·luh·nah** but

그리고 **gu·lee·goh** and

그리다 **gu·lee·dah** paint

그림 **gu·leem** painting

그림자 **gu·leem·jah** shadow

극장 **guk·tzahng** theater

근사한 **gun·sah·hahn** great

근시 **gun·see** near-sighted [short-sighted BE]

근육 **gu·nyook** muscle

근처에 **gun·chuh·eh** nearby

글루텐 **gul·loo·tehn** gluten

금 **gum** gold

금고 **gum·goh** n safe

금속 **gum·sohk** metal

금액 **gu·mehk** amount

금연 **gu·myuhn** non-smoking

금지된 **gum·jee·dwehn** prohibited

급류 **gum·nyoo** rapids

급한 **gu·pahn** urgent

기내 휴대 수하물 **gee·neh hyoo·deh soo·hah·mool** carry-on luggage

기념관 **gee·nyuhm·gwahn** n memorial

기념품 **gee·nyuhm·poom** souvenir

기념품 가게 **gee·nyuhm·poom kkah·geh** souvenir store

기념품 안내 **gee·nyuhm·poom ahn·neh** souvenir guide

기다리다 **gee·dah·lee·dah** wait

기름 **gee·lum** gas [petrol BE], oil

기름통 **gee·lum·tohng** gas tank

기본회화집 **gee·bohn hweh·hwah·jeep** phrase book

기부 **gee·boo** contribution, donation

기어 **gee·uh** gear

기억하다 **gee·uh·kah·dah** remember

기저귀 **gee·juh·gwih** diaper [nappy BE]

기절하다 **gee·juhl·hah·dah** v faint

기차 **gee·chah** train

기차역 **gee·chah·yuhk** train [railway BE] station

기침 **gee·cheem** *n* cough

기침하다 **gee·cheem·hah·dah** *v* cough

기타 **gee·tah** guitar

기호 **gee·hoh** symbol

긴 **geen** long

긴급 서비스 **geen·gup ssuh·bee·su** emergency service

길 **geel** route, street, way

길이 **gee·lee** length

깊은 **gee·pun** deep

까지 **kkah·jee** until

깔개 **kkahl·geh** groundcloth [groundsheet BE]

깡통 **kkahng·tohng** *n* can

깨우다 **kkeh·oo·dah** wake

꽃 **kkoht** flower

꽃가루 알레르기 **kkoht·kkah·loo ahl·leh·lu·gee** hay fever

꽃가루 지수 **kkoht·kkah·loo jee·soo** pollen count

꿰매다 **kkweh·meh·dah** sew

끄다 **kku·dah** turn off

끊임없는 **kku·neem·uhm·nun** continuous

끔찍한 **kkum·tzee·kahn** terrible, awful

끝 **kkut** end

끼는 **kkee·nun** tight

ㄴ

나라 **nah·lah** country

나무 **nah·moo** tree

나무 못 **nah·moo moht** peg

나쁜 **nah·ppun** bad

나아지다 **nah·ah·jee·dah** improve

나중에 **nah·joong·eh** later

낚시 **nahk·ssee** fishing

난방 **nahn·bahng** heat [heating BE]

날씨 **nahl·ssee** weather

날카로운 **nahl·kah·loh·oon** sharp

남자 **nahm·jah** male, man

남자애 **nahm·jah·eh** boy

남자 종업원 **nahm·jah johng·uh·bwuhn** waiter

남자 친구 **nahm·jah cheen·goo** boyfriend

남자 형제 **nahm·jah hyuhng·jeh** brother

남쪽 **nahm·tzohk** south

남편 **nahm·pyuhn** husband

납 **nahp** *n* lead

낭만적인 **nahng·mahn·juh·geen** romantic

낮은 **nah·jun** low

낮추다 **naht·choo·dah** turn down

내기 **neh·gee** bet

내리다 **neh·lee·dah** get off (bus)

내선 번호 **neh·suhn buhn·hoh** extension (phone)

내일 **neh·eel** tomorrow

냄비 **nehm·bee** pot, saucepan

냄새 맡다 **nehm·seh maht·ttah** smell

냅킨 **nehp·keen** napkin

냉방 **nehng·bahng** air conditioning

냉동고 **nehng·dohng·goh** freezer

냉장고 **nehng·jahng·goh** refrigerator

너무 **nuh·moo** too

넓은 **nuhl·bun** wide

넓적다리 **nuhp·tzuhk·ttah·lee** thigh

넣다 **nuh·tah** put

네 **neh** yes

네트워크 **neh·tu·wuh·ku** network

넥타이 **nehk·tah·ee** tie

년 **nyuhn** year

노 **noh** *n* row

노상 강도 **noh·sahng gahng·doh** mugging

노선 **noh·suhn** line

노인 **noh·een** senior citizen

노 젓는 배 **noh juhn·nun beh** rowboat

녹이다 **noh·gee·dah** dissolve, defrost

놀라운 **nohl·lah·oon** amazing

놀이 공원 **noh·lee gohng·wuhn** amusement park

놀이터 **noh·lee·tuh** playground

농구 **nohng·goo** basketball

농담 **nohng·dahm** joke

농장 **nohng·jahng** farm

높은 **noh·pun** high

높은 의자 **noh·pun u·jah** highchair

높이다 **noh·pee·dah** turn up

뇌진탕 **nweh·jeen·tahng** concussion

누구 **noo·goo** who

누구의 **noo·goo·eh** whose

누군가 **noo·goon·gah** anyone, someone

누출 **noo·chool** *n* leak

눈 **noon** eye, snow

눈썹 **noon·ssuhp** eyebrow

뉴스 **nyoo·su** news

뉴질랜드 **nyoo·jeel·lehn·du** New Zealand

느끼다 **nu·kkee·dah** feel

느린 **nu·leen** slow

늙은 **nul·gun** old (person)

늦다 **nut·ttah** late

ㄷ

다듬다 **dah·dum·ttah** trim

다른 **dah·lun** another, alternate

다리 **dah·lee** leg, bridge

다리미 **dah·lee·mee** iron

다림질하다 **dah·leem·jeel·hah·dah** press

다소 **dah·soh** some

다스 **dah·su** dozen

다음 **dah·um** next

다이빙하다 **dah·ee·beeng·hah·dah** dive

다이아몬드 **dah·ee·ah·mohn·du** diamond

다이어트 **dah·ee·uh·tu** diet

다치게 하다 **dah·chee·geh hah·dah** injure

닦다 **dahk·ttah** wipe

단 한번도 **dahn hahn·buhn·doh** never

단계 **dahn·geh** level

단체 **dahn·cheh** group

단추 **dahn·choo** button

닫다 **daht·ttah** close, shut

닫힌 **dah·cheen** *adj* shut

달 **dahl** month

달러 **dahl·luh** dollar

달력 **dahl·lyuhk** calendar

달콤한 **dahl·kohm·hahn** sweet (taste)

담배 **dahm·beh** cigarette, tobacco

담배 가게 **dahm·beh kkah·geh** tobacconist

담배를 피우다 **dahm·beh·lul pee·oo·dah** smoke

담요 **dahm·nyo** blanket

당기다 **dahng·gee·dah** pull

당뇨병 **dahng·nyo·ppyuhng** diabetes

당뇨병 환자 **dahng·nyo·ppyuhng hwahn·jah** diabetic

당일치기 여행 **dahng·eel·chee·gee yuh·hehng** day trip

대걸레 **deh·guhl·leh** mop

대기실 **deh·gee·seel** waiting room

대기표 **deh·gee·pyo** standby ticket

대사 **deh·sah** ambassador

대사관 **deh·sah·gwahn** embassy

대신에 **deh·see·neh** instead

대회 **deh·hweh** contest, tournament

더 많이 **duh mah·nee** more

더 적은 **duh juh·gun** less

더러운 **duh·luh·oon** dirty

더빙된 **duh·beeng·dwehn** dubbed

데님 **deh·neem** denim

도 **doh** degree

도난 **doh·nahn** theft

도난 당한 **doh·nahn dahng·hahn** stolen

도둑 **doh·dook** thief

도로 **doh·loh** road

도서관 **doh·suh·gwahn** library

도움 **doh·oom** help, assistance

도자기 **doh·jah·gee** pottery, ceramics

도착 **doh·chahk** arrivals

도착하다 **doh·chah·kah·dah** arrive, v land

독 **dohk** poison

독감 **dohk·kkahm** flu

돈 **dohn** money, currency

돌다 **dohl·dah** turn

돌아가다 **doh·lah·gah·dah** v return

돕다 **dohp·ttah** v help

동굴 **dohng·gool** cave

동료 **dohng·nyo** colleague

동물 **dohng·mool** animal

동물원 **dohng·moo·lwuhn** zoo

동상 **dohng·sahng** statue

동안 **dohng·ahn** while, during

동전 **dohng·juhn** coin

동쪽 **dohng·tzohk** east

되풀이하다 **dweh·poo·lee·hah·dah** repeat

두꺼운 **doo·kkuh·oon** thick

두드러기 **doo·du·luh·gee** rash

두드리다 **doo·du·lee·dah** knock

두통 **doo·tohng** headache

둘러보다 **dool·luh·boh·dah** browse

뒤에 **dwih·eh** behind

드라이 **du·lah·ee** blow dry

드라이버 **du·lah·ee·buh** screwdriver

드라이 클리닝하다 **du·lah·ee kul·lee·neeng·hah·dah** dry clean

드러내다 **du·luh·neh·dah** expose

드레스 **du·leh·su** dress

듣다 **dut·ttah** hear

들다 **dul·dah** v cost

들어가지 않다 **du·luh·gah·jee ahn·tah** keep out

들판 **dul·pahn** field

등 **dung** back

등급 **dung·gup** class

등기 우편 **dung·gee oo·pyuhn** registered mail

등대 **dung·deh** lighthouse

등록 용지 **dung·noh gyong·jee** registration form

등산로 **dung·sahn·noh** trail

디젤 **dee·jehl** diesel

디지털 **dee·jee·tuhl** digital

따뜻한 **ttah·ttu·tahn** warm

따라가다 **ttah·lah·gah·dah** follow

따로 **ttah·loh** separate

따분한 **ttah·boon·hahn** boring

딱딱한 **ttahk·ttahk·kahn** hard

땅 **ttahng** n land

때문에 **tteh·moo·neh** because

떠나다 **ttuh·nah·dah** leave
떨어뜨리다 **ttuh·luh·ttu·lee·dah** drop
떨어져 **ttuh·luh·jyuh** away
떨어진 **ttuh·luh·jeen** dead (battery)
떼어내다 **tteh·uh·neh·dah** tear off
또는 **ttoh·nun** or
또한 **ttoh·hahn** also
똑바른 **ttohk·bah·lun** straight
뚝뚝 떨어지다 **ttook·ttook ttuh·luh·jee·dah** drip
뜨거운 **ttu·guh·oon** hot
뜻하다 **ttu·tah·dah** v mean

ㄹ

라운드 **lah·oon·du** round (of golf)
라이터 **lah·ee·tuh** lighter
라켓 **lah·keht** racket (tennis)
랩 **lehp** plastic wrap [cling film BE]
러시 아워 **luh·ssee·ah·wuh** rush hour
레이스 **leh·ee·su** lace
렌즈 **lehn·ju** lens
렌터카 **lehn·tuh·kah** car rental [car hire BE]
로비 **loh·bee** lobby
록 **lohk** rock
룸 서비스 **loom ssuh·bee·su** room service
리터 **lee·tuh** liter
립스틱 **leep·ssu·teek** lipstick

ㅁ

마 **mah** linen
마사지 **mah·ssah·jee** massage
마시다 **mah·see·dah** v drink
마을 **mah·ul** village
마지막 **mah·jee·mahk** adj last

마취제 **mah·chwih·jeh** anesthetic
마티네 **mah·tee·neh** matinee
막간 **mahk·kkahn** intermission
만나다 **mahn·nah·dah** meet
많이 **mah·nee** many
말 **mahl** horse
말도 안 돼 **mahl·doh ahn dweh** no way
말리다 **mahl·lee·dah** dry
말하다 **mahl·hah·dah** say, tell
맛 **maht** flavor
맛보다 **maht·ppoh·dah** taste
맛있는 **mah·seen·nun** delicious
망치 **mahng·chee** hammer
맞는 **mahn·nun** correct
맞다 **maht·ttah** fit
맞은편 **mah·jun·pyuhn** opposite
맞춤 **maht·choom** custom made
매니저 **meh·nee·juh** manager
매니큐어 **meh·nee·kyoo·uh** manicure
매력적인 **meh·lyuhk·tzuh·geen** attractive
매우 **meh·oo** very
매일 **meh·eel** daily
매주 **meh·joo** weekly
매진 **meh·jeen** sold out
매트리스 **meh·tu·lee·su** mattress
매표소 **meh·pyo·soh** ticket office
맹도견 **mehng·doh·gyuhn** guide dog
머리 **muh·lee** hair, head
먹다 **muhk·ttah** eat
먹이다 **muh·gee·dah** feed
먼 **muhn** far
멀미 **muhl·mee** motion sickness
멋진 **muht·tzeen** stunning
멍 **muhng** bruise
메뉴 **meh·nyoo** menu

메모리 카드 **meh·moh·lee kah·du** memory card

메스꺼움 **meh·su·kkuh·oom** nausea

메시지 **meh·ssee·jee** message

메신저 **meh·sseen·juh** instant messenger

면 **myuhn** cotton

면도 크림 **myuhn·doh ku·leem** shaving cream

면도날 **myuhn·doh·nahl** razor blade

면도칼 **myuhn·doh·kahl** razor

면도하다 **myuhn·doh·hah·dah** shave

면세 **myuhn·seh** duty-free

명세 **myuhng·seh** itemized

명함 **myuhng·hahm** business card

몇 개 **myuht kkeh** how many

모기 물린 데 **moh·gee mool·leen deh** mosquito bite

모닝콜 **moh·neeng·kohl** wake-up call

모두 **moh·doo** all

모든 **moh·dun** every

모래 **moh·leh** sand

모양 **moh·yahng** shape

모으다 **moh·u·dah** collect

모자 **moh·jah** hat

모조품 **moh·joh·poom** imitation

모터 **moh·tuh** motor

모터 보트 **moh·tuh boh·tu** motor boat

모퉁이 **moh·toong·ee** corner

목 **mohk** neck

목걸이 **mohk·kkuh·lee** necklace

목격자 **mohk·kkyuhk·tzah** witness

목구멍 **mohk·kkoo·muhng** throat

목마르다 **mohng·mah·lu·dah** thirsty

목발 **mohk·ppahl** crutches

목 아픈 데 **moh gah·pun deh** sore throat

목욕 **moh·gyok** bath

목적 **mohk·tzuhk** purpose

목적지 **mohk·tzuhk·tzee** destination

못생긴 **moht·ssehng·geen** ugly

묘사하다 **myo·sah·hah·dah** describe

무거운 **moo·guh·oon** heavy

무게 **moo·geh** weight

무게를 달다 **moo·geh·lul dahl·dah** weigh

무례한 **moo·leh·hahn** rude

무릎 **moo·lup** knee

무선 **moo·suhn** wireless

무언가 **moo·uhn·gah** anything, something

무엇 **moo·uht** what

묵다 **mook·ttah** stay

문 **moon** door

문구류 **moon·goo·lyoo** stationery

문자 **moon·tzah** text

문제 **moon·jeh** problem

묻다 **moot·ttah** ask

물 **mool** water

물건 **mool·guhn** thing

물 내리다 **mool neh·lee·dah** flush

물안경 **moo·lahn·gyuhng** goggles

물에 빠지다 **moo·leh ppah·jee·dah** drown

물집 **mool·tzeep** blister

미국 **mee·gook** United States

미국인 **mee·goo·geen** American

미니바 **mee·nee·bah** mini-bar

미사 **mee·sah** mass

미술관 **mee·sool·gwahn** art gallery

미안하다 **mee·ahn·hah·dah** sorry

미용사 **mee·yong·sah** hairdresser

미용실 **mee·yong·seel** nail salon

미혼 **mee·hohn** single (marital status)

믿을 만한 **mee·dul mahn·hahn** reliable

밀다 **meel·dah** push

ㅂ

바 **bah** bar

바가지 쓴 **bah·gah·jee ssun** overcharged

바구니 **bah·goo·nee** basket

바꾸다 **bah·kkoo·dah** alter, change, exchange, replace

바다 **bah·dah** sea

바라다 **bah·lah·dah** wish

바람 **bah·lahm** wind

바람이 부는 **bah·lah·mee boo·nun** windy

바쁜 **bah·ppun** busy

바지 **bah·jee** pants [trousers BE]

박물관 **bahng·mool·gwahn** museum

밖 **bahk** out

밖에 **bah·kkeh** outside

반 **bahn** half

반바지 **bahn·bah·jee** shorts

반응 **bah·nung** reaction

반지 **bahn·jee** ring

반창고 **bahn·chahng·goh** plaster

받다 **baht·ttah** accept, receive

발 **bahl** foot

발가락 **bahl·kkah·lahk** toe

발레 **bahl·leh** ballet

발음하다 **bah·lum·hah·dah** pronounce

밤 **bahm** night

밤새 **bahm·seh** overnight

밧줄 **baht·tzool** rope

방 **bahng** room

방광 **bahng·gwahng** bladder

방문 **bahng·moon** *n* visit

방문 시간 **bahng·moon see·gahn** visiting hours

방문하다 **bahng·moon·hah·dah** *v* visit

방수 **bahng·soo** waterproof

방해 **bahng·heh** interference

방해하다 **bahng·heh·hah·dah** disturb

방향 **bahng·hyahng** direction

방화문 **bahng·hwah·moon** fire door

배 **beh** ship

배고픈 **beh·goh·pun** hungry

배고픔 **beh·goh·pum** hunger

배구 **beh·goo** volleyball

배낭 **beh·nahng** backpack

배달 **beh·dahl** delivery

배달하다 **beh·dahl·hah·dah** deliver

배우다 **beh·oo·dah** learn

배우자 **beh·oo·jah** spouse

백금 **behk·kkum** platinum

백랍 **behng·nahp** pewter

백화점 **beh·kwah·juhm** department store

밸브 **behl·bu** valve

뱃멀미 **behn·muhl·mee** seasick

버스 **buh·su** bus

버스 정류장 **buh·su juhng·nyoo·jahng** bus stop

버스 터미널 **buh·su tuh·mee·nuhl** bus station

버스표 **buh·su·pyo** bus ticket

버전 **buh·juhn** version

번역 **buh·nyuhk** translation

번역사 **buh·nyuhk·ssah** translator

번역하다 **buh·nyuh·kah·dah** translate

번쩍이다 **buhn·tzuh·gee·dah** flash

번호 **buhn·hoh** number

벌금 **buhl·gum** *n* fine

벌레 **buhl·leh** bug, insect

벌레 물린 데 **buhl·leh mool·leen deh** insect bite

법원 **buh·bwuhn** courthouse

벗다 **buht·ttah** take off (clothing)

베개 **beh·geh** pillow

벨트 **bel·tu** belt

벼룩시장 **byuh·look·ssee·jahng** flea market

벽 **byuhk** wall

변기 뚫는 것 **byun·gee ttool·nun guht** plunger

변비 **byun·bee** constipation

변호사 **byuhn·hoh·sah** lawyer

별거한 **byuhl·guh·hahn** separated

별장 **byuhl·tzang** cottage

병 **byuhng** bottle, jar

병동 **byuhng·dohng** ward (hospital)

병따개 **byuhng·ttah·geh** bottle opener

병원 **byuhng·wuhn** clinic, hospital

보내다 **boh·neh·dah** send

보다 **boh·dah** look, see

보도 **boh·doh** sidewalk [pavement BE]

보루 **boh·loo** carton (cigarettes)

보석 **boh·suhk** jewelry

보석상 **boh·suhk·ssahng** jeweler

보습 크림 **boh·sup ku·leem** moisturizer (cream)

보여주다 **boh·yuh·joo·dah** show

보유하다 **boh·yoo·hah·dah** keep

보증 **boh·jung** guarantee

보증서 **boh·jung·suh** certificate

보청기 **boh·chuhng·gee** hearing aid

보통 **boh·tohng** regular

보통 예금 계좌 **boh·tohng yeh·gum geh·jwah** savings account

보트 **boh·tu** ferry

보트 관광 **boh·tu gwahn·gwahng** boat trip

보행자 **boh·hehng·jah** *n* pedestrian

보행자 전용 구역 **boh·hehng·jah juh·nyong goo·yuhk** pedestrian zone [precinct BE]

보험 **boh·huhm** insurance

보험 카드 **boh·huhm kah·du** insurance card

보험금 청구 **boh·huhm·gum chuhng·goo** insurance claim

보호 구역 **boh·hoh goo·yuhk** conservation area

복권 **boh·kkwuhn** lottery

복사하다 **bohk·ssah·hah·dah** copy, photocopy

복용량 **boh·gyong·nyahng** dosage

복장 규정 **bohk·tzang gyoo·juhng** dress code

복통 **bohk·tohng** stomachache

볼링장 **bohl·leeng·jahng** bowling alley

봉사료 **bohng·sah·lyo** service charge

봉사하다 **bohng·sah·hah·dah** serve

부가가치세 **boo·gah·gah·chee·sseh** sales tax [VAT BE]

부동액 **boo·dohng·ehk** antifreeze

부두 **boo·doo** dock

부록 **boo·lohk** appendix

부르다 **boo·lu·dah** call

부모님 **boo·moh·neem** parents

부수다 **boo·soo·dah** break

부엌 **boo·uhk** kitchen

부은 **boo·un** swollen

부은 데 **boo·un deh** swelling

부인과 **boo·een·kkwah** gynecologist

부작용 **boo·jah·gyong** side effect

부츠 **boo·chu** boots

부탄가스 **boo·tahn·kkah·su** butane gas

부터 **boo·tuh** from

북쪽 **book·tzohk** north

분 **boon** minute

분량 **bool·lyahng** portion

분수 **boon·soo** fountain

분실물 센터 **boon·seel·mool sehn·tuh** lost-and-found [lost property office BE]

분유 **boo·nyoo** formula (baby)

불 **bool** fire

불면증 **bool·myuhn·tzung** insomnia

불법 **bool·ppuhp** illegal

붕대 **boong·deh** bandage

붙들다 **boot·ttul·dah** hold

브래지어 **bu·leh·jee·uh** bra

브레이크 **bu·leh·ee·ku** brake

브로치 **bu·loh·chee** brooch

블라우스 **bul·lah·oo·su** blouse

비 **bee** *n* rain

비 내리다 **bee neh·lee·dah** *v* rain

비누 **bee·noo** soap

비디오 게임 **bee·dee·oh geh·eem** video game

비밀번호 **bee·meel·buhn·hoh** password, PIN

비상 **bee·sahng** emergency

비상 브레이크 **bee·sahng bu·leh·ee·ku** emergency brake

비상구 **bee·sahng·goo** emergency exit

비수기 **bee·soo·gee** off-peak (ticket)

비싼 **bee·ssahn** expensive

비옷 **bee·oht** raincoat

비용 **bee·yong** *n* cost

비자 **bee·jah** visa

비즈니스 센터 **bee·jee·nee·su ssehn·tuh** business center

비즈니스석 **bee·jee·nee·su·suhk** business class

비키니 **bee·kee·nee** bikini

비틀다 **bee·tul·dah** twist

비행기 **bee·hehng·gee** plane, flight

비행기 멀미 **bee·hehng·gee muhl·mee** airsickness

빈 **been** vacant

빌려주다 **beel·lyuh·joo·dah** lend

빌리다 **beel·lee·dah** borrow, rent

빗 **beet** comb

빗자루 **beet·tzah·loo** broom

빚지다 **beet·tzee·dah** owe

빛깔 **beet·kkahl** tint

빠른 **ppah·lun** fast, quick

빨래방 **ppahl·leh·bahng** laundromat [launderette BE]

빼앗다 **ppeh·aht·ttah** rob

뻣뻣한 **ppuh·ppuh·tahn** stiff

뼈 **ppyuh** bone

뽑아내다 **ppoh·bah·neh·dah** extract

뿔 **ppool** horn

삐다 **ppee·dah** dislocate, sprain

ㅅ

사고 **sah·goh** accident

사과하다 **sah·gwah·hah·dah** apologize

사냥하다 **sah·nyahng·hah·dah** hunt

사다 **sah·dah** buy

사다리 **sah·dah·lee** ladder

사람 **sah·lahm** person

사랑하다 **sah·lahng·hah·dah** *v* love

사무실 **sah·moo·seel** office

사발 **sah·bahl** bowl

사분의 일 **sah·boo·neh eel** quarter

사슬 **sah·sul** chain

사실 **sah·seel** true

사업 **sah·uhp** business

사용자명 **sah·yong·jah·myuhng** username

사용하다 **sah·yong·hah·dah** use

사우나 **ssah·oo·nah** sauna

사이에 **sah·ee·eh** between

사이즈 **ssah·ee·ju** size

사적인 **sah·tzuh·geen** private

사전 **sah·juhn** dictionary

사진 **sah·jeen** photograph

사탕 가게 **sah·tahng kkah·geh** candy store

삭제하다 **sahk·tzeh·hah·dah** delete

산 **sahn** mountain

산소 **sahn·soh** oxygen

산책로 **sahn·chehng·noh** nature trail

살다 **sahl·dah** live

삼키다 **sahm·kee·dah** swallow

삽 **sahp** shovel

삽입하다 **sah·bee·pah·dah** insert

상가 **sahng·gah** shopping area, shopping mall [centre BE]

상가 안내 **sahng·gah ahn·neh** store directory

상급자 **sahng·gup·tzah** expert

상담하다 **sahng·dahm·hah·dah** consult

상대 **sahng·deh** partner

상업 지구 **sahng·uhp tzee·goo** business district

상온 **sahng·ohn** room temperature

상자 **sahng·jah** box

상표 **sahng·pyo** label

새 **seh** bird

새기다 **seh·gee·dah** engrave

새다 **seh·dah** v leak

새로운 **seh·loh·oon** new

색 **sehk** color

샌들 **ssehn·dul** sandals

생각하다 **sehng·gah·kah·dah** think

생년월일 **sehng·nyuh·nwuh·leel** date of birth

생리 **sehng·nee** period (menstrual)

생리대 **sehng·nee·deh** sanitary napkin [pad BE]

생리통 **sehng·nee·tohng** menstrual cramps

생명 **sehng·myuhng** life

생일 **sehng·eel** birthday

샤워 **syah·wuh** shower

샴푸 **syahm·poo** shampoo

서두르다 **suh·doo·lu·dah** hurry, rush

서명하다 **suh·myuhng·hah·dah** v sign

서점 **suh·juhm** bookstore

서쪽 **suh·tzohk** west

서핑보드 **ssuh·peeng·boh·du** surfboard

선글라스 **ssuhn·gul·lah·su** sunglasses

선물 **suhn·mool** gift, present

선물 가게 **suhn·mool kkah·geh** gift store

선불 전화 카드 **suhn·bool juhn·hwah kah·du** prepaid phone card

선탠 크림 **ssuhn·tehn ku·leem** suntan lotion

선풍기 **suhn·poong·gee** fan

설명서 **suhl·myuhng·suh** instructions

설사 **suhl·ssah** diarrhea

성 **suhng** sex

성냥 **suhng·nyahng** matches

성당 **suhng·dahng** cathedral

세관 **seh·gwahn** customs

세관 신고서 **seh·gwahn seen·goh·suh** customs declaration form

세금 **seh·gum** duty (tax)

세면대 **seh·myuhn·deh** sink

세미나 **sseh·mee·nah** seminar

세우다 **seh·oo·dah** v stop

세제 **seh·jeh** detergent

세탁 가능 **seh·tahk kkah·nung** washable

세탁기 **seh·tahk·kkee** washing machine

세탁기로 빨 수 있는 **seh·tahk·kkee·loh ppahl ssoo een·nun** machine washable

세탁 서비스 **seh·tahk ssuh·bee·su** laundry service

세탁 시설 **seh·tahk see·suhl** laundry facilities

세탁소 **seh·tahk·ssoh** dry cleaner

세탁하다 **seh·tah·kah·dah** clean

셀프서비스 **ssehl·pu·ssuh·bee·su** self-service

셔츠 **syuh·chu** shirt

소개하다 **soh·geh·hah·dah** introduce

소독액 **soh·doh·gehk** sterilizing solution

소독약 **soh·dohng·nyahk** antiseptic

소매 **soh·meh** sleeve

소방서 **soh·bahng·suh** fire department [fire brigade BE]

소아과 의사 **soh·ah·kkwah u·sah** pediatrician

소유하다 **soh·yoo·hah·dah** v own

소켓 **soh·keht** socket

소포 **soh·poh** package [parcel BE]

소형 **soh·hyuhng** mini

소화기 **soh·hwah·gee** fire extinguisher

소화불량 **soh·hwah·bool·lyahng** indigestion

속 **sohk** filling

속도 **sohk·ttoh** n speed

속하다 **soh·kah·dah** belong

손 **sohn** hand

손가락 **sohn·kkah·lahk** finger

손가방 **sohn·kkah·bahng** hand luggage

손상 **sohn·sahng** damage

손톱 **sohn·tohp** nail

손톱줄 **sohn·tohp·tzool** nail file

쇼핑 **syo·peeng** shopping

쇼핑센터 **syo·peeng·ssehn·tuh** mall

쇼핑 카트 **syo·peeng kah·tu** shopping cart [trolley BE]

수건 **soo·guhn** towel

수공예품 **soo·gohng·yeh·poom** handicrafts

수도꼭지 **soo·doh·kkohk·tzee** faucet [tap BE]

수돗물 **soo·dohn·mool** tap water

수면제 **soo·myuhn·jeh** sleeping pill

수상스키 **soo·sahng·su·kee** water skis

수선하다 **soo·suhn·hah·dah** mend (clothes)

수송 **soo·sohng** transport

수수료 **soo·sso·lyo** commission

수술 **soo·sool** operation

수업 **soo·uhp** lesson

수영복 **soo·yuhng·bohk** swimsuit, swimming trunks

수영장 **soo·yuhng·jahng** pool

수영하다 **soo·yuhng·hah·dah** swim

수유하다 **soo·yoo·hah·dah** breastfeed

수정 **soo·juhng** crystal

수집 **soo·jeep** collection

수표 **soo·pyo** check [cheque BE]

수하물 **soo·hah·mool** luggage

수하물 찾는 곳 **soo·hah·mool chan·nun goht** baggage claim

수하물 카트 **soo·hah·mool kah·tu** luggage cart [trolley BE]

숙박 시설 **sook·ppahk see·suhl** accommodations

숙소 **sook·ssoh** guesthouse

숙취 **sook·chwih** hangover

순수한 **soon·soo·hahn** pure

순은 **soo·nun** sterling silver

숟가락 **soot·kkah·lahk** spoon

술 **sool** drink (alcoholic)

술집 **sool·tzeep** pub

숨막히는 **soom·mah·kee·nun** breathtaking

숨쉬다 **soom·swih·dah** breathe

숲 **soop** forest

쉬다 **swih·dah** rest

쉬운 **swih·oon** easy

슈퍼마켓 **syoo·puh·mah·keht** supermarket

스웨터 **su·weh·tuh** sweater

스카프 **su·kah·pu** scarf

스코틀랜드 **su·koh·tul·lehn·du** Scotland

스쿠버 다이빙 장비 **su·koo·buh dah·ee·beeng jahng·bee** diving equipment

스키장 **su·kee·jahng** ski slope

스타일 **su·tah·eel** style

스테인레스 **su·teh·een·leh·su** stainless steel

스파 **su·pah** spa

스포츠 용품점 **su·poh·chu yong·poom·juhm** sporting goods store

스포츠 클럽 **su·poh·chu kul·luhp** sports club

스폰지 **su·pohn·jee** sponge

슬리퍼 **sul·lee·puh** slippers

습한 **su·pahn** damp

승강장 **sung·gahng·jahng** platform

승객 **sung·gehk** passenger

승마 **sung·mah** horseback riding

승무원 **sung·moo·wuhn** flight attendant

시 **see** o'clock

시가 **ssee·gah** cigar

시각 장애인 **see·gahk jahng·eh·een** visually impaired

시간 **see·gahn** hour, time

시간 있는 **see·gah neen·nun** available, free

시간표 **see·gahn·pyo** schedule [timetable BE]

시계 **see·geh** clock, watch

시끄러운 **see·kku·luh·oon** loud, noisy

시내 **see·neh** town

시대 **see·deh** period (historical)

시디 **ssee·dee** CD

시디플레이어 **ssee·dee·pul·leh·ee·uh** CD player

시설 **see·suhl** facility

시원한 **see·wuhn·hahn** cool

시작하다 **see·jah·kah·dah** begin, start

시장 **see·jahng** market

시차 **see·chah** jet lag

시큼한 **see·kum·hahn** sour

시트 **see·tu** sheet (bed)

시합하다 **see·hahp·hah·dah** play (sports)

식기 세척기 **seek·kkee seh·chuhk·kkee** dishwasher

식당 **seek·ttahng** dining room

식당차 **seek·ttahng·chah** dining car

식료품점 **seeng·nyo·poom·juhm** grocery store [grocer BE]

식물원 **seeng·moo·lwuhn** botanical garden

식사 **seek·ssah** meal

식사하다 **seek·ssah·hah·dah** dine

식욕 **see·gyok** appetite

식중독 **seek·tzoong·dohk** food poisoning

신고하다 **seen·goh·hah·dah** declare, report

신문 **seen·moon** newspaper

신문 가판대 **seen·moon gah·pahn·deh** newsstand [news agent BE]

신발 **seen·bahl** shoe

신발 가게 **seen·bahl kkah·geh** shoe store

신발 수선 **seen·bahl soo·suhn** shoe repair

신분증 **seen·boon·tzung** identification

신사 **seen·sah** gentleman

신선한 **seen·suhn·hahn** fresh

신어 보다 **seen·uh boh·dah** try on (shoes)

신용카드 **see·nyong·kah·du** credit card

신장 **seen·jahng** kidney

신호등 **seen·hoh·dung** traffic light

신혼여행 **seen·hohn·yuh·hehng** honeymoon

실내 수영장 **seel·leh soo·yuhng·jahng** indoor pool

실수 **seel·ssoo** mistake

실수로 **seel·ssoo·loh** accidentally

실업자 **see·luhp·tzah** unemployed

실외 **seel·weh** outdoor

실외 수영장 **seel·weh soo·yuhng·jahng** outdoor pool

실크 **sseel·ku** silk

심각한 **seem·gah·kahn** serious

심장 **seem·jahng** heart

심장마비 **seem·jahng·mah·bee** heart attack

심장 질환 **seem·jahng jeel·hwahn** heart condition

싸다 **ssah·dah** v pack, wrap

싸움 **ssah·oom** fight

싼 **ssahn** cheap

쌍안경 **ssahng·ahn·gyuhng** binoculars

쑤시는 **ssoo·see·nun** sore

쓰다 **ssu·dah** spend, write

쓰러지다 **ssu·luh·jee·dah** collapse

쓰레기 **ssu·leh·gee** trash [rubbish BE]

쓰레기 봉투 **ssu·leh·gee bohng·too** garbage bag

쓰레기통 **ssu·leh·gee·tohng** trash can

쓴 **ssun** bitter

쓸다 **ssul·dah** sweep

씨름 **ssee·lum** Korean wrestling

아기 **ah·gee** baby

아기 놀이울 **ah·gee noh·lee·ool** playpen

아기용 물휴지 **ah·gee·yong mool·hyoo·jee** baby wipe

아기용 침대 **ah·gee·yong cheem·deh** crib [child's cot BE]

아내 **ah·neh** wife

아니다 **ah·nee·dah** not

아니요 **ah·nee·yo** no

아래 **ah·leh** under

아래층 **ah·leh·chung** downstairs

아로마테라피 **ah·loh·mah·teh·lah·pee** aromatherapy

아름다운 **ah·lum·dah·oon** beautiful

아마 **ah·mah** perhaps, maybe

아무 것도 아님 **ah·moo guht·ttoh ah·neem** nothing

아버지 **ah·buh·jee** father

아세트아미노펜 **ah·seh·tu·ah·mee·noh·pehn** acetaminophen

아스피린 **ah·su·pee·leen** aspirin

아이스 스케이트 **ah·ee·su su·keh·ee·tu** ice skating

아이스 스케이트장 **ah·ee·su su·keh·ee·tu·jahng** ice skating rink

아이스 하키 **ah·ee·su hah·kee** ice hockey

아일랜드 **ah·eel·lehn·du** Ireland

아주 작은 **ah·joo jah·gun** petite

아직 **ah·jeek** *adj* still

아침 **ah·cheem** morning

아침식사 **ah·cheem·seek·ssah** breakfast

아파트 **ah·pah·tu** apartment

아픈 **ah·pun** sick [ill BE]

아프다 **ah·pu·dah** hurt

악단 **ahk·ttahn** band

안개 **ahn·geh** fog

안경 **ahn·gyuhng** glasses

안경점 **ahn·gyuhng·juhm** optician

안내 **ahn·neh** information

안내 데스크 **ahn·neh deh·su·ku** information desk

안내 책자 **ahn·neh chehk·tzah** guide book

안내원 **ahn·neh·wuhn** guide (tour)

안녕하세요 **ahn·nyuhng·hah·seh·yo** hi, hello

안녕히 가세요 **ahn·nyuhng·hee gah·seh·yo** bye, goodbye (to someone leaving)

안녕히 계세요 **ahn·nyuhng·hee geh·seh·yo** bye, goodbye (to someone staying)

안다 **ahn·ttah** hug

안에 **ah·neh** inside, within

안전 **ahn·juhn** safety

안전 벨트 **ahn·juhn behl·tu** seat belt

안전핀 **ahn·juhn·peen** safety pin

안전한 **ahn·juhn·hahn** *adj* safe

앉다 **ahn·ttah** sit

알다 **ahl·dah** know, understand

알레르기 **ahl·leh·lu·gee** allergy

알레르기가 있다 **ahl·leh·lu·gee·gah eet·ttah** allergic

알약 **ahl·lyahk** pill, tablet

암 **ahm** cancer

앞 **ahp** front

애 봐주는 사람 **eh bwah·joo·nun sah·lahm** babysitter

애인 **eh·een** boyfriend

애프터셰이브 로션 **eh·pu·tuh·syeh·ee·bu loh·syuhn** aftershave

야구 **yah·goo** baseball

야생 **yah·sehng** wildlife

약 **yahk** medicine

약국 **yahk·kkook** pharmacy [chemist BE]

약물 **yahng·mool** medication

약속 **yahk·ssohk** appointment

약혼한 **yah·kohn·hahn** engaged

양동이 **yahng·dohng·ee** bucket, pail

양말 **yahng·mahl** socks

양모 **yahng·moh** wool

양보 **yahng·boh** concession

양보하다 **yahng·boh·hah·dah** yield

양복 **yahng·bohk** suit

양식 **yahng·seek** form

양초 **yahng·choh** candle

얘기하다 **yeh·gee·hah·dah** speak, talk

어깨 **uh·kkeh** shoulder

어댑터 **uh·dehp·tuh** adapter

어두운 **uh·doo·oon** dark

어디서 **uh·dee·suh** where

어딘가 **uh·deen·gah** somewhere

어떤 **uh·ttuhn** any, which

어떻게 **uh·ttuh·keh** how

어려운 **uh·lyuh·oon** difficult

어린이 **uh·lee·nee** child

어린이 수영장 uh·lee·nee soo·yuhng·jahng kiddie pool

어린이용 메뉴 uh·lee·nee·yong meh·nyoo children's menu, children's portion

어린이용 의자 uh·lee·nee·yong u·jah child seat

어머니 uh·muh·nee mother

어제 uh·jeh yesterday

어지러운 uh·jee·luh·oon dizzy

언덕 uhn·duhk hill

언제 uhn·jeh when

얼굴 uhl·gool face

얼굴 마사지 uhl·gool mah·ssah·jee facial

얼리다 uhl·lee·dah freeze

얼마나 ul·mah·nah how much

엄지손가락 uhm·jee·sohn·kkah·lahk thumb

없어진 uhp·ssuh·jeen missing

없이 uhp·ssee without

에 eh at, in, on, per

에나멜 eh·nah·mehl enamel

에메랄드 eh·meh·lahl·du emerald

에스컬레이터 eh·su·kuhl·leh·ee·tuh escalator

엑스레이 ehk·ssu·leh·ee x-ray

엘리베이터 ehl·lee·beh·ee·tuh elevator [lift BE]

여권 yuh·kkwuhn passport

여기 yuh·gee here

여분 yuh·boon extra, spare

여자 yuh·jah female

여자 형제 yuh·jah hyuhng·jeh sister

여자애 yuh·jah·eh girl

여자친구 yuh·jah·cheen·goo girlfriend

여자 종업원 yuh·jah johng·uh·bwuhn waitress

여행 yuh·hehng tour, trip, travel

여행 가방 yuh·hehng kkah·bahng suitcase

여행 가이드 yuh·hehng gah·ee·du tour guide

여행사 yuh·hehng·sah travel agency

여행 안내소 yuh·hehng ahn·neh·soh tourist office

여행자 수표 yuh·hehng·jah soo·pyo traveler's check [traveller's cheque BE]

역사적인 yuhk·ssah·juh·geen historical

연결 yuhn·gyuhl connection

연결하다 yuhn·gyuhl·hah·dah connect

연극 yuhn·guk n play

연락하다 yuhl·lah·kah·dah contact, reach

연료 yuhl·lyo fuel

연못 yuhn·moht pond

연습하다 yuhn·su·pah·dah v practice

연주하다 yuhn·joo·hah·dah play (music)

연주회장 yuhn·joo·hweh·jahng concert hall

열 yuhl fever

열다 yuhl·dah open

열쇠 yuhl·ssweh key

열쇠고리 yuhl·ssweh·goh·lee key ring

염증 yuhm·tzung inflammation

엽서 yuhp·ssuh postcard

영 yuhng zero

영국 yuhng·gook United Kingdom

영국인 yuhng·goo·geen British

영사관 yuhng·sah·gwahn consulate

영수증 yuhng·soo·jung receipt

영어 yuhng·uh English

영업 yuhng·uhp sale [BE]

영업시간 yuhng·uhp·ssee·gahn office [opening BE] hours

영화 **yuhng·hwah** film, movie

영화관 **yuhng·hwah·gwahn** movie theater [cinema BE]

옆에 **yuh·peh** next to

예 **yeh** example

예배 **yeh·beh** service (religious)

예쁜 **yeh·ppun** pretty

예약 **yeh·yahk** reservation, appointment

예약 접수처 **yeh·yahk juhp·ssoo·chuh** reservation desk

예약하다 **yeh·yah·kah·dah** reserve

오늘 **oh·nul** today

오늘밤 **oh·nul·ppahm** tonight

오다 **oh·dah** come

오두막집 **oh·doo·mahk·tzeep** cabin

오락 안내 **oh·lah gahn·neh** entertainment guide

오래된 **oh·leh·dwehn** old (things)

오류 **oh·lyoo** error

오른쪽 **oh·lun·tzohk** right

오븐 **oh·bun** oven

오직 **oh·jeek** only

오케스트라 **oh·keh·su·tu·lah** orchestra

오토바이 **oh·toh·bah·ee** motorcycle

오페라 **oh·peh·lah** opera

오후 **oh·hoo** afternoon

온도 **ohn·doh** temperature

온도계 **ohn·doh·geh** thermometer

옮기다 **ohm·gee·dah** move

옷가게 **oht·kkah·geh** clothing store [clothes shop BE]

옷걸이 **oht·kkuh·lee** hanger

왕복표 **wahng·bohk·pyo** round-trip [return BE] ticket

왜 **weh** why

외국의 **weh·goo·geh** foreign

외부 전화 **weh·boo juhn·hwah** outside line

외에 **weh·eh** except

왼쪽 **wehn·tzohk** left

요금 **yo·gum** charge

요리하다 **yo·lee·hah·dah** v cook

요인 **yo·een** factor

요트 **yo·tu** yacht

우기다 **oo·gee·dah** insist

우산 **oo·sahn** umbrella

우체국 **oo·cheh·gook** post office

우체통 **oo·cheh·tohng** mailbox [postbox BE]

우편요금 **oo·pyuhn·nyo·gum** postage

우편환 **oo·pyuhn·hwahn** money order

우표 **oo·pyo** stamp

운동 **oon·dohng** sport

운동화 **oon·dohng·hwah** sneakers

운전 면허증 **oon·juhn myuhn·huh·tzung** driver's license

운전사 **oon·juhn·sah** driver

운전하다 **oon·juhn·hah·dah** drive

운하 **oon·hah** canal

움직이지 않는 **oom·jee·gee·jee ahn·nun** adj still

웃기는 **oot·kkee·nun** funny

웅장한 **oong·jahng·hahn** magnificent

원 **wuhn** Won (Korean currency)

원시 **wuhn·see** far-sighted [long-sighted BE]

원조 **wuhn·joh** original

위 **wih** top, stomach

위층 **wih·chung** upstairs

위험한 **wih·huhm·hahn** dangerous

윈드브레이커 **wihn·du·bu·leh·ee·kuh** windbreaker

윈드서핑 **wihn·du·ssuh·peeng** windsurfing

유당 불내증 **yoo·dahng bool·leh·tzung** lactose intolerant

213

유대교 음식 **yoo·deh·gyo um·seek** kosher

유대교 회당 **yoo·deh·gyo hweh·dahng** synagogue

유람선 여행 **yoo·lahm·suhn yuh·hehng** cruise

유로 **yoo·loh** euro

유로체크 **yoo·loh·cheh·ku** Eurocheque

유리잔 **yoo·lee·jahn** glass (drinking)

유명한 **yoo·myuhng·hahn** famous

유모차 **yoo·moh·chah** stroller [push-chair BE]

유스호스텔 **yoo·su·hoh·su·tehl** youth hostel

유원지 **yoo·wuhn·jee** theme park

유적 **yoo·juhk** ruins

유제품의 **yoo·jeh·poo·meh** dairy

유효한 **yoo·hyo·hahn** valid

으로 **u·loh** to (place), by (route)

은 **un** silver

은퇴한 **un·tweh·hahn** retired

은행 **un·hehng** bank

은행 수수료 **un·heng soo·soo·lyo** bank charge

음료수 **um·nyo·soo** n drink

음성 안내 **um·suhng ahn·neh** audio guide

음식 **um·seek** dish, food

음식점 **um·seek·tzuhm** restaurant

음악 **u·mahk** music

음악회 **u·mah·kweh** concert

의료 보험 **u·lyo boh·huhm** health insurance

의무적인 **u·moo·juh·geen** mandatory

의사 **u·sah** doctor

의식을 잃은 **u·see·gul ee·lun** unconscious

의식하는 **u·see·kah·nun** conscious

이다 **ee·dah** be

이동식 주택 **ee·dohng·seek joo·tehk** mobile home

이륙하다 **ee·lyoo·kah·dah** take off (plane)

이름 **ee·lum** name

이메일 **ee·meh·eel** e-mail

이메일 주소 **ee·meh·eel joo·soh** e-mail address

이미 **ee·mee** already

이발소 **ee·bahl·soh** barber

이부프로펜 **ee·boo·pu·loh·pehn** ibuprofen

이빨 **ee·ppahl** tooth

이사 **ee·sah** director

이상 **ee·sahng** over (more than)

이상한 **eee·sahng·hahn** bizarre

이슬람교 식용육 **ee·sul·lahm·gyo see·gyong·nyook** halal

이십사 시간 약국 **ee·seep·ssah see·gahn yahk·kkook** all-night pharmacy

이용할 수 있는 **ee·yong·hahl ssoo een·nun** available

이유식 **ee·yoo·seek** baby food

이인용 **ee·een·nyong** double

이인용 방 **ee·een·nyong bahng** double room

이코노미석 **ee·koh·noh·mee·suhk** economy class

이혼 **ee·hohn** divorce

인기있는 **een·kkee·een·nun** popular

인도하다 **een·doh·hah·dah** v lead

인슐린 **een·syool·leen** insulin

인터넷 **een·tuh·neht** internet

인형 **een·hyuhng** doll

일 **eel** day, work

일하다 **eel·hah·dah** v work (job)

일광 화상 **eel·gwahng hwah·sahng** sunburn

일광욕하다 eel·gwahng·nyo·kah·dah sunbathe

일기 예보 eel·gee yeh·boh weather forecast

일등석 eel·ttung·suhk first class

일방통행 eel·bahng·tohng·hehng one-way (traffic)

일사병 eel·ssah·ppyuhng sunstroke

일어나다 ee·luh·nah·dah happen

일어서다 ee·luh·suh·dah v stand

일인용 ee·leen·yong single (individual)

일인용 방 ee·leen·yong bahng single room

일정한 eel·tzuhng·hahn constant

일찍 eel·tzeek early

일하다 eel·hah·dah v work

일회용 (카메라) eel·hweh·yong (kah·meh·lah) disposable (camera)

읽다 eek·ttah read

잃어버리다 ee·luh·buh·lee·dah lose

잃어버린 ee·luh·buh·leen lost

임신한 eem·seen·hahn pregnant

임자 있는 eem·jah een·nun taken

입 eep mouth

입구 eep·kkoo entrance

입구 경사로 eep·kkoo gyuhng·sah·loh entrance ramp

입국 비자 eep·kkook bee·jah entry visa

입금 eep·kkum deposit

입다 eep·ttah wear

입술 eep·ssool lip

입어 보다 ee·buh boh·dah try on

입장 eep·tzahng entry

입장료 eep·tzahng·nyo entrance fee, cover charge

잊다 eet·ttah forget

ㅈ

자금 jah·gum funds

자기 jah·gee porcelain

자다 jah·dah sleep

자동 jah·dohng automatic

자동차 jah·dohng·chah car, vehicle

자동차 수리공 jah·dohng·chah soo·lee·gohng mechanic

자리 jah·lee place, space

자막 나오는 jah·mahng nah·oh·nun subtitled

자명종 jah·myuhng·johng alarm clock

자물쇠 jah·mool·ssweh lock

자연 jah·yuhn nature

자연 보호 지역 jah·yuhn boh·hoh jee·yuhk nature reserve

자외선 차단 크림 jah·weh·suhn chah·dahn ku·leem sunscreen

자전거 jah·juhn·guh bicycle

자전거 도로 jah·juhn·guh doh·loh bike path, cycle route

자정 jah·juhng midnight

작은 jah·gun small, little

잔돈 jahn·dohn n change

잔디 jahn·dee grass

잘못된 jahl·moht·ttwehn wrong

잠그다 jahm·gu·dah v lock

잠수복 jahm·soo·bohk wetsuit

잠수용 튜브 jahm·soo·yong tyoo·bu snorkle

잠옷 jah·moht pajamas

잡다 jahp·ttah catch

잡지 jahp·tzee magazine

장갑 jahng·gahp gloves

장거리 버스 jahng·guh·lee buh·su long-distance bus

장난감 **jahng·nahn·kkahm** toy

장난감 가게 **jahng·nahn·kkahm gah·geh** toy store

장미 **jahng·mee** rose

장비 **jahng·bee** equipment

장소 **jahng·soh** site

장식 **jahng·seek** decorative

장애 **jahng·eh** barrier

장애인 **jahng·eh·een** handicapped [disabled BE]

잦은 **jah·jun** frequent

재고 정리 **jeh·goh juhng·nee** clearance

재다 **jeh·dah** measure

재떨이 **jeh·ttuh·lee** ashtray

재미 **jeh·mee** fun

재킷 **jeh·keet** jacket

쟁반 **jehng·bahn** tray

저 **juh** me

저녁 **juh·nyuhk** evening

저녁 식사 **juh·nyuhk seek·ssah** dinner

저렴한 **juh·lyuhm·hahn** inexpensive

저수지 **juh·soo·jee** reservoir

저울 **juh·ool** scale

저장하다 **juh·jahng·hah·dah** save

적당한 **juhk·ttahng·hahn** suitable

전경 **juhn·gyuhng** panorama

전구 **juhn·goo** lightbulb

전기 면도기 **juhn·gee myuhn·doh·gee** electric shaver

전기 콘센트 **juhn·gee kohn·sehn·tu** electrical outlet

전등 **juhn·dung** light, lamp

전망 **juhn·mahng** view

전망대 **juhn·mahng·deh** viewpoint

전망이 좋은 곳 **juhn·mahng·ee joh·un goht** overlook

전문의 **juhn·moo·nee** specialist

전염성의 **juhn·yuhm·ssuhng·eh** contagious

전자 **juhn·jah** electronic

전자레인지 **juhn·jah·leh·een·jee** microwave (oven)

전자티켓 **juhn·jah·tee·keht** e-ticket

전쟁 기념관 **juhn·jehng gee·nyuhm·gwahn** war memorial

전적지 **juhn·juhk·tzee** battlesite

전차 **juhn·chah** tram

전통 **juhn·tohng** traditional

전통춤 **juhn·tohng·choom** traditional dance

전형적인 **juhn·hyuhng·juh·geen** typical

전화 **juhn·hwah** phone

전화 걸다 **juhn·hwah guhl·dah** dial

전화 번호 **juhn·hwah buhn·hoh** phone number

전화 번호부 **juhn·hwah buhn·hoh·boo** phone directory

전화 카드 **juhn·hwah kah·du** phone card

전화 통화 **juhn·hwah tohng·hwah** phone call

절단 **juhl·ttahn** *n* cut

절벽 **juhl·byuhk** cliff

젊은 **juhl·mun** young

젊음 **juhl·mum** youth

점심 **juhm·seem** lunch

점원 **juh·mwuhn** shop assistant

접근 **juhp·kkun** access

접는 의자 **juhm·nun u·jah** deck chair

접속을 끊다 **juhp·ssoh·gul kkun·tah** disconnect, log off

접속하다 **juhp·ssoh·kah·dah** log on

접수 **juhp·ssoo** reception (desk)

접수원 **juhp·ssoo·wuhn** receptionist

접시 **juhp·ssee** dishes, plate

정류장 **juhng·nyoo·jahng** *n* stand, stop

정기권 **juhng·gee·kkwuhn** season ticket

정맥 **juhng·mehk** vein

정비공장 **juhng·bee·gohng·jahng** garage

정상 **juhng·sahng** normal

정오 **juhng·oh** noon [midday BE]

정원 **juhng·wuhn** garden

정장 **juhng·jahng** formal dress

정확한 **juhng·hwah·kahn** exact

젖병 **juht·ppyuhng** baby bottle

제거하다 **jeh·guh·hah·dah** remove

제과점 **jeh·gwah·juhm** bakery

제산제 **jeh·sahn·jeh** antacid

제안하다 **jeh·ahn·hah·dah** suggest

제충제 **jeh·choong·jeh** insect repellent

제한 속도 **jeh·hahn sohk·ttoh** speed limit

제한 초과 수하물 **jeh·hahn choh·gwah soo·hah·mool** excess luggage

조각 **joh·gahk** piece, slice

조금 **joh·gum** few

조심 **joh·seem** caution

조심하다 **joh·seem·hah·dah** beware

조용한 **joh·yong·hahn** quiet

조직하다 **joh·jee·kah·dah** organize

족집게 **johk·tzeep·geh** tweezers

졸린 **johl·leen** drowsy

졸음 **joh·lum** drowsiness

좀 **johm** please

좁은 **joh·bun** narrow

종교 **johng·gyo** religion

종류 **johng·nyoo** type

종양 **johng·yahng** tumor

종이 타월 **johng·ee tah·wuhl** paper towel

종종 **johng·johng** often

좋다 **joh·tah** OK

좋아하는 **joh·ah·hah·nun** favorite

좋아하다 **joh·ah·hah·dah** like

좋은 **joh·un** good, nice, fine

좌석 **jwah·suhk** seat (on train, etc.)

주다 **joo·dah** give

주류 **joo·lyoo** alcoholic (drink)

주류 판매점 **joo·lyoo pahn·meh·juhm** liquor store [off-licence BE]

주말 **joo·mahl** weekend

주말 요금 **joo·mahl lyo·gum** weekend rate

주문하다 **joo·moon·hah·dah** order

주방 시설 **joo·bahng see·suhl** cooking facilities

주방용 세제 **joo·bahng·nyong seh·jeh** dishwashing liquid

주사 **joo·sah** injection

주소 **joo·soh** address

주요한 **joo·yo·hahn** main

주유소 **joo·yoo·soh** gas [petrol BE] station

주인 **joo·een** owner

주일 **joo·eel** week

주차 금지 **joo·chah gum·jee** no parking

주차 미터기 **joo·chah mee·tuh·gee** parking meter

주차 서비스 **joo·chah ssuh·bee·su** valet service

주차 위반 딱지 **joo·chah wih·bahn ttahk·jee** parking ticket

주차장 **joo·chah·jahng** parking garage, parking lot [car park BE]

준비된 **joon·bee·dwehn** ready

줄이다 **joo·lee·dah** reduce

중간 **joong·gahn** medium

중심가 **joong·seem·gah** downtown

중요한 **joong·yo·hahn** important

즐거운 **jul·guh·oon** pleasant

즐기다 **jul·gee·dah** enjoy

증상 **jung·sahng** symptom

지갑 **jee·gahp** wallet

지금 **jee·gum** now

지나다 **jee·nah·dah** v pass

지나서 **jee·nah·suh** after

지도 **jee·doh** map

지도자 **jee·doh·jah** leader (group)

지방 **jee·bahng** local

지불 **jee·bool** payment

지붕 **jee·boong** roof

지속하다 **jee·soh·kah·dah** v last

지역 **jee·yuhk** region

지역 번호 **jee·yuhk ppuhn·hoh** area code, code

지연 **jee·yuhn** delay

지점 **jee·juhm** spot (place, site)

지친 **jee·cheen** exhausted

지퍼 **jee·puh** zipper

지하실 **jee·hah·seel** basement

지하철 **jee·hah·chuhl** subway [underground BE]

지하철 노선도 **jee·hah·chuhl noh·suhn·doh** subway [underground BE] map

지하철역 **jee·hah·chuhl·lyuhk** subway [underground BE] station

지휘자 **jee·hwih·jah** conductor

직업 **jee·guhp** job, profession

직원 **jee·gwuhn** staff

직접 만든 **jeek·tzuhp mahn·dun** homemade

직행 **jee·kehng** direct, non-stop

진공 청소기 **jeen·gohng chuhng·soh·gee** vacuum cleaner

진열장 **jee·nyuhl·tzahng** display case

진정제 **jeen·juhng·jeh** sedative

진주 **jeen·joo** pearl

진짜 **jeen·tzah** genuine, real, authentic

질 **jeel** quality, vagina

질긴 **jeel·geen** tough

짐 **jeem** luggage [baggage BE]

짐꾼 **jeem·kkoon** porter

집 **jeep** home, house

짓다 **jeet·ttah** build

짧은 **tzahl·bun** short

짧은 여행 **tzahl·bun yuh·hehng** excursion

쯤 **tzum** around (time)

찢다 **tzeet·ttah** tear

찢어진 **tzee·juh·jeen** torn

ㅊ

차가운 **chah·gah·oon** adj cold

차고 **chah·goh** garage (parking)

차선 **chah·suhn** lane

착륙하다 **chahng·nyoo·kah·dah** v land

참가하다 **chahm·gah·hah·dh** join

창문 **chahng·moon** window

창문석 **chahng·moon·suhk** window seat

찾다 **chaht·ttah** find

채식주의자 **cheh·seek·tzoo·ee·jah** vegetarian

채우다 **cheh·oo·dah** fill

책 **chehk** book

책임 **cheh·geem** responsibility

처방 **chuh·bahng** prescription

천 **chuhn** fabric

천식 **chuhn·seek** asthma

철 **chuhl** steel

철물점 **chuhl·mool·juhm** hardware store

철자하다 **chuhl·tzah·hah·dah** spell

첫 **chuht** first

청각 장애인 **chuhng·gahk tzahng·eh·een** hearing impaired

청바지 **chuhng·bah·jee** jeans

체크아웃 **cheh·ku·ah·oot** check out

초대하다 **choh·deh·hah·dah** invite

최고 **chweh·goh** superb

추가 **choo·gah** supplement

추천하다 **choo·chuhn·hah·dah** recommend

축구 **chook·kkoo** soccer [football BE]

축소 모형 **chook·ssoh moh·hyuhng** miniature

축하합니다 **choo·kah·ham·nee·dah** congratulations

출구 **chool·goo** exit

출금 **chool·gum** withdrawal

출금하다 **chool·gum·hah·dah** withdraw

출발 **chool·bahl** departures

출발하다 **chool·bahl·hah·dah** depart

춤 추다 **choom choo·dah** dance

충격 **choong·gyuhk** shock

충분한 **choong·boon·hahn** enough

취미 **chwih·mee** hobby, interest (hobby)

취소하다 **chwih·soh·hah·dah** cancel

층 **chung** floor (level)

치과의사 **chee·kkwah·u·sah** dentist

치료 **chee·lyo** treatment

치마 **chee·mah** skirt

치수 **chee·soo** measurement

치실 **chee·seel** dental floss

치약 **chee·yahk** toothpaste

치통 **chee·tohng** toothache

친구 **cheen·goo** friend

친절한 **cheen·juhl·hahn** kind

침 **cheem** acupuncture

침구 **cheem·goo** bedding

침낭 **cheem·nahng** sleeping bag

침대 **cheem·deh** bed

침대차 **cheem·deh·chah** sleeper car (train)

침실 **cheem·seel** bedroom

칫솔 **cheet·ssohl** toothbrush

ㅋ

카누 **kah·noo** canoe

카드 **kah·du** card

카메라 **kah·meh·lah** camera

카시트 **kah·ssee·tu** car seat

카운터 **kah·oon·tuh** counter

카지노 **kah·jee·noh** casino

카페트 **kah·peh·tu** carpet

카트 **kah·tu** cart [trolley BE]

칼 **kahl** knife

칼로리 **kahl·loh·lee** calorie

캐나다 **keh·nah·dah** Canada

캠핑장 **kehm·peeng·jahng** campsite

캠핑하다 **kehm·peeng·hah·dah** camp

캡슐 **kehp·syool** capsule

커브 **kuh·bu** curve

커튼 **kuh·tun** curtain

컨디셔너 **kuhn·dee·syuh·nuh** conditioner

컴퓨터 **kuhm·pyoo·tuh** computer

컵 **kuhp** cup

켜다 **kyuh·dah** turn on

코 **koh** nose

코르크 마개뽑이 **koh·lu·ku mah·geh·ppoh·bee** corkscrew

코스 **koh·su** course (meal)

코트 **koh·tu** coat

콘돔 **kohn·dohm** condom

콘텍트 렌즈 **kohn·tehk·tu lehn·ju** contact lens

콘텍트 렌즈 용액 **kohn·tehk·tu lehn·ju yong·ehk** contact lens solution

콜밴 **kohl·behn** van taxi

쿠킹 호일 **koo·keeng hoh·eel** aluminum [kitchen BE] foil

큰 **kun** large, big

클럽 **kul·luhp** dance club

키 **kee** height (person)

키 큰 **kee kun** tall

키스하다 **kee·ssu·hah·dah** kiss

키카드 **kee·kah·du** key card

E

타이어 **tah·ee·uh** tire

타일 **tah·eel** tile

탈의실 **tahl·ee·seel** fitting room

탈취제 **tahl·chwih·jeh** deodorant

탐폰 **tahm·pohn** tampon

탑 **tahp** tower

탑승 수속 **tahp·ssung soo·sohk** check in

탑승 수속대 **tahp·ssung soo·sohk·tteh** check-in desk

탑승 카드 **tahp·ssung kah·du** boarding card

탑승구 **tahp·ssung·goo** gate

탑승하다 **tahp·ssung·hah·dah** board

태어난 **teh·uh·nahn** born

태우다 **teh·oo·dah** tan

택시 **tehk·ssee** taxi

택시 승차장 **tehk·ssee sung·chah·jahng** taxi stand

터널 **tuh·nuhl** tunnel

터미널 **tuh·mee·nuhl** terminal

턱 **tuhk** jaw

턱받이 **tuhk·ppah·jee** bib

텅 빈 **tuhng been** empty

테니스 **teh·nee·su** tennis

테니스 코트 **teh·nee·su koh·tu** tennis court

테이블 **teh·ee·bul** table

텐트 **tehn·tu** tent

텐트용 기둥 **tehn·tu·yong gee·doong** tent pole

텐트용 쐐기 **tehn·tu·yong sswehg·gee** tent peg

텔레비전 **tehl·leh·bee·juhn** TV

토박이 **toh·bah·gee** native

토하다 **toh·hah·dah** vomit

토할 거 같은 **toh·hahl kkuh gah·tun** nauseous

통로 **tohng·noh** aisle

통보하다 **tohng·boh·hah·dah** notify

통역 **tohng·yuhk** interpreter

통조림 따개 **tohng·joh·leem ttah·geh** can [tin BE] opener

통해서 **tohng·heh·suh** through

트럭 **tu·luhk** truck

트레일러 **tu·leh·eel·luh** trailer

특급 우편 **tuk·kkup oo·pyuhn** express mail

특별한 **tuk·ppyuhl·hahn** special

특징 **tuk·tzeeng** feature

틀니 **tul·lee** denture

티셔츠 **tee·syuh·chu** T-shirt

티스푼 **tee·su·pun** teaspoon

팀 **teem** team

팁 **teep** tip

ㅍ

파도 **pah·doh** wave

파운드 **pah·oon·du** pound, pound sterling

파이프 **pah·ee·pu** pipe

파티 **pah·tee** party

판매세 **pahn·meh·sseh** sales tax

판매용 **pahn·meh·yong** for sale

팔 **pahl** arm

팔다 **pahl·dah** sell

팔찌 **pal·tzee** bracelet

패스트 푸드 **peh·su·tu poo·du** fast food

팩스 **pehk·su** fax

팩스 번호 **pehk·su buhn·hoh** fax number

팩스기 **pehk·su·gee** fax machine

팬티스타킹 **pehn·tee·su·tah·keeng** panty hose

팸플릿 **pahm·pul·leht** brochure

페니실린 **peh·nee·seel·leen** penicillin

페디큐어 **peh·dee·kyoo·uh** pedicure

펜 **pehn** pen

편도표 **pyuhn·doh·pyo** one-way ticket

편두통 **pyuhn·doo·tohng** migraine

편지 **pyuhn·jee** letter

편지 보내다 **pyuhn·jee boh·neh·dah** v mail

편지 봉투 **pyuhn·jee bohng·too** envelope

평상복 **pyuhng·sahng·bohk** informal (dress)

평일 **pyuhng·eel** weekday

평평한 **pyuhng·pyuhng·hahn** flat

폐 **peh** lung

포도밭 **poh·doh·baht** vineyard

포크 **poh·ku** fork

포함하다 **poh·hahm·hah·dah** contain, include

폭포 **pohk·poh** waterfall

폭행 **poh·kehng** attack

폴리에스테르 **pohl·lee·eh·su·teh·lu** polyester

표 **pyo** ticket

표백제 **pyo·behk·tzeh** bleach

표본 **pyo·bohn** specimen

표준 **pyo·joon** standard

표지 **pyo·jee** *n* sign

품목 **poom·mohk** item

프로그램 **pu·loh·gu·lehm** program

프린트하다 **pu·leen·tu·hah·dah** *v* print

플라스틱 **pul·lah·su·teek** plastic

플러그 **pul·luh·gu** plug

피가 나다 **pee·gah nah·dah** bleed

피곤한 **pee·gohn·hahn** tired

피부 **pee·boo** skin

피시방 **pee·ssee·bahng** internet cafe

피임약 **pee·eem·nyahk** contraceptive

피크닉 **pee·ku·neek** picnic

피크닉 구역 **pee·ku·neek kkoo·yuhk** picnic area

필기 용지 **peel·gee yong·jee** writing paper

필수 **peel·ssoo** required

필수적인 **peel·ssoo·juh·geen** essential

필요하다 **pee·lyo·hah·dah** need

필요한 **pee·lyo·hahn** necessary

필터 **peel·tuh** filter

ㅎ

하게 하다 **hah·geh hah·dah** let

하고 같이 **hah·goh gah·chee** with

하다 **hah·dah** do

하이킹 **hah·ee·keeng** hike

하이킹 장비 **hah·ee·keeng jahng·bee** hiking gear

하이힐 **hah·ee·heel** heels

학생 **hahk·ssehng** student

한 번 **hahn buhn** once

한 쌍 **hahn ssahng** pair

할인 **hah·leen** discount

할인매장 **hah·leen·meh·jahng** discount store

합법적 **hahp·ppuhp·tzuhk** legal

합성 **hahp·ssuhng** synthetic

합치다 **hahp·chee·dah** merge

항공기 편명 **hahng·gohng·gee pyuhn·myung** flight number

항공사 **hahng·gohng·sah** airline

항공우편 **hahng·gohng·oo·pyuhn** airmail

항구 **hahng·goo** port, harbor

항상 **hahng·sahng** always

항생제 **hahng·sehng·jeh** antibiotics

해 **heh** sun

해발 **heh·bahl** sea level

해변 **heh·byuhn** beach

해안 **heh·ahn** coast

해안 거리 **heh·ahn guh·lee** seafront

해야 하다 **heh·yah hah·dah** must

핸드백 **hehn·du·behk** purse [handbag BE]

행복한 **hehng·boh·kahn** happy

행사 **hehng·sah** event

허락하다 **huh·lah·kah·dah** allow, approve

허용한도 **huh·yong·hahn·doh** allowance

헐렁한 **huhl·luhng·hahn** loose

헤드라이트 **heh·du·lah·ee·tu** headlight

헤어 브러시 **heh·uh bu·luh·see** hair brush

헬멧 **hehl·meht** helmet

헬스클럽 **hehl·ssu·kul·luhp** gym

혀 **hyuh** tongue

현금 **hyuhn·gum** cash

현금 인출기 **hyuhn·gum een·chool·gee** ATM

현대 **hyuhn·deh** contemporary

현상하다 **hyuhn·sahng·hah·dah** develop

혈압 **hyuh·lahp** blood pressure

혈액 **hyuh·lehk** blood

호수 **hoh·soo** lake

호텔 **hoh·tehl** hotel

혼자 **hohn·jah** alone

화랑 **hwah·lahng** gallery

화상 **hwah·sahng** burn

화장 **hwah·jahng** make-up

화장실 **hwah·jahng·seel** bathroom, restroom [toilet BE]

화장실 휴지 **hwah·jahng·seel hyoo·jee** toilet paper

화장지 **hwah·jahng·jee** tissue

화장품 **hwah·jahng·poom** cosmetic

화재 경보 **hwah·jeh gyuhng·boh** fire alarm

화재 비상 계단 **hwah·jeh bee·sahng geh·dahn** fire escape

화재 비상구 **hwah·jeh bee·sahng·goo** fire exit

확대하다 **hwahk·tteh·hah·dah** enlarge

확실한 **hwahk·sseel·hahn** sure

확인하다 **hwah·geen·hah·dah** check, confirm, validate

환불 **hwahn·bool** refund

환영 **hwah·nyuhng** welcome

환율 **hwah·nyool** exchange rate

환자 **hwahn·jah** *n* patient

환전소 **hwahn·juhn·soh** currency exchange office

회교 사원 **hweh·gyo·sah·wuhn** mosque

회사 **hweh·sah** company

회원 **hweh·wuhn** member

회의 **hweh·ee** conference, meeting

회의실 **hweh·ee·seel** meeting room

회의장 **hweh·ee·jahng** convention hall

회의 장소 **hweh·ee jahng·soh** meeting place

횡단보도 **hwehng·dahn·boh·doh** pedestrian [zebra BE] crossing

후라이팬 **hoo·lah·ee·pen** frying pan

훔치다 **hoom·chee·dah** steal

훨씬 **hwuhl·sseen** much

휠체어 **hwihl·cheh·uh** wheelchair

휠체어 진입로 **hwihl·cheh·uh jee·neem·noh** wheelchair ramp

휴가 **hyoo·gah** vacation [holiday BE]

휴게소 **hyoo·geh·soh** rest area

휴대 변기 **hyoo·deh byuhn·gee** chemical toilet

휴대폰 **hyoo·deh·pohn** cell [mobile BE] phone

휴대품 보관소 **hyoo·deh·poom boh·gwahn·soh** coat check

흡연석 **hu·byuhn·suhk** smoking area

흥정 **hung·juhng** bargain

힘 **heem** power

Don't let a little thing like language come between you and your dreams.

Berlitz®

Berlitz® expands your world with **audio products, dictionaries, phrase books** and **learning tools** in 30 languages

A wide selection of handy **travel guides** lets you explore it.

Available at your local bookseller or www.berlitzpublishing.com